CAMBRIDGE

Official Cambridge Exam Preparation

PREPARE

STUDENT'S BOOK WITH EBOOK

B2

LEVEL 6

James Styring
Nicholas Tims

Second Edition

Cambridge University Press
www.cambridge.org/elt

Cambridge Assessment English
www.cambridgeenglish.org

Information on this title: www.cambridge.org/9781009032223

First published 2015
Second Edition 2019
Second Edition update 2021

20 19 18

Printed in Malaysia by Vivar Printing

A catalogue record for this publication is available from the British Library

ISBN 978-1-00-903222-3 Student's Book with eBook
ISBN 978-1-00-903223-0 Workbook with Digital Pack
ISBN 978-1-00-903224-7 Teacher's Book with Digital Pack

CONTENTS

Key to symbols:
✓ *B2 First for Schools* exam task ▶ Video

Key to symbols:

✓ *B2 First for Schools* exam task ▶ Video

WELCOME TO PREPARE

LEARN ABOUT THE FEATURES IN YOUR NEW STUDENT'S BOOK!

ABOUT YOU

Start each unit by talking about you, your life and the unit topic

PREPARE TO WRITE

Learn useful tips to help you prepare, plan and check your writing

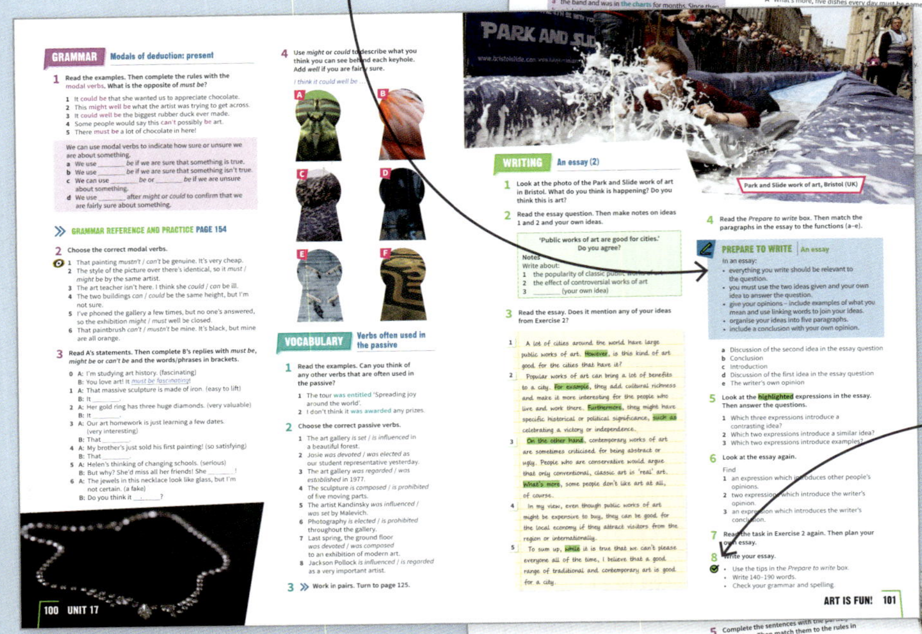

TALKING POINTS

Say what you think about the topic in the text

EASY TO FIND EXAM TASKS

PREPARE TO SPEAK

Learn useful words and phrases for effective communication

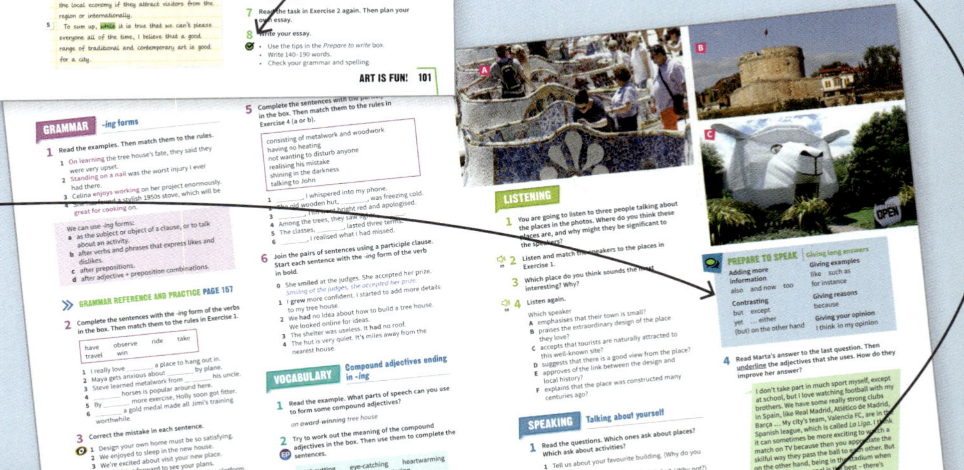

VIDEO

Watch interviews with teenagers like you

CULTURE

Learn about the culture of English-speaking countries and the wider world

VIDEO

Watch interesting documentaries about the culture topics

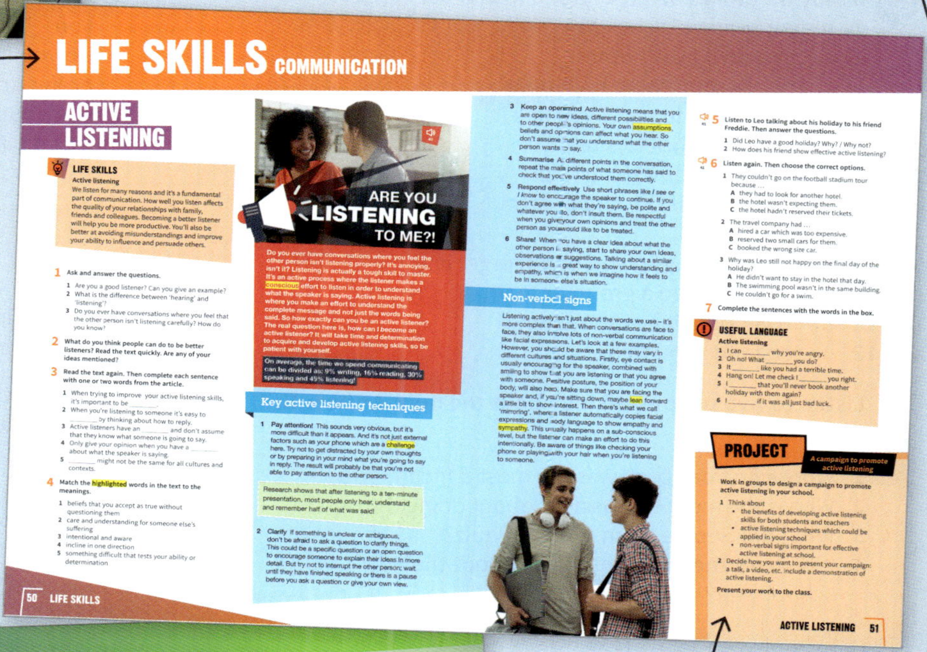

LIFE SKILLS

Develop important skills that you can use in your daily life

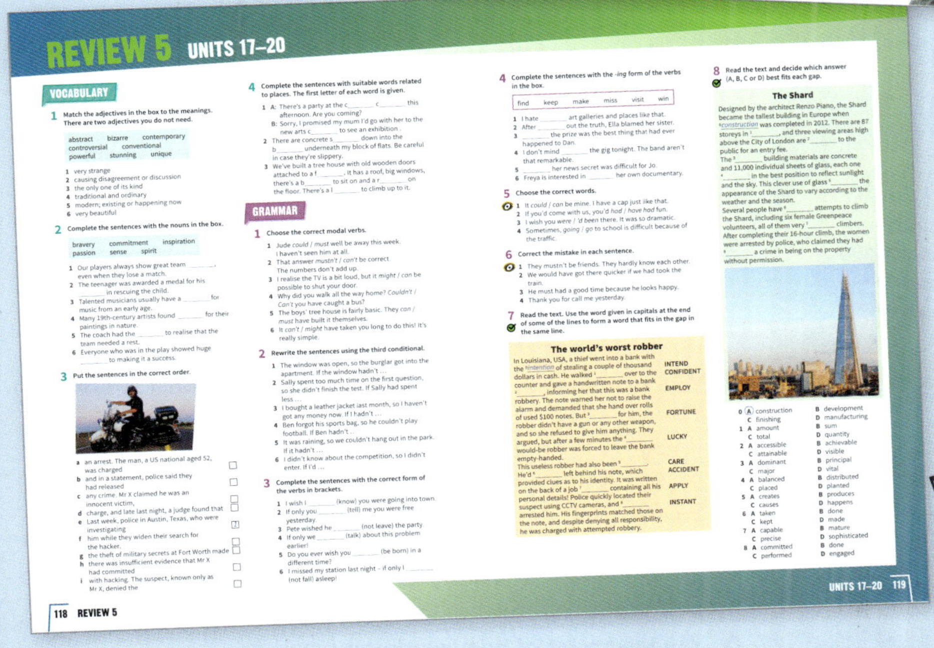

PROJECT

Work together to create something fun and expand your learning

REVIEW

Check your progress

1 NEW YEAR, NEW CHALLENGE

ABOUT YOU

What are your aims and ambitions at school this year? Which subjects do you like the most?

VOCABULARY Education: phrasal verbs

1 Do the quiz below. Compare your answers in pairs.

2 » Turn to page 120 and check your results. Who feels the most optimistic about the new school year? Why?

3 Match the phrasal verbs in the quiz to the meanings.

EP
- **0** say the words of a text aloud *read out*
- **1** remain while others leave
- **2** do an activity with others
- **3** distribute something to people
- **4** do something to see if you like it
- **5** give written work to a teacher
- **6** decide to do something later
- **7** finish classes at the end of term
- **8** make progress
- **9** write something so you don't forget it
- **10** be accepted into a group or team
- **11** try to get or achieve something
- **12** understand something

01 **4** Listen to two people talking about the quiz. Answer the questions.

1. Whose first day back was the most difficult? Why?
2. Who is the most enthusiastic about doing the quiz?
3. What did Sophie learn from the quiz?
4. Who feels the most optimistic about the new school year?

01 **5** Listen again. What are Niall's and Sophie's answers to the quiz?

1 Niall – a Sophie – b

6 Complete the questions with the correct form of the phrasal verbs from the quiz. Then ask and answer the questions.

1. What happens if you ________ homework late at your school?
2. Do you ever have to ________ your work aloud in front of the whole class?
3. Are you generally good at ________ solutions to problems by yourself?
4. Do you ever have to ________ after class? Why?
5. Is there a party or celebration at school when you ________ for the holidays?
6. Do you like ________ group activities or do you prefer doing things independently?
7. Have you ________ to any teams this year?
8. Do you like ________ new experiences or do you tend to stick with what you know?

READING

1 Read the first paragraph of the article on page 11. What is a *mindset*?

2 Read the whole article and tick (✓) the areas of life that your mindset can affect.

- **a** ☐ success at work
- **b** ☐ health
- **c** ☐ friendships
- **d** ☐ education
- **e** ☐ attitude to sports

BACK-2-SCHOOL

Are you the type of person who's into every challenge and new opportunity? Or do you take a more independent, chilled-out approach to life?

DO OUR QUIZ AND FIND OUT!

1 It's the start of the school year. You …
- **a** can't wait until you **break up** for the next holidays.
- **b** feel optimistic – you think you'll **get on** well this year.

2 Your teacher **reads out** some information about an exam. You …
- **a** **note down** all the details in case you forget them.
- **b** don't do anything. You'll **figure** it **out** at the end of term.

3 You see a poster asking people to join the school swimming team. You …
- **a** don't bother trying. You know you won't **get in**.
- **b** decide to **go for** it. It's a cool opportunity.

4 You are asked to fill in a form with some personal information. You …
- **a** agree and promise you'll **hand** it **in** soon.
- **b** **stay behind** and complete it before you go home.

5 Your teacher **gives out** information about clubs and societies at school. You …
- **a** don't listen. You never **join in** after-school activities.
- **b** are pleased. You can't wait to **try out** something new.

6 You have a lot of homework this week. You …
- **a** start right away – you never **put** things **off**.
- **b** relax – there's plenty of time later in the week!

THIS PAGE WILL CHANGE YOUR LIFE

Growth mindset – transform your mind forever

02

Are you wondering how to get on better at school? Have you ever felt that you're good at some things but not at others? Then perhaps it's time to start thinking differently about school, and even yourself. Carol Dweck, a Professor of Psychology from Stanford University, says people may not be aware of their own 'mindset', but mindsets have a huge influence on learning, skills development, personal relationships and professional achievement. Your mindset determines your attitude to your abilities. For example, you might consider yourself to be good (or bad) at sport or maths or languages. Or you might feel that you can be good at anything if you try hard enough.

What mindset do you have? To find out, consider these situations:

1 **You read a short message in English, but it's hard to understand. What would you think?**
- a It's no use! I'm just not very good at languages.
- b I haven't studied English for long, but one day I'll be able to read this.

2 **You try to join a school sports team, but you fail to get in. What do you say to yourself?**
- a It's because I'm not good at sport.
- b I'm not good enough yet, but if I train, I might get in next time.

These situations illustrate the difference between fixed and growth mindsets. People with a fixed mindset tend to answer a) to both questions. People with a growth mindset tend to answer b).

FIXED MINDSET PEOPLE …

- think they are born with the ability to be good at some things and not at others.
- believe that success comes from talent rather than effort.
- don't feel that they can change what they're like as a person.
- dislike failure and focus on what they are 'good' at – they avoid difficult challenges and things they're not 'good' at.
- like doing well at tasks that will get a reward or please their school or parents, for example getting top marks in an exam.

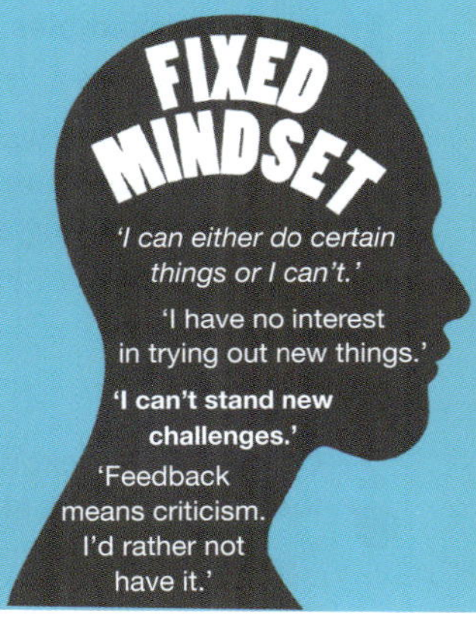

GROWTH MINDSET PEOPLE …

- think they are born with the ability to be good at anything if they try hard enough.
- believe that success comes from effort rather than talent.
- like adapting to new situations and challenges.
- don't mind failure and they learn from it – they'd never think 'I'm no good at this' or 'There's no use even trying.'
- do things for their own sake – for example, they might join a team because they find it personally rewarding, not because they want praise.

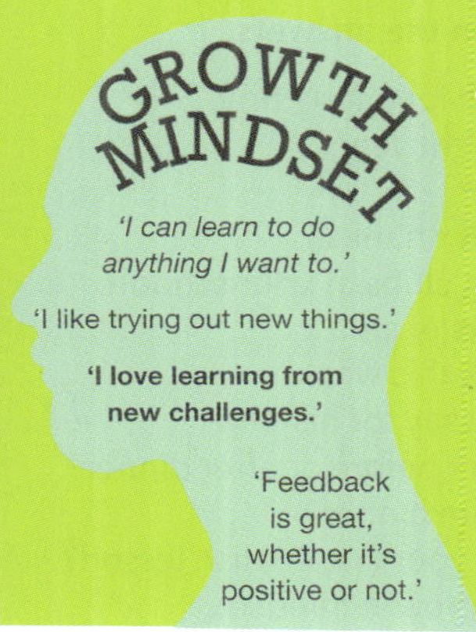

Did you know that when we learn something new, or when we have to concentrate to figure out an answer to a problem, our body creates new nerve connections within the brain? People with a growth mindset are always trying out new things and developing their skills and abilities, and so their brains are always growing.

Do you want to get the most out of your education? Do you want a content and prosperous life? There's no question that adopting a 'growth mindset' is the best decision you could ever make about your future. If you don't already take the growth mindset approach (and most people don't!), the question you should be asking yourself is not 'Should change the way I see myself?' … the big question is 'How quickly can I change?'

3 **Read the article again and answer the questions. Write *Fixed* for people with a fixed mindset or *Growth* for people with a growth mindset.**

1 Who thinks we're born with certain characteristics?
2 Who thinks achievement is a result of working hard?
3 Who thinks we can learn from our mistakes?
4 Who feels it's important to get high scores?
5 Whose brain keeps on growing?

4 **Match the highlighted words and phrases in the article to the meanings. Then write one sentence for each phrase.**

1 do things in a certain way
2 know that something exists
3 getting better at doing things
4 doing well in your career
5 do things simply because you like doing them

5 **Discuss the questions.**

1 What mindset do you have? (Answer the two questions in the article.)
2 Read the five character descriptors for your mindset. Do you agree?

TALKING POINTS

Are there any advantages to having a fixed mindset?

Do you think that this page will change your life?

GRAMMAR Question forms

1 **Read the examples. Then complete the rules with the words in the box.**

1 **Are** you **wondering** how to get on better at school?
2 **Have** you ever **felt** that you're good at …?
3 What mindset **do** you **have**?
4 **Did** you **know** that when we learn something …?
5 **Should** I **change** the way I see myself?
6 How quickly **can** I **change**?

are	before	*does*	*have*

To form questions:
a in simple tenses, we add ________, *do* or *did* before the subject.
b in perfect tenses, we put *has*, ________ or *had* before the subject.
c in continuous tenses, we put *am*, *is*, ________, *was* or *were* before the subject.
d with modal verbs, we put the modal verb ________ the subject.

2 **Complete the questions with *you* and the correct form of the verbs in bold in the answers.**

0 *Have you studied* English for a long time?
Yes, I've **studied** it for eight years.
1 How ________ this term?
I'm **getting on** quite well, thanks.
2 ________ any interesting clubs at your school?
Yes, you can **join** all sorts of clubs.
3 ________ any homework this week?
Yes, I've **handed in** an essay for history.
4 ________ your homework before or after dinner?
I **do** my homework before dinner.
5 What ________ about in your last English lesson?
We **were talking** about growth mindset.

3 **Correct the mistake in each question.**

1 There is a new drama teacher?
2 Did they passed their end-of-year exams?
3 Have you consider my offer yet?
4 What I should study next?
5 How much the extra classes do cost?

Subject and object questions

4 **Read the examples. Then complete the rules with *statement* or *question*.**

Subject question
1 **Who** helps you? **My teacher** helps me.

Object question
2 **Who** do you help? We help **younger children**.

a Object questions ask about the object. They use the same word order as a ________.
b Subject questions ask about the subject. They use the same word order as a ________.

» GRAMMAR REFERENCE AND PRACTICE PAGE 138

5 **Complete the questions with the words given.**

1 do you know / knows you
a 'Who ________ in this class?' 'I only know you.'
b 'Who ________ in this class?' 'Only you know me.'
2 did Carl call / called Carl
a 'Who ________?' 'He called a few classmates.'
b 'Who ________?' 'A classmate called him.'
3 damaged their car / did their car damage
a 'What ________?' 'It damaged a wall.'
b 'What ________?' 'A tree that fell on it.'

6 **Write two questions about each sentence: one with *what* and one with *who*.**

0 Suzanne Collins wrote *The Hunger Games* books.
What did Suzanne Collins write?
Who wrote The Hunger Games *books?*
1 Gary Ross directed *Ocean's Eight*.
2 Elon Musk started SpaceX and Tesla.
3 Brazil has won the FIFA World Cup five times.
4 Cristiano Ronaldo has been voted the world's best male football player five times.

VOCABULARY Education: *-ion* nouns

1 **Read the examples. Then form nouns with *-ion* from the verbs.**

educate: Do you want to get the most out of your **education**?
decide: Adopting a 'growth mindset' is the best **decision** you could ever make.

1 act 3 prepare 5 permit
2 invent 4 discuss 6 register

2 **Complete the text with the singular or plural noun form of the verbs given in capitals.**

Getting the best out of yourself

There's a new book out about self- [0]*motivation* and how to get the best out of yourself. The [1]________ has some interesting facts about the human brain, and the [2]________ between learning and brain development. There's also a glossary where you can read [3]________ of key terms such as 'self-efficacy' and 'growth mindset'. The glossary's useful because you really need to know these [4]________ as you read the book. I've read the whole book now and I've tried a [5]________ of the techniques it mentions. It's definitely helped me with my [6]________ and my ability to focus on reaching certain goals I've set for myself. There are a few case studies of specific issues that people have had, with [7]________ of how they overcame those issues. It ends with [8]________ for simple exercises you can try out to see what works for you.

MOTIVATE
INTRODUCE
CONNECT
DEFINE
EXPRESS
SELECT
CONCENTRATE
EXPLAIN
RECOMMEND

3 » Work in pairs. Turn to page 120.

WRITING An essay (1)

1 **Read the sample essay. Then read the essay task. Does the writer agree or disagree with the essay title?**

In your English class you have been talking about the importance of learning English. Now your English teacher has asked you to write an essay.
Write your essay using **all** the notes and giving reasons for your point of view.

> **'Everyone should learn English.'**
> **Do you agree?**
>
> **Notes**
> Write about:
> 1 finding a job
> 2 travelling
> 3 .... (your own idea)

'Everyone should learn English.' Do you agree?

1 English is the international language for business, travel and culture, and so it makes sense that everyone should learn it.

2 In order to get many jobs, candidates need to be able to speak English. Even if your company doesn't have clients in English-speaking countries, you'll still need English to communicate with business partners from everywhere else in the world.

3 Similarly, when you go abroad, have you noticed that restaurant menus, visitor information and street signs are often in English as well as the national language? Even if you don't speak the language of that country and they don't speak yours, you can always use English to get what you need.

4 Finally, I think that English is important if you're a film or music fan. Many of my favourite songs, shows and films are American or British, so speaking English really helps me to appreciate and enjoy them. I particularly dislike watching films with subtitles! And when I hear a cool song, it's satisfying to be able to work out the lyrics on my own.

5 These three examples illustrate why everyone needs English to get on in different areas of life.

2 **Read the essay again. Then match each paragraph to its function.**

a Write up your ideas for the second note (*travelling*).
b Summarise your ideas in a conclusion.
c Write up your ideas for the third note (*your own idea*).
d Directly address the essay question.
e Write up your ideas for the first note (*finding a job*).

3 **Discuss the questions.**

1 According to the essay, why is English important?
2 What would you write for the third note?
3 What might you write as your conclusion for this essay?

4 **Read the *Prepare to write* box. What examples can you find in the essay? Then rewrite the sentences below as a single paragraph with the correct punctuation.**

PREPARE TO WRITE | Punctuation

We use capital letters:

- at the beginning of all sentences.
- for the personal pronoun *I*.
- for days and months.
- for the names of people, places, nationalities and languages.

We use:

- full stops at the end of most sentences.
- exclamation marks at the end of sentences to show surprise or anger.
- question marks at the end of questions.
- commas to separate items in a list, and before or after certain words to separate clauses.
- apostrophes to show possession and contractions.

i dont see why everyone should learn english just because thats what they speak in the united states

american culture and technology are the most popular at the moment but will it always be that way

it would be better if we all learned chinese because there are more speakers of chinese than any other language

it doesnt make sense for a chinese and a german businessperson to speak english when they meet

wouldnt it make more sense if they just spoke one of their own languages

5 **Read the essay task below. Then discuss the questions.**

1 What could you write for the first note?
2 What could you write for the second note?
3 What could you add for the third note?
4 What would your conclusion be?

In your English class you have been talking about being successful in life. Now your English teacher has asked you to write an essay.
Write your essay using **all** the notes and giving reasons for your point of view.

> **'Being successful in life depends more on a person's ability than on how hard a person tries.'**
> **Do you agree?**
>
> **Notes**
> Write about:
> 1 studies
> 2 sport
> 3 .... (your own idea)

6 **Write your essay.**

- Write your essay using five paragraphs, like the sample essay.
- Pay attention to punctuation.
- Write 140–190 words

2 LIVE MUSIC

ABOUT YOU

01 Watch the video. Then answer the questions.

Which singers or bands have you seen live in concert?

Who would you most like to see in concert?

VOCABULARY Music phrases

03 **1** **Listen and identify the eight types of music you hear. Use the words in the box.**

classical	folk	hip-hop	jazz
opera	pop	reggae	rock

2 **Put the parts of sentences in order to make the first paragraph of two concert reviews. The first line of each review is given.**

LIVE MUSIC REVIEW: Phoebe White

a last month, was unexpected. Her choice of **concert venue** last
b no surprise, but her **debut album**, which came out
c Blue Lines' popularity as **background music** on TV shows
d and her **musical talent** was at its best in the cosy atmosphere.
e night matched her new, quieter sound perfectly, though,
f apparently hated. Her decision to **go solo** last year was
g was something that former **lead singer**, Phoebe White,

1 c Blue Lines' popularity as background music on TV shows …

LIVE MUSIC REVIEW: The Scene

a the band and was in **the charts** for months. Since then,
b might just have heard! *Lucky* was a **massive hit** for
c their home town to just a thousand **devoted fans**, who
d The Scene **released a track** in the summer which you
e they've been **touring the world**, playing to crowds of
f were definitely in the mood for dancing.
g over 50,000. Last night, they **gave a performance** in

1 d The Scene released a track in the summer which you …

04 **3** **Listen and check.**

4 **Match the phrases in each review to the meanings.**

EP Review 1

1 the main vocalist in a band
2 a natural ability related to music
3 leave a band to follow a music career by yourself
4 songs that are playing quietly while you are doing something else
5 a place where musicians play live
6 a singer or group's first collection of songs

Review 2

7 a very popular and successful song
8 an official weekly list of the most popular songs
9 people who like a singer or band very much
10 giving live concerts internationally
11 made a song available for people to buy
12 acted or played music in public

5 **Discuss the questions.**

1 Who is the lead singer of your favourite band?
2 Do you put on some background music when you study?
3 Are there any good concert venues where you live?
4 What is number one in the charts in your country at the moment?

READING

1 **Read the first paragraph of the article, ignoring the gap. What are *riders*?**

2 **Which artist in the photos do you think made these requests in their riders? Read the article quickly and check.**

1 white rooms, white flowers, white furniture
2 crisps, sweets, fruit
3 recycling facilities and locally grown food
4 eight local postcards and stamps

3 **Six sentences have been removed from the article. Choose from the sentences A–G the one which fits each gap (1–6). There is one extra sentence which you do not need to use.**

A What's more, five dishes every day must be named after his songs.
B This is usually where a backstage rider begins.
C There will be no exceptions to this rule, the rider states.
D Some of these concern technical issues, such as sound equipment or lighting that is needed.
E In this case, the venue was trying to save money.
F Although leather and meat are banned from backstage, his rider requests 240 clean towels at each concert!
G However, perhaps the most famous remains one made by American rock band Van Halen.

4 **Imagine you are in a band. Write your own rider.**

CRISPS, SWEETS AND WHITE KITTENS?

Jennifer Lopez

When musicians go on tour, they have a contract with each of the venues that they play at. A 'rider' is part of that contract. It's a list of requests that a singer or band make before they agree to perform. [1] ________ However, the more interesting ones are backstage riders – things that musicians specially request backstage during their performances.

Bands often tour for months, visiting numerous cities. At each venue, the stars need to get ready for their show in a dressing room. They want to be comfortable as they prepare themselves for the performance ahead, so it's natural they need some things. [2] ________ Beyoncé's rider once specified that it must be exactly 28.5°C backstage. And Jennifer Lopez once demanded that all her dressing rooms were white, with white flowers, white candles and white sofas.

Live performances are hard work, so musicians need feeding, too. Some of them make their own arrangements. One young Canadian singer sometimes has his own personal chef while on tour. [3] ________ Others are easier to satisfy, but there are more clues about their working lifestyles in these areas of a rider. Rihanna seems to love snacks: her rider asks for a wide range of crisps, sweets and fruit to be on offer. Lady Gaga used to ask for a whole roast chicken and ten different types of soft drink. She's obviously eating more healthily nowadays: her more recent riders have included soup, fruit juice and tea. And remember to feed her 150-person team exactly on time at 5 pm or the concert will be cancelled!

Some performers are aware that large tours can have a significant environmental impact. Maroon 5 have a 'green' section in their rider, encouraging venues to recycle and to use locally grown food where possible. They even set up stalls for fans attending the concert so they can learn about trying to reduce their carbon footprint. Let's hope a certain former member of The Beatles is seeing them live soon. [4] ________

A few requests reveal a generous and thoughtful side to performers' personalities. Since she started touring, Adele has insisted that people with free tickets to her concerts must make a donation to charity. [5] ________ And even massive bands like Coldplay clearly never stop thinking about their friends and family while they are away. Their rider once asked for eight local postcards and stamps.

On the whole, most musicians' requests are reasonable, but some can be outrageous. One promoter remembers receiving a demand from an extremely famous female singer for 20 white kittens! Another male singer stated that no one at the venue could talk to or even look at the star directly. [6] ________ They would only play on condition that they were given a large bowl of M&M sweets, but without any brown ones. Furthermore, if just one of these sweets were found anywhere backstage, the band would not play. It turned out that there was a good reason behind their bizarre request. The safety section of the band's rider was long and complicated, so they hid the request about sweets among these details to make sure it was being read carefully!

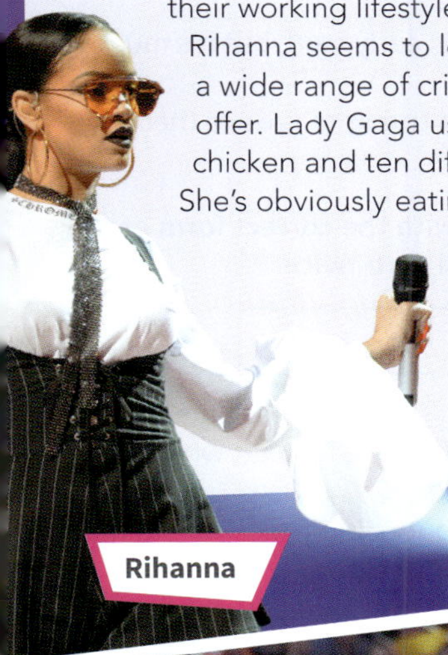

Rihanna

TALKING POINTS

Why do you think some singers/bands make unreasonable demands in their riders?

What's the typical price of a ticket to a concert by an internationally famous band?

Do you think concert tickets are good value in general? Why? / Why not?

Coldplay

Adam Levine from Maroon 5

Adele

GRAMMAR Present tense review

1 Read the examples and name the tenses. Then match the examples to the rules.

1 Live performances **are** hard work.
2 Bands often **tour** for months.
3 Since she started touring, Adele **has insisted** that people with free tickets must make a donation to charity.
4 She**'s** obviously **eating** more healthily nowadays.
5 Let's hope a certain former member of The Beatles **is seeing** them live soon.
6 Rihanna **seems** to love snacks.

We use the present simple:
a for habits and routines.
b with verbs that describe states (*like*, *want*, *need*, *seem*, etc.).
c for permanent situations or facts.

We use the present continuous:
d for things that are happening right now or about now.
e for arrangements in the future.

We use the present perfect:
f with *for/since* for something that started in the past and continues in the present.

» GRAMMAR REFERENCE AND PRACTICE PAGE 139

2 Complete the conversation with the present simple, present continuous or present perfect form of the verbs in brackets. Use contractions if possible.

Eva: What [0]*are you doing* (you, do) on that phone? You [1] ________ (be) on it for ages.
Sam: I [2] ________ (try) to buy some tickets to a concert.
Eva: Who [3] ________ (play)?
Sam: Daft Punk.
Eva: Wow! They [4] ________ (not play) live very often.
Sam: Exactly. It [5] ________ (seem) like everyone [6] ________ (try) to buy a ticket. The website [7] ________ (be) really slow. [8] ________ (you, want) me to get you a ticket, too?
Eva: Yes, please. I [9] ________ (listen) to Daft Punk a lot! What about calling the ticket office?
Sam: Lauren [10] ________ (wait) in a queue on the phone now. She [11] ________ (be) on the phone since ten! Wait … this message is from her. Oh, she's got two tickets … but now they're sold out.
Eva: Oh.
Sam: Sorry, Eva. Sometimes people [12] ________ (sell) their tickets online. You might find one there.

3 Correct the mistake with the verb form in each sentence.

1 I'm really pleased you come to the concert tomorrow.
2 He is needing money very badly.
3 We have the same English teacher for three years.
4 I'm liking this song.
5 Remember that we meet at the shopping centre later.
6 I know her since 2010.

4 Work in pairs. Tell your partner …

1 an interesting fact about you.
2 what you think everyone in your family is doing right now.
3 something you do every week.
4 something interesting you are doing this weekend.
5 how long you've been a fan of your favourite band.
6 something you need at the moment.

VOCABULARY Verb + infinitive/-*ing* with a change in meaning

1 Read the examples. Then discuss the different meanings of the verbs in each pair.

EP

1 A **Remember to feed** her 150-person team on time.
B One promoter **remembers receiving** a demand for 20 white kittens.
2 A The lead singer **stopped to drink** some water.
B Coldplay clearly never **stop thinking** about their friends and family.
3 A I **tried listening** to his early stuff, but it's much heavier music.
B Fans can learn about **trying to reduce** their carbon footprint.

2 Complete the sentences with the correct form of the verbs in the box. Use each verb twice.

forget	remember	stop	try

1 Here's your phone. ________ not to lose it again!
2 I ________ going to my first live concert when I was 14.
3 I saw Jamie at the gig, but I didn't ________ to talk. I was in a hurry to find my seat!
4 ________ listening to their second album. It's much better than the first.
5 Don't ________ to bring your camera. I want to take lots of photos.
6 ________ to print the tickets or we can't get in.
7 You should ________ cycling with headphones on! It's really dangerous.
8 I'll never ________ meeting the band backstage. It was incredible!

3 » Work in pairs. Turn to page 120.

LISTENING

06 **1** **Listen to a girl, Alex, talking about a live music experience. Which statement describes what she says about her experience?**

A I wish I'd known more of the lyrics to the songs.
B I was disappointed not to hear many songs I knew.
C It inspired me to write my own music.

06 **2** **Read and listen again to Alex's experience. Was your answer correct in Exercise 1? Underline two sentences that explain your answer. Why are the other two statements incorrect?**

> Some friends wanted to go to the concert and the venue's close to my house. I've hardly listened to any of the band's albums, so I'm not surprised I only recognised a few of the songs. But it was absolutely amazing to watch the crowd. Thousands of devoted fans sang every song and they knew every word! It must be an incredible feeling to hear all those people singing your lyrics. I'm in a band with some friends and it really made me think that we need to do more original stuff. I've already started writing some songs and I'm quite pleased with a few so far. Writing original music is harder than you think, though!

07 **3** **Listen to four more people talking about a live music experience. Choose from the list A–F what each person says about their experience. There are two extra letters which you do not need to use.**

A I felt proud of the performance.
B I was nervous because it was my first concert.
C It was special because the venue wasn't very big.
D It encouraged me to learn a musical instrument.
E I was impressed by the musical talent.
F It was annoying to miss part of the concert.

SPEAKING Talking about your taste in music

08 **1** **You will hear a student answering four questions. Match his answers to four of the questions.**

a Do you ever go to concerts?
b How important is music to you?
c What sort of music do you listen to?
d Where do you like listening to music?
e Do you play a musical instrument?
f Do you ever listen to the radio?

2 **Do you think they were good answers to the questions? Why? / Why not?**

08 **3** **Read the *Prepare to speak* box. Then listen again to each of the student's answers. What is the problem with each answer?**

PREPARE TO SPEAK

Common mistakes in exam interviews

When you answer questions in an exam interview, you should avoid …

a very brief answers – try to speak for at least 30 seconds for each question.
b listing things – instead, try to give a few examples and justify your answers.
c talking about unrelated things – don't include irrelevant information.
d leaving your answers unfinished – finish sentences properly.

09 **4** **You are going to hear another student answer the question: *What sort of music do you listen to?* Choose three music phrases you might hear. Then listen and check.**

background music	concert venue
devoted fan	release an album
the charts	tour the world

5 **Make notes about the questions in Exercise 1 for you.**

Think about:

- avoiding making the common mistakes in the *Prepare to speak* box.
- which vocabulary related to music you can include.

6 **Ask and answer the questions in Exercise 1. Did your partner make any of the common mistakes in their answers?**

CULTURE

MUSIC FESTIVALS

1 **Ask and answer the questions.**

1 Do you prefer listening to music at home or seeing it live at concerts?
2 Have you ever been to a music festival? Where and when?
3 Are there any music festivals where you live? Are there any you'd like to go to?

2 **Read the article quickly and complete the timeline for when the four festivals first started.**

3 **Read the article again. Are the sentences true (T), false (F) or not mentioned (NM)?**

1 Editions of Lollapalooza have been held in four European capital cities.
2 The Pyramid stage at Glastonbury Festival is the largest in the UK.
3 Splendour in the Grass takes place in late summer.
4 Visitors to the festival in Byron Bay will only find food from the local area.
5 Before Rock in Rio, there had never been anything similar in South America.
6 1.5 million people attended Rock in Rio on each day of its first edition.

4 **Match the highlighted words in the article to their meanings.**

1 the area where actors or entertainers perform
2 people attending a festival
3 the place where a public event or meeting happens
4 very famous or popular
5 group of people performing at an event

10 **5** **Listen to a talk about how to organise a music festival. Number the topics in the order you hear them.**

a groups that will perform at the festival ☐
b the main idea for the festival ☐
c how green the festival will be ☐
d money needed to organise the festival ☐
e services for tickets holders ☐
f deciding on the venue for the festival ☐
g a good time to have the festival ☐

10 **6** **Listen again. Complete the sentences with information from the talk.**

1 Rachel's vision is that Summerfest festival should be ....
2 Summerfest takes place in mid-July because of the ....
3 The .... for Summerfest was London's Battersea Park.
4 *LondonScene* magazine and LON Radio are two of Summerfest's ....
5 The final point Rachel suggests thinking about is a festival's ....

7 **Complete the sentences with the words in the box.**

facilities	funding	headliners
sponsors	venue	vision

USEFUL LANGUAGE

Organising an event

1 Let's choose a .... that will be easy for most people to get to.
2 If we get more ...., we can book some really well-known bands.
3 The .... is key – I think our aim should be to have the best new music.
4 There are lots of potential .... who want to be linked to our festival.
5 We need .... who different types of festivalgoers will enjoy.
6 The .... we provide will be important for a positive overall experience.

TALKING POINTS

Which of the festivals would you prefer to go to? Why?
Do you think that five days for a music festival like Glastonbury is too long? Why? / Why not?

ON THE WORLD STAGE:

FOUR OF THE BEST MUSIC FESTIVALS

For many people around the world, holiday time is when they go to their favourite music festivals. And more often than not, music isn't the only thing on offer. **Festivalgoers** will find lots of ways to enjoy themselves and make their experience a memorable one!

11

LOLLAPALOOZA

This world-famous festival takes place at the historic Grant Park in the city of Chicago, Illinois. It hosts a diverse **line-up** of music and artists, from alternative rock to electronic, dance performances and comedy shows. Started in 1991, Lollapalooza lasts two or three days, during which time more than 160,000 people go wild listening to their favourite bands. In 2010, the festival celebrated its first edition outside the United States, in Santiago, Chile. Since then, there have been versions of the event in different South American countries, as well as in European capitals like Paris and Berlin.

The word *Lollapalooza* itself comes from an old American English phrase which means 'something outstanding or unusual'.

GLASTONBURY FESTIVAL

Glastonbury Festival is considered to be a major event in British culture. The five-day event combines contemporary music, dance, circus, comedy and theatre. It's held on a farm in the English county of Somerset. The festival has seen some of the world's biggest stars from rock, dance and pop music performing there since it began in 1970, many on its **iconic** Pyramid stage. In its first summer, tickets cost just £1 and that included milk from the farm! Around 1,500 people went to the festival that year, compared to the 135,000 tickets sold in recent years.

SPLENDOUR IN THE GRASS

This Australian event, which has been going since 2001, is much smaller than many festivals in other parts of the world. It takes place in late July or early August, which is actually Australia's winter. It attracts 30,000 people to Byron Bay, a popular beachside town in New South Wales. This music and arts festival also offers a Comedy Club and a Science tent, both with music, of course! There's also International Street Eats and the Global Village, both for hungry festivalgoers looking for some food from beyond Australia's shores.

ROCK IN RIO

Rock in Rio began in 1995 in Rio de Janeiro, Brazil, and was the first event of its kind in a South American country. The **venue** was the City of Rock, a huge stadium that was built especially for the festival and could hold 250,000 people! At the time, its 80-metre wide **stage** was the biggest in the world. This was a festival on a massive scale, and in total nearly 1.5 million music-lovers attended the festival over ten days and nights of performances. Rock in Rio festivals have also been held in Las Vegas, Madrid and Lisbon. Around 350,000 people visited the festival in the Portuguese capital's Bela Vista Park. Not bad for a city with a population of 500,000!

PROJECT

Create your own music festival

Use the topics in Exercise 5 and the *Useful language* to help you. Answer the questions.

1 What will be the vision for your festival?
2 Where and when will you hold the event?
3 How will you get the money you need to run the festival?
4 Which bands would you like to play?
5 What will you call your festival?
6 What will there be in addition to live music?
7 What might the environmental impact of your festival be, and how could you reduce it?

Make a poster to promote the event. Present your poster to the class and tell them about your festival. Would they like to go?

02 NOW WATCH THE CULTURE VIDEO

3 FAMILY MATTERS

ABOUT YOU

Which members of your family do you get on best with? Why?
Do you think family is more important than friends?

VOCABULARY Verbs of communication

12 **1 Listen to four conversations. Then match them to the pictures.**

12 **2 Listen again. Then match two quotes to each conversation.**

a 'Not me. I promise. They don't even fit me.'
b 'Why did you delete all the apps on my tablet?'
c 'If you don't reply to my texts, I'll take it away.'
d 'But I did answer it, Dad.'
e 'Well, don't leave it all until Sunday night.'
f 'Give me the tablet, Jack!'
g 'Sorry, you were out and I needed something to wear to a party.'
h 'Why not do it now?'

3 Match the sentences to the quotes in Exercise 2.

EP
1 Amy **confessed to** borrow**ing** her sister's red top.
2 Lily's dad **threatened to** take her phone away.
3 Alice's mum **suggested that** she should do some of her homework now.
4 Jack **accused** his brother **of** delet**ing** his apps.
5 Lily **claimed that** she had answered her dad's text message.
6 Alice's mum **warned** her **not to** leave all her homework until Sunday night.
7 Jack's mum **ordered** him **to** give her the tablet.
8 Amy **denied** borrow**ing** her sister's jeans.

4 Match the verbs in Exercise 3 to the meanings.

EP
a give someone an instruction that they must do
b express an idea or plan for someone to consider
c tell someone that you will cause problems for them if they do not do what you want
d make someone aware of a possible danger or problem, especially one in the future
e admit you have done something bad
f say that someone has done something bad
g say that something is true or is a fact, although you cannot prove it and other people might not believe it
h say that something is not true

5 Discuss the questions in groups. Use the verbs in Exercise 3.

1 Has anyone ever wrongly accused you of doing something? What was it?
2 Have you ever denied doing something to avoid getting into trouble? What was it?
3 When was the last time your parents ordered you to do something?
4 What kind of things do your parents warn you not to do?
5 When you need a helpful suggestion, who do you ask?

READING

1 Read the first part of the article, ignoring the gaps. Choose the best answer to complete the statement.

The article is positive news for
A all children with brothers or sisters.
B just children who have older brothers or sisters.
C all children without brothers and sisters.

2 Complete the first part of the article with the words in the box. There are two extra words that you do not need.

are	at	despite	each	few
more	of	or	out	to

3 Read the second part of the article. Complete the sentences with names. Then choose the correct words.

1 .... has got at least *two* / *three* older sisters.
2 .... has got one *older* / *younger* brother.
3 .... has got two younger *brothers* / *sisters*.
4 .... almost hurt herself because of her *brother* / *sister*.
5 .... *is more popular* / *gets better marks* because of his *brothers* / *sisters*.
6 .... got better at *maths* / *English* because of her eldest *sister* / *brother*.

BROTHERS AND SISTERS

We see them every morning. We eat with them every evening. We sometimes even share our bedrooms with them. They're our very best friends and, [0] *from* time to time, our worst enemies.

Very [1] ______ people would claim that they never fall [2] ______ with their brothers or sisters. However, according to research, this sometimes difficult relationship can actually be good for you.

When brothers and sisters quarrel with [3] ______ other, they practise social skills that [4] ______ key in adult life. They learn to understand their own feelings and they become more aware [5] ______ other people's feelings. The youngest child benefits even [6] ______. They develop better language skills for their age, compared [7] ______ other children without older brothers or sisters. Lastly, brothers and sisters are naturally competitive in everything they do. This competition often encourages them to try harder, whether they're doing sport [8] ______ schoolwork.

What are your experiences with your brothers and sisters? What do you think you've learned from them?

COMMENTS (3)

ADAM

I remember being quite mean to my youngest brother. We picked on him all the time because we were so much older than him. For instance, he used to get terrified while watching horror films. One day, while we were watching one, my other brother and I quietly left the room. Soon the film got slightly scary, and he suddenly realised he was all on his own. We'd both gone. He started screaming like a baby!

As the eldest child of three, I think I'm good at identifying with children younger than me. It's also made me more patient with younger kids at school – which means I tend to make a lot of friends.

SARA

My brother takes after my dad in that he has always been good at fixing things. One day (I was 11, he was 13), my parents were really impressed when he fixed the brakes on his bike himself. The next day, I was riding my bike down a steep hill near our house. Once I reached the bottom, I found out how he'd done it. He'd taken the brakes off my bike! Fortunately, I just managed to stop without injuring myself, but I learned something from that day – I always check my bike before I use it!

LUCY

When I was four, my sisters and I had very little money. I can't imagine I really understood what it was. But sometimes we used to get a few coins from relatives, like our grandparents. My eldest sister was 11 and she used to talk me into swapping my old, dirty coins for her new, shiny ones. What I didn't realise, of course, was that the coins she was giving me were worth less than the ones that I was giving her! I learned two things: how to count and never to depend on my eldest sister's honesty!

TALKING POINTS

What are the advantages of coming from a large family?
What are the advantages of being an only child?

GRAMMAR Past tense review

1 Match the examples to the rules.

1 He **fixed** the brakes on his bike himself.
2 The next day, I **was riding** my bike down a steep hill near our house.
3 Once I reached the bottom, I found out how he**'d done** it.
4 He **used to get** terrified while watching horror films.
5 One day, while we **were watching** one, my other brother and I quietly left the room.
6 When I **was** four, my sisters and I **had** very little money.

> We use the past simple:
> **a** for completed actions in the past.
> **b** for states in the past.
>
> We use the past continuous:
> **c** for longer events in the past.
> **d** to talk about events that were in progress when another shorter action happened.
>
> We use *used to*:
> **e** to talk about past habits.
>
> We use the past perfect:
> **f** for events that happened before another event in the past.

» GRAMMAR REFERENCE AND PRACTICE PAGE 140

2 Choose the correct verb forms.

> Both Andy Murray and his brother Jamie [1] *were / had been* good at tennis from a very young age, but when they [2] *were playing / used to play* against each other, Jamie [3] *was always winning / always won*. Then, one day, at a tournament for under-12s, Andy finally [4] *beat / used to beat* his brother. He was really pleased. He'd played against his brother hundreds of times before, but he [5] *didn't win / hadn't won* a match against him. While they [6] *were travelling / used to travel* home from the match that day, Andy [7] *started / had started* teasing Jamie about the game. Soon they [8] *fought / were fighting*. Twenty years later, Andy still has a scar on his finger from that fight!

3 Complete the story with the correct form of the verbs in brackets.

> One day, my sister Daisy and I [1] ________ (play) in the living room when suddenly my dad started shouting my sister's name. He was furious because my sister [2] ________ (write) on the walls in our bedroom. My sister [3] ________ (deny) doing it and [4] ________ (blame) me. [5] ________ (I, do) it? Of course I hadn't. I was only two and I [6] ________ (not know) how to write!

4 Correct the mistake with the verb form in each sentence.

1 Last week, I was needing some new clothes.
2 I used to work at a festival last summer.
3 The phone rang while I had dinner.
4 When we were kids, we use to go away together.
5 He choose the film that we saw.
6 We went to my house and we were watching TV.

VOCABULARY Phrasal verbs: relationships

1 Read the examples from the article on page 21. Then match the verbs to the meanings.

EP

1 We **picked on** him all the time because we were so much older than him.
2 As the eldest child of three, I think I'm good at **identifying with** children younger than me.
3 Very few people would claim that they never **fall out with** their brothers or sisters.
4 My brother **takes after** my dad in that he has always been good at fixing things.
5 She used to **talk** me **into** swapping my old, dirty coins for her new, shiny ones.
6 I learned two things: how to count and never to **depend on** my eldest sister's honesty!

a feel that you can understand someone or be able to share their feelings
b persuade someone to do something
c be similar to an older member of your family
d argue with someone and stop being friendly with them
e trust someone or something to help you
f choose a person and criticise or treat them unfairly

2 Complete the second sentence so that it has a similar meaning to the first sentence, using the word given. Do not change the word given. You must use between two and five words, including the word given.

1 My brother isn't like either of my parents. **TAKE**
My brother ________ either of my parents.
2 Lucy isn't talking to her brother because he lost her phone. **FALLEN**
Lucy has ________ her brother because he lost her phone.
3 It was hard for me to understand how the main character felt. **IDENTIFYING**
I had difficulty ________ the main character.
4 Did you persuade your parents to let you stay over? **TALK**
Did you ________ you stay over?
5 The other girls treated Maria unfairly because she was clever. **PICKED**
Maria ________ by the other girls because she was clever.
6 Michael can be trusted in a crisis. **DEPEND**
________ Michael in a crisis.

3 » Work in pairs. Turn to page 120.

WRITING An informal email

1 **Discuss the questions.**

1. Have you ever looked after a younger relative? What did you do together?
2. What activities did you enjoy when you were about 12?

2 **Read the task below. Then read Jen's email opposite. What are her suggestions?**

You have received this email from your English-speaking friend Cate.

> Hi!
>
> My 12-year-old cousin is staying with us during the holidays and I have to look after him for a few days while my parents are at work. You have a brother about that age, don't you? Have you got any suggestions? I'm sure the weather will be bad, so I'm looking for ideas for things to do indoors – at home or somewhere else.
>
> Write soon,
>
> Cate

Write your **email**.

3 **Read the *Prepare to write* box. Then read Jen's email again. Match the tips (a–f) to the underlined phrases or sentences. Some tips match two sentences.**

PREPARE TO WRITE

Informal emails and letters

- **a** Use an informal opening expression: *Dear X, Hi X, I hope you're well., How's it going?*
- **b** Use contracted forms.
- **c** Use informal language and phrasal verbs.
- **d** Use expressions for making suggestions: *What/How about … ?, You might (not) want to … , Why not … ?*
- **e** Use phrases such as *because (of), since, as* to give reasons.
- **f** Use an informal closing expression: *Have fun!, Take care, Keep in touch*

4 **Look at phrase 7 in Jen's email. What type of word do we use after *because of*?**

5 **Rewrite the sentences to give reasons. Use the words in brackets. Make any other changes necessary.**

1. I'd lost my keys, so I couldn't get into the house. (because)
2. The traffic was terrible. I was an hour late. (because of)
3. It was getting late. So we decided to stay in. (since)
4. Transport problems meant the match was cancelled. (because of)
5. Jen suggested that we went climbing, so we gave it a go. (as)

[1]Hey, Cate

[2]It's great to hear from you. Yes, my brother's exactly the same age as your cousin, so I can definitely give you some ideas.

[3]First of all, you might want to try some computer games. Most kids that age love gaming. My brother and I avoid competitive games, though, as otherwise [4]we fall out pretty quickly. He takes after me – he can't stand losing!

What about cooking something together? Since your parents will be at work all day, [5]I'm sure they'd appreciate it if you made dinner for them.

[6]If you fancy something more active, I really recommend going to an indoor climbing centre. It's a good sport to do with kids because everyone can climb at their own level. Just warn your cousin not to go too high!

And finally, [7]if you have to stay in because of the weather, a great project for a day is to make a film together. My brother is quite imaginative and he loves acting. All you need is a smartphone. And there are tons of apps that can help you.

[8]Have fun!

Jen

6 **Read the task and make notes.**

You have received this email from your English-speaking friend Seb.

> Hi!
>
> I need some help with a school project. I have to write about activities that families from different countries enjoy doing together and why they do them. Can you tell me about any activities that you and your family enjoy doing together? How do you think they help to improve your relationship with your family?
>
> Hope you can help!
>
> Seb

7 **Write your email to Seb.**

- Use the tips in the *Prepare to write* box.
- Write 140–190 words.
- Check your grammar and spelling.

4 FORCES OF NATURE

ABOUT YOU

03 Watch the video. Then answer the questions.

What examples of extreme weather have you seen on the news recently?

What kinds of extreme weather have you experienced?

Have you seen any of the extreme weather shown in the photos in your country? If so, where and when?

VOCABULARY Natural disasters: verbs

14 **1** **Read the sentences and match them to three of the photos. Then listen and check.**

EP

1. During this event, the ground shakes, sometimes so violently that buildings collapse and roads crack.
2. When it erupts, lava runs from the top down its side, and clouds of dust and toxic gas float into the air.
3. It's a huge wave that is big enough to knock over trees and smash buildings, before the water flows back out to sea and drags everything with it.

15 **2** **Discuss what has happened in photo D. Use some of the verbs from Exercise 1. Then listen and check.**

3 **Use verbs from Exercise 1 to describe some of the natural disasters in the box. Do not say which it is. Can your partner guess?**

floods	heavy snow	rainstorms
tornados	wildfires	

READING

1 **Read the article quickly, ignoring the gaps. Choose the best answer.**

The purpose of the article is to

A explain the science behind objects that enter the atmosphere.
B inform readers about the danger of asteroids crashing into Earth.
C ask readers to join in the search for dangerous asteroids.

2 **Look at the gaps in paragraph 1 and at the options at the bottom of page 25. Decide which answer (A, B, C or D) best fits each gap.**

3 **Read the article again. Then discuss the questions.**

1. Why do you think Jaime Nomen was looking at telescope images?
2. Whose telescopes do you think started following Asteroid 2012 DA14?
3. What are the pros and cons of destroying an asteroid rather than pushing it away?
4. How dangerous are asteroids to the average person? Why?

4 **Find information in the article about four different asteroids. Then compare them.**

Talk about

1. their size.
2. when they hit the Earth or passed close by.
3. where they hit or nearly hit the Earth.
4. their effects.

5 **Find an adjective in each paragraph that means** ***extremely big*****.**

ASTEROID ATTACK

16

1 **IT COULD EASILY BE THE [0] *plot* FOR A HOLLYWOOD DISASTER MOVIE:** in February 2012, a young dentist called Jaime Nomen was sailing [1] ______ the Mediterranean coast of Spain, checking images on his laptop from a telescope 600 kilometres away. Suddenly, he [2] ______ a dot of light racing through space. Nomen knew [3] ______ what it was. He warned the International Astronomical Union, which [4] ______ information about asteroids, and telescopes around the world immediately started following the new asteroid's orbit. They [5] ______ a spectacular discovery: on 15th February 2013, 'Asteroid 2012 DA14' would [6] ______ the Earth just 27,700 kilometres above our heads. In space terms, that is close – very close. Asteroid 2012 DA14 was 30 metres across, which is enormous, but not quite as large as the asteroid that [7] ______ in 1908 over the remote Tunguska region of Siberia, Russia. The Tunguska event destroyed 80 million trees across 2,000 square kilometres and even people over 60 kilometres away were [8] ______ over.

2 **STRANGELY ENOUGH,** on the same day in February 2013 that Asteroid 2012 DA14 passed the Earth, a slightly smaller asteroid suddenly appeared over the Chelyabinsk region of Russia. It was travelling at 70,000 km/h and was apparently almost as bright as the Sun. It was around 17 metres across, easily the largest object to enter the Earth's atmosphere since 1908. It exploded before it hit the Earth, and a massive shock wave cracked glass and ruined buildings hundreds of kilometres away.

3 **IN TERMS OF POTENTIAL DAMAGE,** a Tunguska-sized asteroid (50–100 metres across) would be a good deal worse. It could easily destroy a city, and at sea it would trigger a terrible tsunami. Some asteroids are far bigger than that – up to 10 kilometres across – and would generate such a powerful explosion that clouds of dust would cover the Earth for years. This means life on Earth could even be in danger. A huge asteroid like this crashed in the Yucatán Peninsula in Mexico 65 million years ago and contributed to the death of a lot of plant and animal life on Earth – including the extinction of the dinosaurs.

4 **SO HOW CAN WE PREDICT FUTURE ASTEROID CRASHES** and, more importantly, can we prevent them? Asteroid scientists believe they have identified 90% of the giant space rocks with the potential to hit the Earth, but the smaller the asteroids are, the harder it is to spot them. However, smaller asteroids are likely to cause less destruction if they hit the Earth.

5 **TO PREVENT A MAJOR DISASTER LIKE YUCATÁN,** it would be far too risky to blow up an asteroid with a bomb. This would break it into millions of pieces, but thousands of smaller rocks would still hit the Earth. In the long term, the best way to avoid a serious incident is to use a spacecraft to push an asteroid in a different direction, over a period of five to ten years. But the pushing technique is so slow that an asteroid might hit the Earth before its orbit has moved far enough away. Scientists need more time to find faster ways of protecting Earth from asteroids, which is why, in the short term, it is so vital that we keep an eye on every single asteroid heading for the Earth.

6 **IF THIS ALL SOUNDS RATHER TERRIFYING, RELAX.** There are no confirmed reports of human death being caused by rocks from space. The vast majority of the Earth's surface is unpopulated, so the chances of something landing on your head are pretty small.

	A	B	C	D
0	A concept	(B) plot	C review	D report
1	A along	B amongst	C beneath	D throughout
2	A blinked	B displayed	C searched	D spotted
3	A absolutely	B actually	C completely	D exactly
4	A browses	B broadcasts	C collects	D observes
5	A did	B got	C had	D made
6	A cover	B pass	C travel	D tour
7	A burned	B exploded	C erupted	D smashed
8	A fallen	B knocked	C run	D taken

TALKING POINTS

Do you think we should be worried about asteroids crashing into Earth? Why? / Why not?

What warning systems have you heard of for other natural disasters?

GRAMMAR Making comparisons

1 **Read the examples. Then complete the rules with the words in the box.**

1 The asteroid was **not quite as large as** the one that exploded in 1908.
2 A **slightly smaller** asteroid suddenly appeared.
3 It was apparently **almost as bright as** the Sun.
4 It was **easily the largest** object to enter the Earth's atmosphere since 1908.
5 In terms of potential damage, this asteroid would be **a good deal worse**.
6 Some asteroids are **far bigger than** that.
7 **The smaller** asteroids are, **the harder** it is to spot them.

almost	easily	far	good	quite	~~slightly~~

We can use these patterns to make comparisons:
a *slightly* bigger (than) • a bit bigger (than) • a little bigger (than)
b ________ as big as • nearly as big as
c a ________ deal bigger than • much bigger than • ________ bigger than • a lot bigger than
d ________ the biggest • by far the biggest
e not ________ as big as
f the bigger, the better

» GRAMMAR REFERENCE AND PRACTICE PAGE 141

2 **Look at the rules again.**

Which patterns are used to describe a
1 small difference? 2 big difference?

3 **Choose the correct words.**

1 Asia is *easily* / *far* the largest continent.
2 Australia is slightly *than smaller* / *smaller than* Europe.
3 Antarctica is *far* / *far more* colder than anywhere else.
4 K2 is 8,611 metres high, but Mount Everest is a *slightly* / *little* higher.
5 The *more hot* / *hotter* the climate, the more you have to drink.

4 **Complete the text with the phrases in the box.**

a lot less harmful	almost as active as	by far the strongest
bigger than	powerful than	the smaller

Last night's earthquake in Hawaii, measuring 6.9 on the Richter scale, is [1] ________ earthquake recorded in the North Pacific in recent years. It was [2] ________ the last earthquake in the area ten years ago. Forecasters have predicted that a second earthquake is likely to follow, certainly no more [3] ________ the first and possibly [4] ________. Of course, a major landslide into the sea could cause a tsunami, but the weaker the earthquake, [5] ________ the risk of a landslide. Hawaii is no stranger to the forces of nature, being home to one of the most active volcanoes on Earth, Kilauea. Kilauea is [6] ________ Stromboli in Italy, which has erupted continuously for almost 2,000 years.

5 **Write sentences with the adjectives in brackets to compare these things. Then check your answers on page 120.**

1 the River Amazon / the River Thames (long)
2 the Red Sea / the Pacific Ocean (small)
3 Tokyo / São Paulo / New York (big)
4 the Sahara Desert / the Atacama Desert / the Dry Valleys in Antarctica (dry)

VOCABULARY *too … to, so … that, such … that*

1 **Complete the examples with the phrases in the box. Check your answers in the article on page 25.**

far too risky **to**	so vital **that**
such a powerful explosion **that**	
so slow **that**	

1 Some asteroids would generate ________ clouds of dust would cover the Earth for years.
2 To prevent a major disaster like Yucatán, it would be ________ blow up an asteroid with a bomb.
3 The pushing technique is ________ an asteroid might hit Earth before its orbit had moved far enough away.
4 That is why in the short term, it is ________ we keep an eye on every single asteroid heading for Earth.

2 **Complete the sentences using** ***too … to, so … that*** **or** ***such … that*** **and the words in brackets.**

0 There are far *too many people to* (people) fit on the bus.
1 The last exam was ________ (hard) I could only answer half of it.
2 I'm going to get the bus. It'd cost far ________ (money) go home by taxi.
3 This is ________ (a boring book) I stopped reading it halfway through.
4 This soup is boiling. It's far ________ (hot) eat.
5 There are ________ (films) choose from. I can't decide which to watch.
6 My teammates always need ________ (help) I might as well be in a one-person team.

3 » **Work in pairs. Student A, turn to page 121. Student B, turn to page 127.**

LISTENING

1 **Look at the pictures of sinkholes. What is a sinkhole, and why do you think they appear?**

New York, USA

Fukuoka City, Japan

17 **2** **Listen to a news broadcast and check.**

17 **3** **Are the sentences true or false? Correct the false ones. Then listen again and check.**

1 The New York sinkhole was nearly 20 feet across.
2 Cars were damaged when the sinkhole opened up.
3 Sinkholes are far more common in Florida than in New York.
4 Sinkholes are always caused by natural events.
5 Most sinkholes occur outside urban areas.
6 When windows crack, it is a warning that a sinkhole is about to appear.
7 The Fukuoka sinkhole hurt around 100 people.
8 They fixed the enormous Fukuoka sinkhole in five days.

SPEAKING Discussing options

1 **Look at the items in an emergency survival kit. When might you need these things?**

18 **2** **Listen to two people talking about the survival kit. Which two of the three things do they do?**

1 Describe each item in the picture.
2 Talk about why you might need these things after a disaster.
3 Decide which three are the most important.

18 **3** **Read the *Prepare to speak* box. Then listen again. Which expressions do you hear?**

PREPARE TO SPEAK | Discussing options

Bear in mind that …
Don't forget that …
What if there's no … ?
If you think about it, …
It seems pretty obvious that …
Surely … is by far the most essential one.
I'd have thought that …
We're bound to need … because …

4 **Discuss what you would and would not need in the situations, and what you would do to survive.**

- Bear in mind that you're together rather than alone.
- Include the items in the emergency survival kit and more items of your own choice.
- Use phrases from the *Prepare to speak* box.

1 You're driving off-road in the Simpson Desert, Australia. It's 45°C and the nearest town is 500 km away. Suddenly, your car breaks down.
2 You go diving off a boat in the Andaman Sea, 20 km off the coast of Thailand. Unfortunately, you lose sight of the other divers in your group and when you get back to the surface, the dive boat has gone.
3 You're skiing off-piste in the Austrian Alps. Unexpectedly, a heavy snow storm starts. Soon you can't see further than about 5 metres and all around you, big piles of snow are getting deeper.

LIFE SKILLS PHYSICAL WELL-BEING

PERSONAL SAFETY

1 **Ask and answer the questions.**

1 Can you remember any recent natural disasters? Which ones and where?
2 What should you do in case of a fire at home?
3 How can we plan for the possibility of a fire at home and prevent one from happening?

2 **Read the text quickly. Are any of your ideas from questions 2 and 3 in Exercise 1 mentioned?**

3 **Read the text again. Then answer the questions.**

1 How often should you check that a smoke alarm is working correctly?
2 What shouldn't you do with a microwave? Why?
3 Should you always disconnect an electrical device which is burning? Why? / Why not?
4 What should you do if you have visitors staying with you?
5 What should you do when you first discover a fire?

4 **Match the highlighted words in the text to the meanings.**

1 something which is not covered / not protected
2 the grey or black gas that is produced when something burns
3 make it difficult to pay attention
4 place to connect a plug to an electricity supply
5 stop a fire

LIFE SKILLS

Personal safety

Knowing how to keep yourself safe in a dangerous situation can mean the difference between life and death. This involves careful planning to ensure your personal safety in the event of a problem, as well as knowing how to react and recover from an event. These skills can be applied in any emergency situation, not just when natural disasters strike.

FIRE SAFETY AT HOME: what you need to know!

19

Even a small fire in the home can have serious consequences. Luckily, a little knowledge about what to do in the event of a fire can help to keep you safe. It's important to know how to minimise the risk of fire and how to get out of your home quickly and safely. Here are some simple tips to follow.

1 Your family can install smoke alarms at different levels in your house. If there's a fire, these will give you a few minutes' warning. The batteries in alarms should be checked regularly, at least once a month.

2 Many fires at home start in the kitchen. Try not to distract anyone who is cooking and be extra careful when you cook with oil, because it can catch fire easily. It's a good idea to have a fire blanket in the kitchen to help extinguish fires. And don't put anything with metal parts in the microwave, because it can start a fire.

3 Always put candles in a stable candle-holder and on a heat-resistant surface. And don't place them near curtains or furniture. You should never leave burning candles unattended in a room – a naked flame can easily start a fire.

5 Listen to a radio interview with a safety expert. Then answer the questions. (20)

1 What is the interview about?
2 What is the last thing that needs to be done with a plan?

6 Listen again. Are the sentences true (T), false (F) or not mentioned (NM)? (20)

1 We should only plan for emergencies which we know have happened before.
2 The first step in creating a plan involves the prediction and prevention of emergencies.
3 It's also important to protect wildlife when a natural disaster strikes.
4 Having a planned escape route is part of responding to an emergency.
5 Recovery from an emergency is normally quite fast.

4 It's better to have only one device connected to each wall socket. Too many devices in the same socket can cause overheating. If a fire starts with an electrical device, never try to extinguish it with water! Disconnect the device, but only if you can do so safely.

5 Plan a fire escape route with your family and make sure that you tell any visitors who are staying for the night what the route is. Always remember to leave door and window keys in an accessible place for everyone. If your building has one, never use a lift to escape.

6 If you discover a fire, you should always try to find an adult to help you. If you're alone and it's only a small fire, try to put it out yourself using a fire blanket or extinguisher. But if it's a big fire, it's a job for the professionals! So leave your home immediately and call the emergency services. Make sure you know the number you need to call. And never go back into a building that's on fire. It can put your safety and the safety of others at risk.

7 Complete the sentences with the words in the box.

critical	procedure	recover
reduce	respond	scenario

USEFUL LANGUAGE

Describing a plan

1 Any actions which are taken in the first few minutes are ________.
2 We should make plans for any potential emergency ________ where there is a threat or risk to personal safety.
3 The key here is to identify things which will ________ injuries, deaths or damage to property.
4 The next important area to consider is: how can we ________ to the emergency situation?
5 There needs to be a clear ________ for contacting and coordinating with emergency services.
6 There's one final area to include, and that's how to ________ from the emergency.

PROJECT

An emergency response plan

Work in groups to create an emergency or disaster response plan for your school. Use these steps to help you.

1 Brainstorm possible natural disasters or emergency events which could happen at your school and decide on one together.
2 Create an emergency response plan (ERP). Give group members different parts of the plan to work on and then coordinate your ideas:
   - predicting or preventing an emergency or event
   - protecting people and reducing the impact
   - procedures for responding to the emergency
   - recovering from the event.

   Use the phrases from *Useful language* when you discuss your ideas.
3 Decide on a format to present your work: poster, presentation, physical demonstration, video, etc.

Present your ERP to the class.

REVIEW 1 UNITS 1–4

VOCABULARY

1 Complete the sentences with the correct phrasal verbs. Use a word from A and a word from B.

A break figure get x2 go hand note put

B down for in x2 off on out up

1 Do you know when we ______ for the summer holidays?
2 Please ______ the details in case you need them later.
3 We had to ______ three essays yesterday.
4 I hope you ______ OK this term; you have a very full timetable!
5 I can't ______ how to change my password.
6 Sam has ______ meeting us again. I'm beginning to think he doesn't want to see us!
7 I was nervous when Georgia asked me to make a speech at our graduation party, but later I decided to ______ it.
8 I've trained for the hockey team for ages, so I hope I ______!

2 Complete the text with suitable music nouns. The first letter of each word is given to help you.

The band Bad Buildings have just released the third [1] t______ from their debut [2] a______, *A Pocket of Slow Blinks*, and now they're on a [3] w______ tour. The band are giving a special [4] p______ in Prague for 100 devoted [5] f______ who won tickets in a competition. The gig is at the famous Klub 007, 'probably the best small concert [6] v______ in Western Europe,' says Steven Hay, the band's lead [7] s______.

3 Complete the second sentence so that it has a similar meaning to the first. Use two words from the box in each sentence.

accused be confessed denied losing not of ordered suggested that to wait

1 'Why don't you study a bit harder?' said the teacher.
The teacher ______ ______ we should study a bit harder.
2 'Don't be late!' my dad said.
My dad warned us ______ to ______ late.
3 'Stay there a moment!' said the police officer.
The police officer ______ us to ______.
4 'I didn't lose your glasses. It wasn't me!' said Tommy.
Tommy ______ ______ the glasses.
5 'You've broken my phone,' Ted said to his sister.
Ted ______ his sister ______ breaking his phone.
6 'I'm sorry, I took £5 from the drawer,' Isla said.
Isla ______ ______ taking £5 from the drawer.

4 Complete the texts using two of the three natural disaster verbs in brackets.

The earthquake started at around 10 pm local time. The ground [1] ______ violently and a wall next to me [2] ______. (knocked over / shook / collapsed)

The River Thames has burst its banks. River water is flooding into the busy town centre, [3] ______ trees and vehicles with it. Cars are [4] ______ down the main street. (cracking / dragging / floating)

Whenever the volcano [5] ______, lava [6] ______ down the northern side of the volcano into the sea, but the urban areas to the south tend not to be affected. (runs / erupts / smashes)

GRAMMAR

1 Choose the correct option, a or b.

1 Who helped you with the homework?
a No one, I did it all myself.
b I didn't help anyone.

2 Wait a moment, …
a my phone rings.
b my phone is ringing.

3 When I was younger, …
a I used to ride a bike all the time.
b I was riding a bike all the time.

4 Since the start of this year, …
a I've been to the cinema about 15 times.
b I went to the cinema about 15 times.

5 Look at these phones.
a Which are you preferring?
b Which do you prefer?

6 Once I got to college, I realised …
a I'd forgotten my tablet.
b I forgot my tablet.

7 I've arranged to meet Danielle. We …
a meet next Thursday at 6 pm.
b 're meeting next Thursday at 6 pm.

8 What did Anna's car damage?
a It damaged a bus stop.
b A bus drove into it.

9 Kevin dropped his laptop while …
a he had run for the bus.
b he was running for the bus.

10 When we lived in New York, …
a I was speaking English all the time.
b I spoke English all the time.

2 Complete the questions using the correct form of the verbs in brackets.

1 '______ (visit) London?'
'Yes, I have. I've visited London twice.'
2 'What ______ (say)?'
'I didn't say anything.'
3 'Who ______ (know) at the party?'
'I didn't know anyone.'
4 'What ______ (do)?'
'I'm not doing anything.'
5 'Who ______ (email)?'
'Simon emailed the school.'
6 'Who ______ (give) this number?'
'I was given this number by a friend.'

3 Complete the conversation with the words and phrases in the box.

almost as	as	easily	good deal
not quite	than	the	the better

Sam: Although my laptop's brand new, it's [1] ______ as fast [2] ______ yours. It's still a [3] ______ faster [4] ______ the last one I had, though.
Amy: Yours is the 8GB model, so it's [5] ______ quick as mine, isn't it?
Sam: No, yours is [6] ______ the fastest.
Amy: Well, [7] ______ faster [8] ______, I always say!

4 Choose the correct words.

1 'Who *called you* / *did you call* at lunchtime?'
'I called Marc. Why?'
2 I *go* / *'ve been* to three birthday parties this month.
3 I don't play football as much as I *had done* / *used to do*.
4 I think my town will be *bigger* / *more bigger* in 20 years' time.

5 Correct the mistake in each sentence.

1 How much it costs exactly?
2 My cousin is visiting me sometimes.
3 He studied there since September.
4 The second restaurant was far better as the first.

6 Read the text and think of the word which best fits each gap. Use only one word in each gap.

SCHOOLING VS UNSCHOOLING

It's 8.45 am on a school day, and whilst millions of schoolchildren are sitting [0] *down* in class, Natasha and Toby Lewis are in their kitchen making models of kangaroos. Natasha (14) and Toby (9) don't go to school, but they aren't 'home-schooled' [1] ______. Natasha and Toby are 'unschooled'. It all started two years ago, when they were being picked [2] ______ at school. The siblings were never going to [3] ______ on there, so their parents decided to [4] ______ out unschooling. Unschooled children have complete freedom to decide what they want to do. As long [5] ______ parents can prove the children are learning, this is allowed. It was Toby's suggestion [6] ______ make kangaroos – his inspiration came from a recent zoo visit, and his kangaroo is a painted pottery model. Natasha's a fan of animatronics, and inside her cardboard kangaroo there's a tiny motor [7] ______ allows it to move [8] ______ a robot.

7 Read the text and decide which answer (A, B, C or D) best fits each gap.

Ahead in music

Following a sports accident, a teenager has [0] *discovered* a hidden musical talent and can now play 13 different instruments.

Lianne Woodson, 19, was once a keen lacrosse player, but she had little [1] ______ in music. However, after a particularly bad sports [2] ______, she ended up in hospital having [3] ______ the back of her head on the ground.

Lianne was really upset when doctors [4] ______ her to stay off the sports field. But soon after, she discovered her new musical abilities. [5] ______ having no musical training, Lianne suddenly found she could play a [6] ______ of instruments, including the guitar and the piano.

Doctors believe the accident [7] ______ a previously unused part of Lianne's brain – one which controls musical skill. Lianne can't play lacrosse for her school any more, but she's [8] ______ use of her new skills by playing in the school band.

	A	B	C	D
0	detected	(B) discovered	located	revealed
1	affection	enthusiasm	interest	passion
2	injury	pain	scar	wound
3	beaten	broken	collapsed	smashed
4	demanded	requested	suggested	ordered
5	Although	Despite	Even	Just
6	figure	number	sum	total
7	attracted	inspired	motivated	stimulated
8	taking	making	having	keeping

5 VIRTUAL ACTION

ABOUT YOU

Which video games do you enjoy playing? Why?
What devices do you prefer to play games on? (PC, games console, phone, tablet, etc.) Why?

VOCABULARY Video gaming: verbs

1 Look at photos A–D. What types of game are they?

21 **2 Listen to Michelle and Zach talking about video games. Then answer the questions.**

1. Which game from Exercise 1 do they not mention?
2. Which game does Zach initially think is boring?
3. Which game is Zach playing the most at the moment?
4. Which is Michelle's favourite game at the moment?

22 **3 Complete the paragraphs with the verbs in the boxes. Then listen and check.**

EP

constructing exchanging gathering interacting

You can do stuff like [1] ______ whole towns if you want to. I love that whole process of [2] ______ everything I need, buying it or just [3] ______ stuff with villagers. And because there are about ten of us playing, I'm [4] ______ with friends the whole time.

balance dive roll slide

You can [5] ______ down a roof, jump off it and [6] ______ along the ground in seconds. If someone is shooting, you can react in lots of different ways, like you can build a wall really quickly and [7] ______ behind it. You can even do tricks, like you can jump on top of a moving rocket and [8] ______ on it as it flies along.

brake chase overtake reverse steer

I can [9] ______ round obstacles that appear without ever crashing. I can [10] ______ most of the cars I come across. I can even [11] ______ to get away from people. If another car starts to [12] ______ me and it's catching up, I [13] ______ to slow down, and then turn the steering wheel really quickly, and the car spins around and then I'm reversing. You just have to be careful that you don't roll it over.

4 Imagine you are playing a game. Read the problems. What would you do in each case? Answer using the verbs in Exercise 3.

1. You're driving very fast and suddenly you realise you're about to crash into a wall.
2. You're hungry and you don't have any food, but you have some gold coins.
3. You need to get past a massive wall. You can see a tiny window high up. You're standing next to a tree with a long branch that passes a few metres from the window.
4. It's cold and you need somewhere to cook your dinner and then sleep. There are a lot of pieces of wood around you in the forest.
5. You're chasing a car, but a slow truck has appeared in front of you.

5 Describe what happens in your favourite games. Use the verbs in Exercise 3.

READING

1 Look at the title of the article. Then discuss the questions.

1. In what ways might video games be good for you?
2. How might playing video games make you smarter?

2 Read the article quickly and check your ideas.

3 Read the article again. Are the sentences true or false, according to the article?

1. Playing games can help your brain to work faster.
2. Playing fitness games can help you learn how to make decisions.
3. Games can teach you that sometimes things are too difficult to achieve.
4. Playing role-playing games can help you become a successful leader.
5. Playing games can make you more unfit.
6. There is no evidence that violent games can have a bad effect on you.

4 Discuss your own opinions about the sentences in Exercise 3.

23

VIDEO GAMES

Have fun and get smarter?

We all know about the pleasure and satisfaction that you can get from playing video games. There's the sense of achievement when you finally reach the last level of a game after months of trying, or the feeling of pride when you beat your best friend for the first time. But some experts now say that, as well as offering fantastic entertainment, video games might also be good for you. Too good to be true? Read on and find out!

It seems that when you play video games, you might be acquiring some very important skills. For a start, games are great for your concentration. Being able to focus on a task for an extended period of time is definitely a skill you can use at school or later, in a job. Because you have to think incredibly quickly, video games can also stimulate your brain and improve the speed at which you react. Fitness games, which are still very popular, allow you to practise sports techniques like balancing or hitting balls from the comfort of your living room. A lot of games also teach decision-making skills. For example, when you have to choose the best way to escape from a trap in a game, you're learning how to solve problems and use your judgment quickly, and under pressure – skills that will be very useful later in life. Gaming teaches you about success and failure, too. The fact that a lot of games are difficult, and you have to work hard to reach the top level, teaches you determination. In life and in games, you can succeed if you keep on trying.

Some psychologists believe that role-playing games are particularly valuable. In the virtual environment, young people can take on roles that are often not available to them in real life. This can help develop character; for example, someone whose natural character is quiet and shy might find that, in a role-play situation, they find the confidence to be outgoing and brave. You can become a leader who has to inspire and encourage a team, or lead them against players who are attacking your group. By dealing with these situations, you can develop social skills that might help you in the real world when you're older.

Gaming does have its downsides, of course. Playing for a while is great, but people who play for hours on end can have problems. Physically, it can stop you from getting enough exercise, which is unhealthy. Psychologically, there is evidence that players can become addicted to their games and begin to prefer their 'virtual' lives, where they are always in control. It is sometimes claimed that very violent games can have a negative effect on players and lead to violence in real life. Although there isn't much evidence to support it, this is an argument that will go on and on.

Overall, the message is that playing video games is not harmful, unless you spend too much time on them. And while you're constructing your city, gathering valuable items, defeating your enemies or making your fortune in a game, you're also developing useful skills that will stay with you for the rest of your life.

5 Find the words in the article.

1. the opposites of *harmless*, *healthy*, *positive*
2. the adverbs related to the adjectives *incredible*, *physical*, *psychological*
3. the noun forms of *concentrate*, *entertaining*, *violent*

TALKING POINTS

What are some other advantages of video games?
Is there a connection between violence in video games and violence in real life?
How easy is it to become addicted to video games?

GRAMMAR Relative clauses

1 **Read the examples. Then complete the rules with the words in the box.**

Defining relative clauses

1 People **who play for hours on end** can have problems.
2 This is an argument **that will go on and on.**
3 Someone **whose natural character is quiet and shy** might find that in a role-play situation …

Non-defining relative clauses

4 Fitness games**, which are still very popular,** allow you to practise sports techniques.
5 Players can begin to prefer their 'virtual' lives**, where they are always in control**.

that	where	which	who	whose

a A defining relative clause explains who, what or where we are talking about.
We use:
[1] ________ or *that* for people
which or [2] ________ for things
[3] ________ for places
[4] ________ for possession.

b A non-defining relative clause gives extra information about a noun. The main clause makes sense with or without the relative clause. We use a comma before and after the clause. We can't replace *who* or [5] ________ with *that*.

» GRAMMAR REFERENCE AND PRACTICE PAGE 142

2 **Match the sentence halves. Add *who*, *which*, *whose* or *where*.**

0 f – I've got to the level where you get another life.

0 ~~I've got to the level~~	a you mustn't forget.
1 I don't like people	b I lent you?
2 What's the website	c brother broke my Wii.
3 I'll give you a password	d cheat at video games.
4 I like computer games	e you usually buy games?
5 He's the guy	f ~~you get another life.~~
6 Can you return the game	g are really exciting.

3 **Write definitions for the words in the box. Use the sentence beginnings below to make defining relative clauses.**

~~blog~~ chatroom email gamer the internet keyboard mouse password programmer screen social media site webcam

This is a person who / a thing which / a place where …

blog: This is a short article which someone writes about their opinions or experiences and posts online.

4 **Work in pairs. Read your definitions from Exercise 3. Can your partner guess the words?**

5 **Rewrite the pairs of sentences with a non-defining relative clause at the place marked *.**

0 *Pong* * was my uncle's favourite game. It was first sold in 1972.
Pong, which was first sold in 1972, was my uncle's favourite game.
1 Simon * sits next to me in class. He is brilliant at driving games.
2 Cupertino * is in California. Apple Computers is based there.
3 My brother * is brilliant at *Rocket League*. He is only seven.
4 *Minecraft* * still has millions of players. It's quite an old game.

6 **Choose the correct options.**

1 I was playing against my mates, *that* / *who* are much better than me.
2 This game's about a character *has* / *who has* to get back to Earth.
3 We visited a web page *which* / *where* they give game hints.
4 Is Ali the guy *which* / *whose* Instagram was hacked?
5 This is an area *that* / *where* you can use public wi-fi.

VOCABULARY Nouns: *-ness* and *-ment*

1 **Read the examples. Which ending can we add to adjectives to make nouns? Which can we add to verbs to make nouns?**

1 It's important to keep **fit**. **Fitness** games allow you to practise sports techniques like balancing or hitting balls.
2 People will **argue** about this a lot. The **arguments** will go on and on, I think.

2 EP **Make nouns from the adjectives and verbs in the boxes. Then use them to complete the sentences.**

dark	friendly	tired	weak

1 Asking for help isn't a sign of ________.
2 The lights went out and we were left in total ________.
3 ________ meant we made a few mistakes in the test.
4 What I love about this school is the ________ of all the students.

arrange	embarrass	encourage	treat

5 Who made all the ________ for the party?
6 My dog received very prompt ________ at the vet's.
7 My parents and teachers gave me a lot of ________ to apply to university.
8 I can't get over the ________ of my dad singing at my party. It was dreadful!

3 » **Work in pairs. Student A, turn to page 121. Student B, turn to page 127.**

WRITING A review

1 Read the exam task. What should you include in your review?

1. a description of the game
2. the good and bad points about the game
3. where you bought the game
4. your opinion, and whether or not you recommend the game

You see this notice on a school website.

> **Reviews wanted**
>
> We are looking for reviews of computer games. Write a review of a computer game you have played. What happens in the game? What do you like or dislike about it? Would you recommend it to other people of your age?
>
> We will publish the best reviews on our website.

Write your **review**.

2 Read the review of *DeepSpace*. Does it include all the points from Exercise 1? Is the review positive, negative or mixed?

DeepSpace

a *DeepSpace* is a multi-player game that you can play with other gamers online. Your spaceship has crash-landed on an ancient planet called Awaba, which is full of disgusting creatures called Magnatrons. The aim of the game is to find the parts you need to mend your spaceship so you can escape. At the same time, of course, you have to make sure the Magnatrons don't get you!

b As you go through the levels, you can get new skills to help you, but you can also lose points if the Magnatrons catch you. The game is packed with surprises, so it's never boring. The graphics are superb, too, especially once you get inside the Magnatrons' city.

c There are a few ridiculous things which are a bit annoying, for example you lose points when you can't complete a challenge the first time you try. And there are a few bugs, which can slow you down.

d Overall, *DeepSpace* is a fun game with some fantastic features. I'd recommend it to anyone who enjoys action fantasy games.

3 Read the *Prepare to write* box. Match paragraphs a–d in the review of *DeepSpace* to the four functions below.

> **PREPARE TO WRITE** A review
>
> In a review:
> - organise your ideas into paragraphs.
> - write in an informal style.
> - use extreme adjectives, e.g. *disgusting*, *superb*, to show how positive or negative you feel.
> - end the review with a recommendation.

1. positive points about the game
2. conclusion and recommendation
3. introduction
4. negative points about the game

4 Read the review of *DeepSpace* again. Match the extreme adjectives to the meanings.

1 very silly 2 very old 3 very full 4 really horrible 5 very good

5 Read a review of *Megalopolis*. Is the review positive or negative about the game?

MEGALOPOLIS 2025

In this game, you have to construct a city and help it develop. It's a game for solo gamers playing offline. The aim of the game is to keep your city running smoothly, but lots of things can go wrong. You might find the weather is **freezing** for two weeks and you can't move any goods in or out of the city, so you run out of food. Or you might get a strange illness in the city, which makes everyone so **exhausted** that they can't work.

There are some good ideas in the game, which make it challenging. Planning and constructing your city is fun, and I guess in some ways it's **fascinating** to see how your city changes over time.

There are a few problems, though. The biggest is that there isn't enough action. The game is too slow! Sometimes nothing seems to happen for ages, so the game can feel **endless**. Some of the graphics are **dreadful**, too. The characters look old-fashioned and not realistic at all.

The game has some interesting ideas, but I wouldn't recommend it. There are much better city-building games out there!

6 Look at the extreme adjectives in bold in the *Megalopolis* review. What do they mean?

7 Read the task in Exercise 1 again. Then plan your review.

- Choose a game that you know, or invent one.
- Make notes about
  - what happens in the game
  - why you like the game
  - what you don't like about the game.

8 Write your review.

- Use the tips in the *Prepare to write* box.
- Write 140–190 words.
- Check your grammar and spelling.

6 LIVE TO EAT!

ABOUT YOU

04 Watch the video. Then answer the questions.

What types of restaurant do you typically go to?

Are you adventurous with food or do you always eat the same things?

Do you eat to live or live to eat? Why?

VOCABULARY Food and drink: phrasal verbs

1 Match the question halves.

You and food

1 How often do you eat out
2 Do you tend to live on
3 Do you wait for coffee to cool down or
4 Have you had to cut out
5 Do you ever fill up on
6 Were you made to eat up
7 When your parents are out, do you cook properly or just heat up
8 If you think something might have gone off,

a a ready meal or leftovers?
b do you like to drink it hot?
c any food from your diet for any reason?
d with your friends?
e all your vegetables as a child?
f just one type of food, like pasta?
g do you ever risk eating it?
h snacks between meals?

2 Match the phrasal verbs in Exercise 1 to the meanings.

EP

a eat in a restaurant
b eat all the food you have been given
c make food hot so it can be eaten
d stop being good to eat because it is too old
e become less hot
f only eat a particular type of food
g become full and unable to eat more
h stop eating or drinking something completely, often for health reasons

3 Ask and answer the questions in Exercise 1.

24 **4** Listen to two people talking about food. Do you think they eat to live or live to eat? Which person do you think you are most similar to? Why? Use some of the phrasal verbs in Exercise 1 in your answer.

READING

1 Look at the photo opposite and answer the questions. Then read the article quickly to check.

1 Do you recognise this person?
2 What do you think he is doing?
3 What does it mean if a video *goes viral*?
4 Can you remember any videos that have gone viral over the past few years?

2 You are going to read an article about someone who reviews restaurants. For questions 1–6, choose the answer which you think fits best according to the text.

1 What do we learn about fried-chicken restaurants in London in the first paragraph?
A They are particularly popular because of their low cost.
B They have just become more popular than burger restaurants.
C Many of them are starting to change the way they cook.
D One in a thousand Londoners visits them frequently.

2 Elijah was inspired to start making the videos because he
A saw an opportunity to do something that nobody else was doing.
B wanted to help his friends find the cheapest places to eat.
C was encouraged to do so by a friend.
D thought he could do better than the presenter on a TV show he saw.

3 What particularly impressed the writer about the first video?
A the serious tone of Elijah's review
B how well it had been filmed
C the range of things Elijah talked about
D the consideration for people on a tight budget

The Chicken Connoisseur

Elijah Quashie found fame online when his chicken shop review went viral. ***Alice Kirby*** *reports.*

Elijah Quashie has always been a big fan of fried chicken and has eaten out at fried chicken restaurants for many years. In London, Elijah's home town, there are 8,000 fried chicken shops – that's one for every thousand people. The popularity of these shops is explained by the fact that millions of people love fried chicken and, of course, its price. While nowadays some fried chicken shops use better-quality ingredients, cooked in healthier ways, the majority of them are cheaper than any other fast-food shops, including the burger chains.

Looking back, Elijah says he got the idea while watching a competitive cooking show online. A critic was reviewing a contestant's dish, which looked like the kind of food you'd get at a top restaurant. Elijah rarely ate food like this and started wondering why there weren't reviews of restaurants that he and his friends went to. People like him were far more interested in finding the best places for cheap fried chicken, he thought. After chatting with a friend and video producer, who agreed to help him, Elijah decided to review these restaurants himself and post the videos on YouTube. He called his channel 'The Chicken Connoisseur'.

For the first review, Elijah reviewed a chicken shop in East London. The Chicken Connoisseur gave a detailed account of his opinion of the chicken, from its appearance to how spicy it was, along with his assessment of the chips and even the sauces. Special emphasis was given to value for money. But what struck me about this six-minute video was the quality of its production. Elijah and his friend weren't messing about. With lively music and cool special effects, the review looked like a professionally made show.

Then there was Elijah himself. With his boyish looks, many people significantly underestimated his age. Indeed, the idea of a teenager producing these videos probably helped with the story's initial appeal. Elijah was actually in his early twenties. But he was a *born* presenter. Dressed smartly, he was relaxed, confident and funny. And the reviews' success has mainly come from those qualities. Other elements helped, of course. Elijah introduced many viewers to slang they had never heard before. Words like *peng* (meaning 'good') and *gassed* (meaning 'very excited'). And the *crep check* (*crep* means 'shoes'), part of the show where Elijah gets to show off one of his pairs of rare trainers, is definitely *peng*.

When Elijah posted the sixth episode of *The Pengest Munch*, some 15 months later, the videos typically had around 700 views each and there were merely 150 subscribers to the channel. Then, out of nowhere, the sixth review went viral, spreading quickly across social networks. Hundreds of new people were subscribing to his YouTube channel every minute. Soon the story was all over the news, and requests for TV interviews started to come in from all over the world. In one of them, Elijah admitted that since everything had taken off, he had been extremely busy. 'It's kind of what I wanted, *just not necessarily at this scale*,' he said. *line 55*

Six months later, interest might have faded in 'The Chicken Connoisseur'. However, Elijah's enthusiasm and hard work made sure it didn't. In that time, he presented nine more video reviews, including one in New York. He also sensibly did some, no doubt well-paid, advertising work for a mobile-phone maker and launched an app for finding the best chicken shops. Since then, he's written a book of his reviews and, if that wasn't enough, he's just made his own show for UK television. On *The Peng Life*, Elijah finds the essential things to do in London, beyond fast food, and then samples them at the lowest and the highest prices. It's a simple but brilliant idea. I suspect that, with local hosts alongside Elijah himself, it will be a recipe for success all over the world.

4 What does the writer suggest has contributed most to the popularity of Elijah's reviews?
- **A** the idea of reviewing clothing as well as food
- **B** Elijah's accent and pronunciation
- **C** the talent Elijah has for presenting the reviews
- **D** the fact that he looks younger than he actually is

5 Elijah says 'just not necessarily at this scale' in line 55 to show that he
- **A** hadn't wanted to become internationally famous through the videos.
- **B** was nervous about appearing on international television.
- **C** felt under pressure to make more reviews very quickly.
- **D** was surprised by the level of reaction to his videos.

6 What attitude does the writer express in the final paragraph?
- **A** She's pleased that Elijah is not only reviewing fast-food restaurants now.
- **B** She's impressed how Elijah is making the most of his success.
- **C** She's concerned that Elijah is in danger of doing too many things at once.
- **D** She's convinced Elijah will become internationally well-known soon.

TALKING POINTS

How do you decide where to eat out with your friends? Do you read reviews?

If you were a restaurant critic, what types of restaurant would you like to review?

GRAMMAR Present perfect and past simple

1 **Complete the examples with the correct form of the verbs in brackets. Then check in the article on page 37.**

1 He ______ (eat out) at fried chicken restaurants for many years.
2 He ______ just ______ (make) his own show for UK television.
3 He ______ (write) a book of his reviews.
4 When Elijah ______ (post) the sixth episode of *The Pengest Munch*, some 15 months later, …
5 Elijah Quashie ______ always ______ (be) a big fan of chicken.

2 **Match the examples in Exercise 1 to the rules.**

We use the present perfect:
a for something that happens in a period of time which is not finished.
b for past events at an unknown or irrelevant time.
c with time markers *still*, *just*, *yet*, *already*.
d for events repeated over a period of time until the present.

We use the past simple:
e to talk about completed actions that happened in a time which is now finished.

» **GRAMMAR REFERENCE AND PRACTICE PAGE 143**

3 **Read the first part of the article. Then choose the correct verb forms.**

Alessandra Peters [1] *wasn't / hasn't been* a 'foodie' her whole life. Her interest developed out of necessity when she [2] *found out / 's found out* that she was allergic to 72 different types of food. It meant her diet had to change dramatically, and straight away Alessandra [3] *cut out / has cut out* all junk food and even ice cream. However, she [4] *quickly became / has quickly become* bored of living on the same few 'safe' meals all the time. So, over the next few months, she [5] *taught / 's taught* herself to cook tasty and nutritious food.

Since then, Alessandra [6] *launched / 's launched* her own blog, sharing her recipes for healthier eating. When she first started the blog, she [7] *only expected / has only expected* her friends and family to read it. But over the past few years, she [8] *received / 's received* 'thank you' emails from teenagers like her all over the world.

4 **Complete the second part of the article with the past simple or present perfect form of the verbs in brackets.**

When Alessandra was 17, she [1] ______ (get) an email from a publishing company who [2] ______ (be) interested in publishing a book of her recipes. She thought it was her brother messing about at first, but as soon as the editor [3] ______ (phone), she knew it was real. So while revising for her end-of-school exams, she [4] ______ (write) her first book. She's deeply proud of it, but she feels it's the blog that [5] ______ (have) the greatest impact on her. 'Since starting a blog, my life [6] ______ (change) so much for the better,' she says. 'I [7] ______ (have) the amazing opportunity to connect with an incredible number of people all over the world.'

Alessandra [8] ______ (just, start) university, studying biology and chemistry.

5 **Correct the mistake with the verb form in each sentence.**

1 Last year, I've decided to cut out meat from my diet.
2 I went to that restaurant three times – I love it.
3 We didn't eat out for ages. Let's eat out tonight.
4 A few weeks ago, I've launched my own food blog.
5 Did you ever taste milk that has gone off?
6 On my last birthday, I've had a party.

VOCABULARY Forming adverbs with *-ly*

1 EP **Complete the table with the adverb forms of the adjectives. Check your answers in the articles about Elijah and Alessandra.**

Adjective	Adverb
deep	[0] *deeply*
mere	[1]
typical	[2]
necessary	[3]
sensible	[4]
dramatic	[5]

2 **Complete the sentences with the adverb forms of the adjectives in brackets.**

1 Sorry. I ______ (accidental) left the milk out and it's gone off.
2 We never eat out in the centre. ______ (basic), it's too expensive.
3 The restaurant was ______ (incredible) crowded.
4 My sister would ______ (happy) live on crisps if my parents let her.
5 I feel ______ (physical) sick when I eat fried food.
6 I've cut out dairy products ______ (complete).
7 My mum gets ______ (extreme) annoyed if we fill up on snacks and don't eat dinner.
8 The meal wasn't ______ (terrible) difficult to cook. I just heated it up in the microwave!

3 » **Work in pairs.** **Turn to page 121.**

LISTENING

1 **These words appear in a podcast about a TV show. Answer the questions.**

amateur chef
contestant knock out

1 What do you think the TV show is about?
2 What do you think happens on the show each week?
3 Have you seen any similar shows?
4 Would you like to participate in a show like this?

26 **2** **Listen to the first part of the podcast and check.**

27 **3** **Listen to the rest of the podcast. For questions 1–7, choose the best answer (A, B or C).**

1 How is the TV programme *Teenage Get Cooking!* different from the adult cookery programme?
- **A** Inexperienced cooks are encouraged to apply.
- **B** The tasks are more appealing to the age group.
- **C** It isn't as challenging because the contestants are younger.

2 What surprises Carrie about the contestants on *Teenage Get Cooking!*?
- **A** They are nervous about taking part.
- **B** They are often quite creative.
- **C** They usually have good kitchen skills.

3 Last year's winner of *Teenage Get Cooking!* is
- **A** learning to cook professionally.
- **B** preparing food at a relative's food business.
- **C** working full-time in a restaurant.

4 One thing Carrie mentions as enjoyable about presenting the show is that she
- **A** sees the contestants' ability improve.
- **B** is able to try a wide range of food.
- **C** doesn't have to cook when she gets home.

5 While the show is being recorded, the contestants
- **A** mustn't talk to their friends.
- **B** still have to do schoolwork.
- **C** mainly live at home.

6 In their video application, Carrie suggests that potential applicants should
- **A** get an experienced person to make the video.
- **B** prepare a simple dish.
- **C** express their personality.

7 According to Carrie, in July fans of the TV show can
- **A** find out who wins the competition.
- **B** watch the new series being made.
- **C** apply to be a contestant.

SPEAKING

Describing photographs (1)

1 **You are going to compare two photos. They show people preparing food in different situations. Make notes on the questions in pairs.**

1 What is similar and different about the two photos?
2 How do you think the people feel in each photo?
3 Have you ever experienced either of these situations? Do/Would you enjoy them?

28 **2** **Listen to Ana comparing the photos. Which similarities and differences in your notes in Exercise 1 does she mention?**

29 **3** **Listen to Ana answering a question about the photos. Which question does she answer?**

1 What do you think people might find difficult about preparing food in these situations?
2 What do you think people might enjoy about preparing food in these situations?

30 **4** **Read the *Prepare to speak* box. Then listen to Ana's complete answer. Which phrases does Ana use?**

PREPARE TO SPEAK | Keeping talking

Gaining time to think
Let me see/think …
That's an interesting question.
It's difficult to say, really.

Saying something in a different way
By that I mean …
What I mean is that …
To put it another way, …
Basically, …

31 **5** **Listen to Felipe answering another question. What do you notice about his answer, compared to Ana's?**

6 **Work in pairs. Turn to page 122 and do the task. Use phrases from the *Prepare to speak* box to keep talking.**

CULTURE

GAMING CULTURE

1 **Ask and answer the questions.**

1. Are you a gamer or do you know any?
2. What do you think about people who spend most of their free time on gaming?
3. What do you think the life of a professional gamer is like?

2 **Work in pairs. Make a list of things you associate with gaming culture. Then read the text quickly. Are any of your ideas mentioned?**

3 **Find these numbers in the text. What do they refer to?**

a 2004 **b** 2015 **c** 100,000,000

4 **Complete the sentences with one or two words from the text.**

1. Initially, gaming wasn't considered to be a form of ________.
2. In ________, a respected organisation started giving prizes to the best video games.
3. Gamers often call a player who hasn't played a game very much a ________.
4. ________ has had a big impact on gaming culture in recent years.
5. Unfortunately, ________ are often bullied in online multiplayer games by other players.

5 **Match the highlighted words in the text to their meanings.**

1. involving real people or animals
2. put on different clothes and pretend to be someone different
3. having a particular value, especially in money
4. causing a lot of harm and unhappiness
5. appeared or became known
6. places containing coin-operated game machines

TALKING POINTS

Why do you think gaming has become so popular?

Do you think teenagers spend too much of their time gaming? Why? / Why not?

How do you think the gaming industry could fight 'toxic' behaviour in gaming?

32 **6** **Listen to the show *Gaming World*. What does Laura say about the negative attitudes she has noticed towards female gamers? Choose the best summary.**

A She gets very annoyed with negative attitudes in gaming and doesn't know how to deal with them.

B She actively challenges negative attitudes, although this is difficult to do at times.

C She tries to respond to negative attitudes in gaming, but feels that nothing changes.

32 **7** **Listen again. Then choose the correct options.**

1. When she was younger, Laura's parents wanted her to play with *a controller* / *a computer* / *their choice of toys.*
2. *A half* / *A third* / *15%* of US gamers are adult females.
3. A typical gamer in the United States is *30* / *33* / *35* years old.
4. The number of female pro gamers is *steadily* / *slowly* / *quickly* going up.

8 **Complete the sentences with the words in the box.**

challenge	hard	irritated
over	respect	respond

USEFUL LANGUAGE

Talking about negative attitudes

1. It's hard not to get ________ when people say that.
2. I take a deep breath and ________ positively.
3. We have to work ________ to change negative attitudes.
4. Dealing with negative attitudes can be a real ________.
5. The good thing is that attitudes change ________ time.
6. It's about maintaining a healthy level of ________.

LET'S PLAY!

Are you a gamer? Over 2.2 billion people around the world play video games. And with so many people playing, it's no surprise that the gaming industry is big business, with an estimated worth of over $100 billion. But should we also be paying attention to gaming's cultural value? And what exactly is *gaming culture*?

33

FROM ARCADE TO THE BIG SCREEN

Early video games in the 1970s and 80s were much simpler than today's games and were mainly popular with children and teenagers, who would spend hours playing them in arcades. Adults didn't take this new form of entertainment very seriously and didn't consider it to be a type of popular culture like books, music or cinema. However, over the decades, as games became more sophisticated and available on a wider range of devices and in a wider range of genres, their appeal grew rapidly and they became popular with people of all ages.

In the past, video games were often based on other forms of entertainment. For example, there were video games based on films such as *Star Wars* and James Bond, or sports such as football and Formula 1. However, this later began to change, and video games started to influence other forms of entertainment and popular culture. Books, cartoons and live-action films based on the stories and characters from famous video games were produced.

The wider appeal of gaming among the general public, and its influence on books, television and cinema, helped change the perception of video games and led to them being more respected and accepted as a form of entertainment and popular culture in their own right. In 2004, the British Academy of Film and Television Arts, best known for its prestigious annual BAFTA Film Awards, held the first British Academy Games Awards, which recognise creative achievement in games. And in 2015, the World Video Game Hall of Fame was opened in New York to celebrate the video games that 'have made an impact on the world'.

GAMING CULTURE

As well as influencing other forms of entertainment, a separate gaming culture has emerged in recent years thanks to social media and online multiplayer games. Electronic sports, or eSports, are an example of this. Players can win massive sums of prize money. The incredibly popular game *Fortnite* provided a total of $100 million in tournament prizes for its first year of competitive play!

Gamers have also developed their own language that they use when playing online. *Noob* is an insult used to describe a new or inexperienced player; the term *pwned*, originally a typing mistake of 'owned', is used to describe a defeat, often when a gamer kills their opponent. And then there are more practical examples like *AFK* (away from keyboard) and *OMW*, a term often used in multiplayer gaming and short for 'on my way'.

Like in many areas of culture nowadays, YouTube also has a massive effect on gaming culture. As well as playing video games, many young people enjoy watching other people play. Gamers such as Fernanfloo, Germán Garmendia and Evan Fong, who upload videos of themselves playing and commenting on video games, have some of the most popular channels on YouTube, with tens of millions of subscribers. And no mention of gaming culture would be complete without *cosplay*, where people dress up to represent their favourite characters from games, comics, films or anime.

TOXIC GAMERS

However, gaming has its dark side, too. Many people in recent years have started to fight against so-called 'toxic' gaming culture. Unfortunately, a number of people in gaming communities use online multiplayer games, internet forums and social media to insult and bully other players, often female gamers. The gaming industry is looking for new ways to make gaming communities safer places and to stop online bullying and other forms of negative behaviour.

PROJECT *Gaming habits*

Work in groups to investigate gaming habits and attitudes towards gaming. Use these steps to help you.

1. Design a questionnaire or online survey.
2. Find out what people think about gamer culture and different groups of gamers.
3. Ask a range of people about themselves and their friends/families.
4. Ask about gaming preferences, habits, attitudes and toxic behaviour.
5. Display your results on a poster or slide presentation and write a brief summary.

Present your work to the class.

05 NOW WATCH THE CULTURE VIDEO

7 TEEN FICTION

ABOUT YOU

What types of thing do you read?
What was the last book you read?
How do you choose new books to read?

VOCABULARY Fiction: adjectives and nouns

1 **Match the phrases from the book reviews to the meanings.**

EP

1 The predictable plot meant I guessed the ending halfway through the book.
2 In this novel, the author raises some complex issues, which are all relevant to us as teenagers.
3 The stunning illustrations are beautifully drawn and give this story life.
4 Despite not having a major role in the novel, the minor characters are all fascinating.
5 From the opening chapter until the last sentence, I could not put this book down.
6 This is an incredibly moving novel, which will bring tears to your eyes.

a beautiful drawings
b sad book
c first part of a book
d a story that happens in a way that you expect
e important purpose
f difficult subjects
g not the main people in a story

2 34 **Listen to four teenagers talking about novels they have read recently.**

Which teenager
A was not impressed by the author's work?
B didn't finish the book?
C says this is their favourite writer at present?
D found the story very emotional?

3 34 **Complete the sentences with adjectives from Exercise 1. Then listen again and check.**

0 This particular story was incredibly *moving* and I didn't want it to end!
1 The ________ chapter was strong and raised several ________ issues, but by the end I was disappointed.
2 It's a familiar story of two friends growing up, so their families also play ________ roles in the tale. But it wasn't at all ________.
3 The ________ illustration on the cover made me buy this book rather than download it.

4 **Talk about a book you have read.**

Describe
- the plot
- any complex issues it deals with
- the illustrations
- the characters who have a major role in the story.

READING

1 **Read the text about an author of teenage fiction, ignoring the gaps. What role did Malorie Blackman have for two years?**

Malorie Blackman – author of teenage fiction

Malorie Blackman is an author and [0]*passionate* fan of teen fiction. Her books are popular worldwide and [1]________ of her work are available in over 15 languages.	PASSION TRANSLATE
[2]________ from doing an English degree by one of her teachers, Malorie actually studied computing after leaving school and became a computer [3]________. After nine years, she decided she wanted to do something more [4]________.	COURAGE PROGRAM CREATE
For her first novel, *Noughts and Crosses*, Malorie took inspiration [5]________ from her own childhood and teenage years.	DIRECT
From 2013 to 2015, Malorie Blackman took over as the Children's Laureate, a [6]________ position that is awarded in the UK every two years to a writer or illustrator, to celebrate outstanding achievement in their field. As Laureate, she made frequent public [7]________, giving talks and visiting schools. She also encouraged other writers to produce stories that were not [8]________ and would appeal to modern teenage readers.	PROFESSION APPEAR CHILD

2 **Look at the example in Exercise 1. How is the word formed?**

3 **Complete the text using the beginnings and endings to form new words from the words in capitals. You may need to make other spelling changes. There is one ending you won't need.**

-al	-ance	~~-ate~~	-er	dis-
-ed	-ion	-ish	-ly	-ive

WRITING for TEENAGERS – we talk to Malorie Blackman

35

A ....

I believe that we have to get them motivated by showing the many new opportunities they will be able to have through reading. And if a child tells me they don't like reading, I always say, 'You haven't found the right books for you yet!' First of all, children should be encouraged to read what they are interested in – comics, football stories, romances … whatever!

B ....

I think it was mainly down to a love of stories and reading. I spent most Saturdays during my early years at the library, reading fairy stories, myths and legends, contemporary stories, fantasy, science fiction and anything else I could lay my hands on. I also wrote stories and poems for my own amusement, but it never, ever occurred to me as a child or teenager that I could become a published writer. But in my mid-20s, after a few years in computing, I decided that I would try really hard to do that, and eventually I managed to get published.

C ....

Because as an audience they show good judgment and their minds haven't yet been closed down. And I like the way they are honest about what they like and don't like.

D ....

When I first started writing, I attended a basic course in writing for children, and then I attended several more workshops run by the same brilliant individual. It was invaluable and very inspiring – a great, supportive atmosphere where you were able to present your own work and listen to the work of others. Also, it was a great place to try to improve my own critical skills. To cut a long story short, yes it did help!

E ....

There wasn't any one thing. It grew out of a lifetime of experiences. Some of the events in the book were based on real events from my own childhood. And I also wanted to play with the idea that 'history is luck' to a certain extent. You put all that together and you have the beginnings of an idea which led to *Noughts and Crosses*.

F ....

No! We must never underestimate teens. As a teen, that kind of attitude used to drive me mad – a belief that I might not be able to understand certain 'grown-up' issues because I was just a teen. If we want mature, responsible teenagers making good decisions about the difficult issues that they face, then they have to be exposed to these subjects early enough to make a difference. We really need to get past this idea that teens can't think for themselves – they can.

4 **Read the interview with Malorie Blackman. Then match the questions to the paragraphs.**

1. Why did you decide to become a writer?
2. Do you ever worry that young people might struggle with the complex questions your books raise?
3. What inspired you to write your first novel?
4. How can teenagers be encouraged to keep reading?
5. Have you ever belonged to a writer's group – and if so, was it useful?
6. Why do you like writing for children and teens?

5 **Read the interview again.**

In which paragraph does Malorie Blackman

1. praise teenagers for being open to different ideas?
2. argue that teenagers need to experience adult topics through reading?
3. mention that she was helped by other authors?
4. talk about a change in her attitude to being an author?
5. explain her views on why some children aren't keen to read?
6. give some details about the ideas behind one of her books?

6 **Match the highlighted words and phrases in the interview to the meanings.**

1. make me extremely annoyed
2. because of someone or something
3. form sensible opinions
4. have experience of seeing, feeling, reading about, etc.
5. person
6. in some ways
7. to say only the final result of a situation or story
8. enjoyable way of spending your time

TALKING POINTS

How important is it for children to start reading at a young age?

What do you think young people can learn from reading fiction?

GRAMMAR Modals of ability and possibility

1 **Read the examples. Then complete the rules with the verbs.**

1 … reading fantasy, science fiction and anything else I **could** lay my hands on.
2 Eventually I **managed to** get published.
3 You **were able to** present your own work and listen to the work of others.
4 … a belief that I **might** not **be able to** understand certain 'grown-up' issues because I was just a teen.
5 … the many new opportunities they **will be able to** have through reading.

To talk about ability or possibility in the past, we use:
a ________ or *was/*________ for general ability.
b ________ or *was/were able to* for a specific situation.

For the future, we use:
c ________ to talk about a definite ability or possibility.
d ________ to talk about a less certain ability or possibility.

» GRAMMAR REFERENCE AND PRACTICE PAGE 144

2 **Choose the correct verbs.**

1 I *managed to* / *could* convince her to read the book.
2 People say that Albert Einstein *couldn't* / *can't* read until he was nine.
3 I'm away this weekend, so I *might not be able to* / *won't be able to* come on Saturday.
4 The homework was really difficult, but I *could* / *managed to* finish it.
5 Do you think you *could* / *might* be able to bring my book back tomorrow?
6 I hope I *was able to* / *could* give you the information you required.
7 My sister *managed to* / *could* read by herself from the age of four.
8 I *could* / *will* be able to write a book review for the website.

3 **Complete the text with the verbs in the box.**

could	managed to x2	wasn't able to
will be able to		

Beth Reekles started writing her first novel, *The Kissing Booth*, because she simply [1]________ find anything good to read about real teenage issues. Every time she finished writing a chapter, she posted it on the story-sharing website *Wattpad*. Within 18 months, she had [2]________ get 19 million views!

Soon a publisher got in touch to offer Beth a contract for three books. Beth couldn't believe it and neither [3]________ her parents. She was just 17 years old and still at school!

Despite her success, Beth didn't want to become a full-time writer. Over the next few years, she [4]________ balance writing and studying for a degree in physics – her other major interest – *and* write three more books. Her first novel was also made into a film. Now, she hopes she [5]________ do two jobs in the future: scientist and writer!

4 **Write sentences about you. Then compare your ideas in pairs.**

Write about something you
1 couldn't do in the past, but can do now.
2 were able to do in the past, but can't do now.
3 can't do now, but might be able to do in the future.
4 won't ever be able to do.
5 managed to do after trying very hard.

I couldn't understand our teacher when I started this class, but I can now.

VOCABULARY Adjective + preposition

1 **Read the example. What other adjectives do you know that are followed by a preposition?**

Children should be encouraged to read what they are ***interested in*** *– comics, football stories, romances … whatever!*

2 **Check you understand the adjectives. Then match the sentence halves.**

1 Were you **disappointed**
2 As a child, I was **nervous**
3 Is this novel **suitable**
4 I'm **addicted**
5 My cousin's really **keen**
6 I sometimes get **annoyed**
7 Are you **surprised**
8 Gabby's **furious**

a **to** reading manga comics.
b **at** the number of novels I've read?
c **by** stories with happy endings.
d **with** me for losing her book.
e **for** children under 12?
f **on** science fiction.
g **with** your test results?
h **about** being late for school.

36 **3** **Listen to eight people. Then complete the sentences to describe each person using an adjective and a preposition from Exercise 2.**

1 He's ________ mystery stories.
2 She thinks the story is ________ both boys and girls.
3 He gets ________ his brother's questions.
4 He's ________ the result of the match.
5 She's ________ listening to audio books.
6 She's ________ Jack for ignoring what she said.
7 He's ________ making a speech in front of the school.
8 She's ________ the popularity of the books.

4 » Work in pairs. Turn to page 123.

WRITING A story (1)

1 Read the task. How do you think the story might continue from the first sentence?

You see this announcement in a magazine.

> **Stories wanted!**
> We are looking for exciting stories by teenagers to publish in our magazine. Your story must begin with this sentence:
> *Billy crawled nervously through the hole in the wall and looked down.*
> Your story must include:
> - a boat
> - a dangerous animal.

Write your **story**.

2 Read the story to see if any of your ideas are mentioned. Then answer the questions.

1 Does the story include a boat?
2 Which dangerous animal did Billy face?
3 How does the story end?

Billy crawled nervously through the hole in the wall and looked down. It was more than three metres to the ground below, but Billy knew he had no choice. He jumped and landed badly, but managed not to hurt himself. Immediately, he started running towards the river, desperately hoping he would be able to find the boat.

And there it was, behind the trees. He climbed in and turned the key. Three times he tried and failed, but eventually, the engine started and Billy was on his way. Once he was in the open water, the biggest danger he faced was the crocodiles. They would easily be able to turn the boat over if they attacked. Billy looked around anxiously, ready to take action if he needed to. He was feeling scared now, but he couldn't turn back.

After what seemed like hours, but was probably only 20 minutes, Billy reached his destination. He tied up the boat hurriedly and ran towards the safety of the house. Every few seconds, he quickly looked over his shoulder towards the river. No one would dare to follow him here, he thought. He had escaped at last.

3 Read the *Prepare to write* box. Then match the highlighted words in the story to four of the phrases in the box. What does the remaining phrase mean?

PREPARE TO WRITE | A story

A good story:
- has a beginning, a middle and an end.
- uses time words and phrases that move the action forward.
- uses adjectives and adverbs of manner to add interest or excitement.
- uses a range of tenses, including the past simple, past continuous and past perfect.

all of a sudden | as soon as | finally | following | without waiting

4 Look at the underlined adverbs of manner in the story. What do they each describe?

5 Complete the sentences with adverbs of manner from the story. In some cases, more than one answer is possible.

1 He .... climbed up the rock, motivated by the thought of being first to the top.
2 I was .... trying to remain calm, even though I was feeling furious with my friend.
3 He looked .... at his watch and felt a little disappointed in himself. Why hadn't he left earlier?
4 I was surprised at getting such a low mark. I didn't expect to do so ....

6 Explain why the writer has used these tenses in the story.

1 Past simple: *He **climbed** in and **turned** the key.*
2 Past perfect: *He **had escaped** at last.*
3 Past continuous: *He **was feeling** scared now.*

7 Read the task and plan your story.

> COMPETITION:
> **Send us your stories!**
> We are looking for interesting stories for our student website. The best will be published on our website and win a prize. Your story must begin with this sentence:
> *Charlie watched the dark clouds anxiously, wondering when the storm would start.*
> Your story must include:
> - a boat
> - a rescue.

8 Write your story.

- Use the tips in the *Prepare to write* box.
- Write 140–190 words.
- Check your grammar and spelling.

8 GETTING AWAY

ABOUT YOU

06 Watch the video. Then answer the questions.

What is your dream holiday destination?

What do you think young people can learn from travelling to other countries?

VOCABULARY Holiday activities

1 What holiday activities do the pictures show? Use some of the words in the quiz to help you.

What's your kind of holiday? QUIZ

1 You're planning a holiday in Thailand. You can't wait to …
- a go trekking in the jungle.
- b try out some authentic Thai food.
- c cool down in the shade by the pool.

2 The most important thing on a summer holiday is to …
- a relax, sunbathe and get a tan.
- b make the most of your time and do as much as possible.
- c socialise with friends and catch up on the latest films.

3 Your ideal holiday accommodation would be …
- a a tent in the middle of nowhere.
- b a luxury hotel where you can chill out.
- c a youth hostel in a major city.

4 On a holiday in the Caribbean, you'd want to …
- a cruise from island to island on a yacht.
- b get involved in a local festival.
- c head straight for the beach and hire a jet ski.

5 You're on a short break to New York City. You …
- a sign up for an organised tour of Manhattan.
- b stay up all night to experience 'the city that never sleeps'.
- c wander around, photograph the sights and take selfies.

2 Do the quiz. Compare and explain your answers in pairs.

3 Turn to page 123 and check your results. Do you agree with them?

4 Complete the sentences with some of the words and phrases in the quiz.

EP

1. I'm going to ______ a motorbike. Do you want to come, or have you ______ for the museum tour?
2. We're going to ______ and climbing in the Pyrenees this year!
3. You'll never ______ if you ______ all night and lie in bed all day! Come outside in the sunshine – you can still ______ by the pool.
4. I have no desire to ______ around the ocean. I'd rather visit a city where I can ______ around interesting areas and ______ the historic buildings.

5 Discuss the questions.

1. Are you a fan of taking selfies on holiday?
2. Do you tend to photograph everything you see?
3. What would you like to try out next time you're abroad?
4. Which cities would you most like to visit? Why?
5. What would you like to do in New York?

READING

1 Look at the article on page 47 and find the three destinations. Can you guess what each person is going to take on their travels?

2 Read the article quickly and check.

3 Read the article again. Who would give the following advice?

1. Don't pack thick clothing.
2. Think about security.
3. Pack as little as possible.
4. Remember your medicines.
5. Liquids can spill inside your bag.
6. Don't take white clothes.
7. Back up your paperwork.
8. Pack clothes in a particular way.

4 Find five adjectives in Javi's section that mean *very important*.

PACK AND GO!

EXPERT BACKPACKERS SHARE THEIR TOP TIPS

'My flight leaves at midday tomorrow and I still haven't packed my bags. Help!'

If that sounds familiar, don't worry! Everyone has a last-minute panic before a trip. Here, three experienced backpackers share their tips for packing.

Alex, 19, Warsaw

DESTINATION: the peaks of the Pyrenees

I'm going trekking, so I'm taking a very light backpack that's comfortable for walking. I'd always suggest taking a few aluminium water bottles. They're stronger than plastic ones and you can refill them in streams. If you plan to get around on foot, remember to take high-energy snacks – you don't want to feel hungry in the middle of nowhere! Leave space for a first-aid kit because you'll always need things like bandages and antiseptic cream. It's definitely worth going high up for the views, but pack something warm, as it can get cold. Last but not least, put shampoos and creams inside a sealed plastic bag and pack it on the outside of your luggage.

Frances, 18, Glasgow

DESTINATION: the beaches of Central America

I'm flying to Costa Rica later this week – I can't wait to get away! The most important advice for any backpacker is PACK LIGHT. The last thing you need is luggage that weighs a tonne when you're wandering around a crowded city. My advice is to get everything you're planning to take, then divide it in two and just take half of what you started with. I'm definitely going to take as few clothes as possible – just enough for five days at a time. And I'm not going to take any pale clothes – they always get dirty when you're out sightseeing. Thinking about it, I probably won't take jeans either – they're heavy and hot. Before I start packing, I roll my clothes – if you do that, they look better when you unpack them! I won't pack trainers – I'll wear them, and I'll put my lightweight sandals in my luggage. A phone's useful, but I always take an old one in case it gets damaged or stolen. You can buy a cheap SIM card in each country you visit.

Javi, 20, Valencia

DESTINATION: the sights and cities of southern India

I first went to India the year before last and I can't wait to get back. My flight for Kerala leaves tomorrow! For me, preparation is key. Most people can work out what clothes to pack, but you're going to need more than just something to wear. I'd recommend taking an LED head-torch in case of power cuts and putting sunglasses in a hard case to protect them. I'd keep the free eye mask from your flight so you can sleep on bus journeys. For solo travellers, having someone to chat to is crucial and fellow travellers will be your main source of company, but hostels can be noisy places, so I'll certainly pack some ear plugs for this trip. Hygiene is critical, especially when you're eating. In India, you often eat with your hands, so I'm going to carry an anti-bacterial gel in my pocket. Backpack zips with locks are really useful, and a travel belt for hiding your passport and cash under your shirt is essential. Scan your ID, tickets and insurance details, and keep details of vital documents in the cloud. Then you can relax and enjoy your trip!

TALKING POINTS

Where would you like to go backpacking?
What are the pros and cons of organised tours compared with independent travel?

GRAMMAR Future (1): plans and intentions

1 **Read the examples. Then complete the rules with *will*, *be going to*, *the present continuous* or *the present simple*.**

1 My flight **leaves** at midday tomorrow.
2 I**'m** certainly **going to take** as few clothes as possible.
3 I**'m flying** to Costa Rica later this week.
4 I**'m not going to take** any pale clothes.
5 Thinking about it, I probably **won't take** jeans either.
6 I**'ll** definitely **pack** some ear plugs.

> We can use *be going to*, *will*, the present continuous and the present simple to talk about future plans and intentions. We use:
> **a** ________ to talk about timetabled events.
> **b** ________ to talk about firm arrangements, usually with a time reference.
> **c** ________ to talk about something we are (not) planning to do.
> **d** ________ when we decide (not) to do something while we are speaking or writing.

» **GRAMMAR REFERENCE AND PRACTICE PAGE 145**

2 **Put the adverbs in brackets in the correct position in the sentences.**

1 Thinking about it, I won't have access to the internet most of the time. (probably)
2 I'm not going to take an expensive camera. (certainly)
3 I'll call you when I get to New York. (definitely)
4 I'm going to visit my cousins in Thailand. (probably)

3 **Complete the email with a future form of the verbs in brackets. Discuss your answers. Sometimes there is more than one possible answer.**

Hi, Markus

My dad and I can't wait to see you again! Our flight [1] ________ (leave) at 9.30 am on Friday, so I'm getting very excited! I know you [2] ________ (study) on Friday afternoon, so we [3] ________ (probably / wait) for you in our hotel. I know we [4] ________ (go) for a bike ride during the day on Saturday, but do you have any plans for the evening? Can we do something together or [5] ________ (you / go) out somewhere? I'm reading an Amsterdam guidebook, but I [6] ________ (not / bring) it with me, so I [7] ________ (definitely / need) you to take us around the city! I'm online now, so I think I [8] ________ (do) an online search to see what recommendations there are.

See you very soon,

Sam

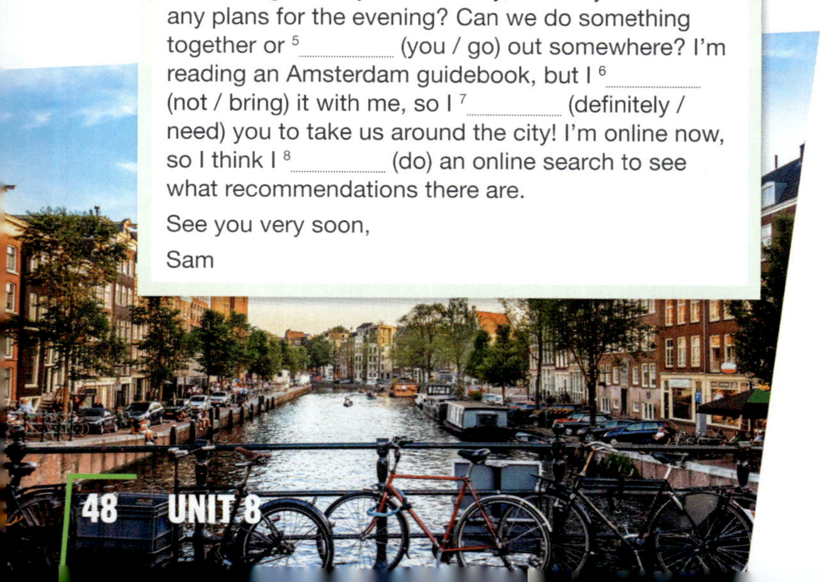

4 **Correct the mistake with the future form in each sentence.**

1 This evening we get the train to my cousins' house.
2 You can visit any time, so just let us know when you will come.
3 I've booked my flights, now I try to book some hostels.
4 Oh no, the forecast is for rain this weekend, so I probably don't go out.
5 I like the sound of Mexico, I think I visit there next.
6 My best friend goes on holiday as soon as term ends.

5 **Discuss the questions.**

1 What are you doing this evening?
2 What are you going to do next weekend?
3 What do you think you'll do later today?

VOCABULARY Phrasal verbs: travel

1 EP **Read the sentences. Then match the phrasal verbs to the meanings.**

1 If you plan to **get around** on foot, take high-energy snacks.
2 Don't carry heavy luggage when you're **looking around** a city.
3 I can't wait to **get away**.
4 I'll definitely need you to **take** us **around** the city.
5 Let's **stop over** in Paris on the way to London.
6 You have to **check out** before midday.
7 I'm going to **stay over** at my friend's house.
8 They came to **see** me **off** at the station.
9 I'll **check in** after 4.30 pm.

a arrive and get the key at a hotel
b show someone the best parts of a certain place
c travel or move from place to place
d pay the bill, return your key and leave a hotel
e stay somewhere briefly during a longer journey
f go to where someone is leaving to say goodbye
g go on holiday, often because you need a rest
h spend the night somewhere other than home
i visit a place and look at the things in it

2 **Complete the text with the correct form of the phrasal verbs in Exercise 1.**

> I'm really looking forward to our holiday in Morocco. I definitely need to [1] ________ at the moment, as I feel quite tired and stressed. I'm [2] ________ at my cousin's tonight, then my uncle is [3] ________ us ________ at Heathrow Airport tomorrow afternoon. Our flight arrives in Marrakesh at about 7 pm local time, so we'll go straight to our hotel and [4] ________. The next day, someone is going to [5] ________ us ________ the city. The following morning, we're going to [6] ________ of our hotel quite early and travel south. We're going to [7] ________ in Fes for one night, and then go up into the mountains. We're going to [8] ________ in a hire car. On the last day, we're going to Casablanca. I really want to [9] ________ the market before we fly home.

3 » **Work in pairs. Turn to page 123.**

LISTENING

1 **Look at the photos. Then read the paragraph about working holidays. Where do you think the people are? What are they doing?**

WORKING ⇆ 'HOLIDAY'?

When you think about going on holiday, you don't usually think about working, but more and more people are choosing to do just that, to combine a holiday with voluntary or paid work in the country they're visiting. Particularly for young people, a working holiday can be a great way to enjoy a trip abroad.

2 **You will hear a report about working holidays. Before you listen, read the sentences and the clues, and predict what the missing information might be.**

0 Working holidays mean people can afford travel, *accommodation* and food in big cities.
(Clue: What do people need or want in a city?)
somewhere to stay

1 As well as getting free meals, Charlie made .... a week working in a hotel in London.
(Clue: What do working people get every week or month?)

2 On the coast in Cornwall, Charlie did conservation work, and on his days off, he decided to ....
(Clue: What leisure activities might people enjoy on the coast?)

3 On the Galapagos Islands, Charlie's job was to ....
(Clue: What work could people do in the Galapagos Islands?)

4 The highlight of Charlie's working holiday in Thailand was ....
(Clue: What might people enjoy in Thailand?)

5 Charlie mentions that people must be .... to work for a year in the Australian 'outback'.
(Clue: What kind of word is missing?)

38 **3** **Listen to the report. Then complete the sentences in Exercise 2 with a word or short phrase.**

SPEAKING Discussing holidays

1 **Read the question and the five ideas related to it. Discuss which is the most important to you.**

Is it a good idea to go away somewhere in the holidays?
- resting after a term at school
- exploring other cultures
- hanging out with old friends
- spending time with your family
- enjoying exciting new experiences

39 **2** **Listen to two students discussing the task. What is their answer to the question?**

39 **3** **Look at the *Prepare to speak* box. Then listen again. Which two phrases do you hear twice?**

PREPARE TO SPEAK | Managing a discussion

Selecting ideas
How about starting with this idea?
Shall we move on to …?
What about this one?

Inviting a response
I don't know about you, but …
Don't you? / How about you?
What do you think?

Responding

Sure, why not?	OK, so you mean …
Yeah, definitely.	I see your point, but …
Exactly/Indeed.	I mean, yes …, but …
Fair enough.	I'm / My family's the same.
I totally agree.	Agreed.

4 **Look at five reasons why young people might be attracted to working holidays. Take one minute to read the task and think about your responses. Then follow the instructions.**

1 • Discuss the question using some (but not necessarily all) of the reasons given.
• Use the language from the *Prepare to speak* box.
• You have two minutes to complete this task.

2 • Decide on an answer to the question.
• You don't need to agree with one other.
• You have one minute to complete this task.

Should all young people try a working holiday?
- having a cheap holiday
- travelling abroad
- getting work experience
- being independent
- earning and saving money

5 **Discuss the questions.**

1 How important is it for teenagers to have experience of working?
2 Is it a good idea for teenagers to earn and save money? Why? / Why not?
3 How can a holiday without your family be good for you?
4 What would be the hardest part of going on a working holiday? Why?
5 Should all young people experience working holidays? Why? / Why not?

LIFE SKILLS COMMUNICATION

ACTIVE LISTENING

LIFE SKILLS

Active listening

We listen for many reasons and it's a fundamental part of communication. How well you listen affects the quality of your relationships with family, friends and colleagues. Becoming a better listener will help you be more productive. You'll also be better at avoiding misunderstandings and improve your ability to influence and persuade others.

1 **Ask and answer the questions.**

1. Are you a good listener? Can you give an example?
2. What is the difference between 'hearing' and 'listening'?
3. Do you ever have conversations where you feel that the other person isn't listening carefully? How do you know?

2 **What do you think people can do to be better listeners? Read the text quickly. Are any of your ideas mentioned?**

3 **Read the text again. Then complete each sentence with one or two words from the article.**

1. When trying to improve your active listening skills, it's important to be ....
2. When you're listening to someone it's easy to .... by thinking about how to reply.
3. Active listeners have an .... and don't assume that they know what someone is going to say.
4. Only give your opinion when you have a .... about what the speaker is saying.
5. .... might not be the same for all cultures and contexts.

4 **Match the highlighted words in the text to the meanings.**

1. beliefs that you accept as true without questioning them
2. care and understanding for someone else's suffering
3. intentional and aware
4. incline in one direction
5. something difficult that tests your ability or determination

ARE YOU LISTENING TO ME?!

Do you ever have conversations where you feel the other person isn't listening properly? It's annoying, isn't it? Listening is actually a tough skill to master. It's an active process where the listener makes a conscious effort to listen in order to understand what the speaker is saying. Active listening is where you make an effort to understand the complete message and not just the words being said. So how exactly can you be an active listener? The real question here is, how can I *become* an active listener? It will take time and determination to acquire and develop active listening skills, so be patient with yourself.

On average, the time we spend communicating can be divided as: 9% writing, 16% reading, 30% speaking and 45% listening!

Key active listening techniques

1 **Pay attention!** This sounds very obvious, but it's more difficult than it appears. And it's not just external factors such as your phone which are a challenge here. Try not to get distracted by your own thoughts or by preparing in your mind what you're going to say in reply. The result will probably be that you're not able to pay attention to the other person.

Research shows that after listening to a ten-minute presentation, most people only hear, understand and remember half of what was said!

2 **Clarify** If something is unclear or ambiguous, don't be afraid to ask a question to clarify things. This could be a specific question or an open question to encourage someone to explain their ideas in more detail. But try not to interrupt the other person; wait until they have finished speaking or there is a pause before you ask a question or give your own view.

3 **Keep an open mind** Active listening means that you are open to new ideas, different possibilities and to other people's opinions. Your own assumptions, beliefs and opinions can affect what you hear. So don't assume that you understand what the other person wants to say.

4 **Summarise** At different points in the conversation, repeat the main points of what someone has said to check that you've understood them correctly.

5 **Respond effectively** Use short phrases like *I see* or *I know* to encourage the speaker to continue. If you don't agree with what they're saying, be polite and whatever you do, don't insult them. Be respectful when you give your own opinions and treat the other person as you would like to be treated.

6 **Share!** When you have a clear idea about what the other person is saying, start to share your own ideas, observations or suggestions. Talking about a similar experience is a great way to show understanding and empathy, which is when we imagine how it feels to be in someone else's situation.

Non-verbal signs

Listening actively isn't just about the words we use – it's more complex than that. When conversations are face to face, they also involve lots of non-verbal communication like facial expressions. Let's look at a few examples. However, you should be aware that these may vary in different cultures and situations. Firstly, eye contact is usually encouraging for the speaker, combined with smiling to show that you are listening or that you agree with someone. Positive posture, the position of your body, will also help. Make sure that you are facing the speaker and, if you're sitting down, maybe lean forward a little bit to show interest. Then there's what we call 'mirroring', where a listener automatically copies facial expressions and body language to show empathy and sympathy. This usually happens on a sub-conscious level, but the listener can make an effort to do this intentionally. Be aware of things like checking your phone or playing with your hair when you're listening to someone.

41 **5** **Listen to Leo talking about his holiday to his friend Freddie. Then answer the questions.**

1 Did Leo have a good holiday? Why? / Why not?
2 How does his friend show effective active listening?

41 **6** **Listen again. Then choose the correct options.**

1 They couldn't go on the football stadium tour because …
A they had to look for another hotel.
B the hotel wasn't expecting them.
C the hotel hadn't reserved their tickets.

2 The travel company had …
A hired a car which was too expensive.
B reserved two small cars for them.
C booked the wrong size car.

3 Why was Leo still not happy on the final day of the holiday?
A He didn't want to stay in the hotel that day.
B The swimming pool wasn't in the same building.
C He couldn't go for a swim.

7 **Read the sentences from the conversation. Then complete them with one word.**

USEFUL LANGUAGE

Active listening

1 I can ________ why you're angry.
2 Oh no! What ________ you do?
3 It ________ like you had a terrible time.
4 Hang on! Let me check I ________ you right.
5 I ________ that you'll never book another holiday with them again?
6 I ________ if it was all just bad luck.

PROJECT

A campaign to promote active listening

Work in groups to design a campaign to promote active listening in your school.

1 Think about
- the benefits of developing active listening skills for both students and teachers
- active listening techniques which could be applied in your school
- non-verbal signs important for effective active listening at school.

2 Decide how you want to present your campaign: a talk, a video, etc. Include a demonstration of active listening.

Present your work to the class.

REVIEW 2 UNITS 5–8

VOCABULARY

1 Complete the review with the verbs in the box.

brake	chase	exchange
gather	interact	steer

TimeThief

In this game, you [1] ______ 'time thieves' around a virtual city set hundreds of years in the future. You can [2] ______ with other 'chasers' and [3] ______ clues with them about the location of the time thieves, but for most of the game you just [4] ______ points and information on your own. You have a car, but be careful – the roads are wet, so it's difficult to [5] ______ and you have to [6] ______ very carefully, otherwise you'll slide everywhere.

2 Complete the phrasal verbs.

1 A: Shall we eat ______ tonight? We could go to that amazing beef restaurant.
B: The Argentinian one? I'd rather not, I'm trying to cut ______ meat from my diet at the moment.

2 A: Eat ______ your salad!
B: Yes, you can't live ______ just chips.

3 A: I'm going to heat ______ this curry so we can eat it before it goes ______.
B: Not again, Dad! That'll be the third day in a row.

3 Complete the sentences with one word from A and one from B.

A

chill	cool	get	sign
stay	take	try	wander

B

around	down	out x2
selfies	tan	up x2

1 We're going to ______ ______ for a yoga class this holiday.
2 I was on my own, so I decided to ______ a few ______.
3 I'd like to ______ a ______ without burning my skin.
4 It's so hot! Let's jump in the pool and ______ ______.
5 Did you ______ ______ all night? You should get to bed early tonight.
6 You've been working too hard. You should ______ ______ for a day.
7 I hope we have time to ______ ______ the markets tomorrow.
8 I've decided to ______ ______ the local food on holiday.

4 Match the sentence halves.

1 The film dealt with some really complex
2 The director discussed the opening
3 I loved the unpredictable
4 It's not a romance, but it's a very moving
5 I got confused between the minor
6 The book won awards for its stunning

a characters because they were all so similar.
b chapter of the novel and how they adapted it for the film.
c novel with some wonderful dialogue.
d issues about childhood and growing up.
e plot and never knowing what would happen next.
f illustrations of the countryside.

GRAMMAR

1 Match the sentence halves. Which sentence does not need a relative pronoun?

1 I've been in a few situations that
2 New York and Los Angeles, which
3 My uncle Barny, who
4 Salerno, where
5 The book which
6 I don't know anyone whose

a grandparents play computer games.
b were quite frightening.
c we're reading at school is fascinating.
d we used to live, is a coastal town in Italy.
e is about 60, has never owned a computer.
f seem so exciting, can actually be quite lonely places.

2 Complete the sentences with the present perfect or past simple form of the verbs in brackets.

A life on two wheels

Amy Patterson [1] ______ (visit) more than 150 countries, making her by far one of the world's most-travelled people. She [2] ______ (leave) her home in Toronto, Canada, in 2015 and she [3] ______ (not return) since. She [4] ______ (ride) out of town on an old Kawasaki motorcycle and she is still riding the same machine today. Since 2015, Amy and her bike [5] ______ (travel) more than 100,000 km. [6] ______ (she / ever / have) any bad experiences? 'Plenty! I [7] ______ (be) ill and lost money – but the worst thing was the time someone [8] ______ (steal) my motorbike. It [9] ______ (happen) last year just outside Sunderland, in the north of England. I [10] ______ (never / feel) so upset. Luckily, the thief [11] ______ (not keep) it, and the police [12] ______ (find) it the following day.'

3 Complete the sentences with the modal verbs in the box.

could	couldn't	managed to
might be able to	wasn't able to	
won't be able to		

1 Is this the best ending they ________ think of?
2 It's a great story, but I haven't ________ finish the whole book yet.
3 I enjoyed the film. I ________ see anything wrong with the plot.
4 This film's in English. Concentrate and you ________ follow it.
5 I ________ join you, I have to do some homework instead.
6 I'm sorry, I ________ get tickets for the opening night. It had sold out.

4 Complete the conversations with a future form of the verbs in brackets.

1 **A:** Oh, no. We've missed the last bus. What shall we do?
B: Well, a taxi ________ (definitely / cost) over £15.
A: My dad ________ (not collect) us because it's too late. Shall we walk?

2 **A:** What's that?
B: A guide book. My parents and I ________ (probably / visit) Paris this summer. At least, I hope so. I ________ (be) seriously disappointed if we don't.

3 **A:** Has the last train left yet?
B: No. It ________ (not leave) until 23:45.

4 **A:** I ________ (not go) to this year's end-of-term party. Are you?
B: Yes, I ________ (help) with the food. You should come. It ________ (be) fun.

5 **A:** ________ (you / do) much this weekend?
B: No. I ________ (not do) anything in particular.

5 Choose the correct words.

1 She has a friend *which* / *who* is like a sister.
2 Last night, I *left* / *'ve left* my phone in the cinema.
3 I hope we *could* / *'ve managed to* persuade you to join the team.
4 What time *are you going to meet* / *will you meet* tomorrow?

6 Correct the mistake in each sentence.

1 Did you like the present wich they gave you?
2 Hi, how are you? I didn't see you for ages.
3 We're sorry we wouldn't be able to go to your party.
4 Jon comes later to lend us his tablet.

7 Read the text. Use the word given in capitals at the end of some of the lines to form a word that fits in the gap in the same line.

The teacher with a secret

John Corcoran was born in 1937 and grew up in New Mexico in the USA. After [0]*graduating* from high school, Corcoran went to university and, in the 1960s, became a teacher. He taught for 17 years and is the author of a book about literacy. But Corcoran spent his entire teaching career keeping an [1] ________ secret. At the age of 48, he was almost [2] ________ illiterate. All he could read and write was his own name. At primary school, while his classmates started to read, Corcoran couldn't understand the letters. He found the problem hard to explain and he was [3] ________ in trouble for messing about. However, he was charming and fun, and his [4] ________ meant his classmates were easily persuaded to do his homework. At college, it became [5] ________ more difficult to conceal his problem, but thanks to some incredible cheating techniques, he managed to pass his exams. And after college, he decided to teach. A friend filled in his [6] ________ form and he began working as a teacher. Finally, aged 48, Corcoran took adult literacy classes and his lifelong [7] ________ was over. It was an incredible relief: 'Adults who can't read are suspended in their [8] ________, emotionally, psychologically, academically, spiritually. We haven't grown up yet.'

GRADUATE (0), BELIEVE (1), COMPLETE (2), CONSTANT (3), POPULAR (4), CONSIDER (5), APPLY (6), EMBARRASS (7), CHILD (8)

8 Complete the second sentence so that it has a similar meaning to the first sentence, using the word given. Do not change the word given. You must use between two and five words, including the word given.

1 The shop won't give a discount to students without an ID card. **ABLE**
Students ________ get a discount without an ID card.
2 I shouldn't eat so much fatty food. **OUT**
I really ________ some of the fatty food I eat.
3 It's uncertain whether the goalkeeper will be involved in future matches. **ANY**
The goalkeeper may not have ________ future matches.
4 This exam will certainly be fairly difficult. **FIND**
You ________ this exam easy.
5 We last went abroad about five years ago. **FOR**
We ________ about five years.
6 We should join the running club. **SIGN**
Why don't we ________ the running club?

9 SPEND OR SAVE?

A

B

C

D

ABOUT YOU

07 Watch the video. Then answer the questions.

What do you spend most of your money on?

Do you ever waste money on things you don't really need?

Do you need money to be happy?

VOCABULARY Money

42 **1 Read and listen to the statements. Then match them to the photos.**

1 I tried to **take out** some money at the **cashpoint**, but something weird happened. I typed in my **PIN**, which is the same four numbers that I've always used, and an error message came up on the screen. After three attempts, the machine kept my **debit card**. Now I can't get any money or even check my **balance** to see how much I have left!

2 I'm on a tight **budget** of about £20 a week. I get a £15 **allowance** and a few extra pounds for doing jobs around the house. I haven't got any **savings**, so that's all I have to **live on**, and I can only afford to go out once or twice a month! How am I expected to have a social life if I can't go out?

3 I feel like I'm always **short of cash**, and I'm *so* tired of asking my parents to give me money. I bet they're tired of it, too. My dream is to be **financially independent**. I mean, I don't need to be **wealthy**, I just want enough to do the things I want to do.

4 I've just been shopping again. I can't resist a **bargain**! I paid with my credit card, which at least means I've got until the end of the month before I have to **pay** it **off**.

2 Complete the questions with the correct form of words and phrases from Exercise 1. Then discuss the questions. EP

1 Do you use a ________, or do you pay for everything with cash? Why?
2 Have you ever had problems ________ money at a ________?
3 Do you get an ________ from your parents?
4 How much money do you need to ________ each week?
5 Do you use the same ________ for more than one debit card?
6 Have you found any good ________ in the shops recently? What were they? How much money did you save?
7 What do you do when you are ________ and don't have money to spend? Do you have any ________ you can use?
8 Would you rather be healthy but poor, or unhealthy but ________?

READING

1 Discuss the questions. Then read the article quickly and check.

1 Why is most teens' budget beyond their control?
2 How can working help you to spend less?
3 How can you sell unwanted possessions?
4 How can you get the best price for something you want to buy?
5 How can you work out a budget for buying something special?

2 Read the article again. Then answer the questions.

1 What are the good and bad things about babysitting, according to Jon?
2 How did Milly save money when she sold her possessions?
3 How did Lawrence get money back from a department store?
4 How did Abbie reduce her spending?

IN THE MONEY

'Money makes the world go round', or so they say, and it's certainly hard to imagine life without it. Most under-20s are financially dependent on parents, but that will change sooner than you think. You're going to spend your entire adult life trying to earn a living, so it's time to think about how money works. We travelled up and down the country asking how you get money and what you do with it.

> **› phrase (informal)**
> ***in the money***
> wealthy, having money
> • *Nicholas is really in the money now.*

HOW TO GET MONEY

Allowances and gifts

Getting an allowance means that you probably have little control over the amount that you receive. But make the most of your freedom – you'll be working fairly soon!

Paid work

If, before you leave school, you get the opportunity of part-time work, take it. Making money is not only highly satisfying, but you might also find you're more careful with your own earnings than with money you've been given.

I babysit a couple of evenings a week. The kids I babysit never wake up, so I basically get paid to watch TV at people's houses. The pay's not great, but because of the number of times I've babysat this month, I'm going to earn nearly £80! It's a good feeling to earn my own money, and I'm never short of cash.

Jon Fletcher, 17, Manchester

Selling possessions

There are probably a number of things lying around your house that you don't really need. Why not collect together anything you haven't used for at least a year and sell it? You may well be amazed by how much there is. You could be making hundreds of pounds every year selling on auction websites.

My dad helped me sell hundreds of old comics on an online auction website. Remember to take into account the website's fees, as well as the cost of postage and packing. I saved money by finding buyers who lived locally, so they could collect the comics themselves.

Milly Lewis, 16, Newcastle

HOW TO LOOK AFTER YOUR MONEY

Getting the best price

If you're looking for something in particular, don't go shopping with a wallet full of cash. Compare prices online first or make a note of what the item costs in various shops before you buy it. Try to wait for the sales and take advantage of special offers and multi-buy discounts.

I bought a tablet from a department store that guarantees it has the best prices. After I bought it, I found the same tablet cheaper online. I love a bargain, so I showed the department store the online deal, and they refunded me the difference. I saved £20!

Lawrence Weston, 16, Plymouth

Small amounts add up

Keep a record of what you spend and look for ways to save. Even small savings are worth it when you add them all up.

I was spending 70p a day on cereal bars from the school vending machine. That's £14 a month! I found that I could buy two dozen bars for under £10 in a supermarket. I decided to buy in bulk from the supermarket and saved £28 in a year, which is quite a lot really.

Abbie Watkins, 17, Peterborough

Saving for special purchases

If you want to buy something expensive, don't get into debt. Save up instead! Work out your weekly income. Then add up your regular expenses, for example bus fares, snacks and so on. Take away your expenses from your income, and the balance is the amount you can save every week. Put that money in a separate pot each week, or open a savings account, and count the weeks until you can afford to buy the item.

3 Match the highlighted words and phrases in the article to the meanings. (Two words have the same meaning.)

1. money that you get for working
2. reductions in price
3. money that you pay to do or use something
4. the money that you spend on something
5. to work to get money to pay bills, buy food, etc.
6. to start owing money that you have borrowed

4 Discuss the questions.

1. Do you keep an eye on what you spend? How?
2. Have you ever saved money? What for?
3. Have you ever got into debt? Why?
4. At what age do you think it's good to become financially independent?

TALKING POINTS

Do you agree with the suggestions for looking after your money? Why? / Why not?

GRAMMAR Future (2): predictions

1 **Read the examples. Then complete the rules with the words in the box.**

1 Because of the number of times I've babysat this month, **I'm going to** earn nearly £80!
2 Most under-20s are financially dependent on parents, but that **will** change sooner than you think.
3 Make the most of your freedom – you**'ll be** working fairly soon.

be	be going to	will

We use:
a .... to make general predictions about the future.
b .... to make predictions based on something we can see or already know.
c the future continuous (*will/won't* + ... + *-ing*) to make predictions about actions and habits in progress in the future.

2 **Choose the correct words.**

1 I've just heard that my parents *are going to increase* / *will increase* my allowance soon.
2 I *won't live* / *won't be living* at home when I'm 20. I *'ll be studying* / *'ll study* at university by then.
3 By the 2030s, no one *is using* / *will be using* cash.
4 Look, there's a really long queue. We *won't get* / *aren't going to get* into the gig.
5 We *'ll be stayed* / *'ll be staying* with my cousins in London, but we *'ll be spending* / *'ll be spend* most of our time at the festival.

3 **Read the examples. Then complete the rules.**

1 You **might** also **find** you're more careful with your own earnings.
2 You **may well be** amazed by how much there is.
3 You **could be making** hundreds of pounds every year selling on auction websites.

a We can also use *might*, ... and *could* instead of *will* to say that something is possible in the future.
b We can use *may/might/could* + ... to express strong possibility.
c We can't make negative predictions with *could*.

» GRAMMAR REFERENCE AND PRACTICE PAGE 146

4 **Choose the correct verb forms.**

Millions of tablets are sold every year, so they [1] *might not disappear* / *aren't going to disappear* any time soon. We [2] *may still use* / *may still be using* them in 20 years' time. Tablets of the future [3] *may not be* / *could not be* so expensive. They [4] *could well weigh* / *will well weigh* less than my phone does now. The batteries [5] *will definitely last* / *may definitely last* longer. Who knows – they [6] *may even replace* / *will even replace* laptops and desktops altogether one day.

5 **Make future predictions about yourself. Use some of the ideas in the box or your own ideas. Then compare your predictions in pairs.**

earn over £1 million a year	get a credit card
go to a concert this year	live in America
live until I'm 100	open a bank account soon
rain this evening	visit Australia
watch TV later	

I probably won't live until I'm 100.

I might well visit Australia when I'm older.

VOCABULARY *a/the number of*

1 **Look at the phrases in the examples. Which one refers to an actual quantity? What is the meaning of the other one?**

1 There are probably **a number of** things lying around your house that you don't really need.
2 Because of **the number of** times I've babysat this month, I'm going to earn nearly £80.

2 **All of the adjectives in the box go with *a number of* and *the number of*. Add them to the table, according to their meaning.**

~~considerable~~	growing	increasing
limited	maximum	minimum
record	reduced	unlimited

Small quantity	Rising quantity	Large quantity
		a/the considerable number of

3 **Complete the sentences with adjectives from Exercise 2. In some cases, more than one answer is possible.**

1 Most tickets will be sold in advance, but a .... number of tickets will be available on the day.
2 Internet banking is becoming more secure, which explains the .... number of people using it.
3 Cloud services allow you as much storage space as you need, so you can back up an .... number of files.
4 The .... number of hours students should spend on homework each week is ten, but ideally you should spend much more than that.
5 This is the best year ever for the band and they've sold a .... number of albums – double their previous best.
6 The over-50s are becoming more interested in video games and the .... number of sales to this age group is changing the industry.

4 » **Work in pairs. Turn to page 123.**

WRITING An article

1 **Discuss the questions.**

1 What kinds of article do you read? Where are they published?
2 Have you, or has anyone you know, ever raised money for a local community project? What was it?

2 **Read the task. Then read the article quickly. Does the article answer the questions in the task?**

You see this notice in an international English-language magazine for teenagers.

Articles wanted

Imagine you want to raise £5,000 to spend on improving facilities for teenagers in the area where you live.

- How would you raise the money?
- What would you spend the money on, and why?

The best articles will be published in the magazine next month. Send us your article, and we might print it!

Write your **article**.

1 The facilities for teenagers at my local community centre are in need of updating. With a group of friends, I'm raising £5,000 to do it up. What's more, we hope to buy some new equipment.

2 How are we raising so much money? We're using our school's social media page as a shop, offering services to people in the neighbourhood, such as washing cars and tidying up gardens. On top of that, the school's parents' association has promised to match whatever we earn. For example, if we make £3,000, they'll give us an additional £3,000!

3 How are we going to spend the money? Mostly on repainting the rooms and repairing windows. We're also going to do up the kitchen. We'll probably have some money left, and we'll use it to buy a smart TV, install wi-fi and buy a pool table.

4 Will we raise enough? Yes! Even though we've only raised £800 so far, this is our dream and we're going to make it happen! It's hard to believe that one day we'll be watching films and playing pool in the community centre.

PREPARE TO WRITE | An article

When you write an article:
- include some opinion or comment as well as facts.
- organise your ideas into paragraphs.
- use linking phrases to connect your ideas.
- use an informal style.
- include questions to address the reader directly.
- think of an interesting title after you've written the article.

3 **Read the *Prepare to write* box. Then choose the best title for the article.**

A Making a dream come true
B Doing up our community centre
C Raising money for a good cause

4 **Match the paragraphs in the article to the topics.**

A Getting the funding
B Changes and purchases
C The end result
D Introduction

5 **Look at the highlighted linking phrases in the article. Then answer the questions.**

1 Which two phrases introduce a similar idea?
2 Which one introduces two contrasting ideas?
3 What other linking words and phrases can you use for these functions?

6 **Find three questions in the article. Why do you think it helps to include questions in an article?**

7 **Read the task in Exercise 2 again. Then plan your own article.**

8 **Write your article.**

- Use the tips in the *Prepare to write* box.
- Write 140–190 words.
- Check your grammar and spelling.

10 GIVE ME A HAND

ABOUT YOU

Do you have to help around the house? What do you have to do?
What is the worst household task you can think of?

VOCABULARY Household tasks

1 Look at the picture. Oliver has had some friends at his house for the weekend. They have just left. Match the tasks in the box to what Oliver needs to do before his parents get home.

EP

clear up the mess on the chair **fix** the leak
fold the towels **load** the dishwasher
put away the shopping **sort** the recycling
sweep the floor **wash up** the pans
water the plants **wipe** the surfaces

1 He has to wash up the pans.

2 Complete the sentences with the correct form of verbs in bold from Exercise 1.

1 Before I take out the rubbish, I have to ________ the glass and metal items for recycling.
2 My mum wants me to ________ her bike. The brakes aren't working.
3 You've spilled the sugar! Now you'll have to ________ the floor.
4 Can you ________ all the clothes that are on your bed? You need to ________ them first.
5 Be careful when you ________ the plants. Last time, you spilled the water and I had to ________ the table.
6 I have to ________ all the junk in my room before I can go out.

3 Discuss the questions.

Which of the tasks in Exercise 1
1 do you do regularly?
2 do you not have to do?
3 do you give others a hand to do?
4 are done by a parent or by someone else?

READING

1 Read the web post. Then choose the best summary.

A Teenagers should be paid for doing housework.
B Whether teenagers should do housework and be paid for it.
C Teenagers shouldn't be forced to do housework.
D Allowances should be earned by doing housework.

2 Read paragraph A and decide which answer (A, B, C or D) best fits each gap.

	A	B	C	D
0	choices	decisions	(C) priorities	preferenc
1	needed	obligatory	urgent	vital
2	after	for	on	with
3	losing	missing	misusing	wasting
4	expect	hope	suppose	wait
5	away	up	out	from
6	does	has	is	makes
7	already	always	still	yet
8	companion	member	partner	representati

3 Answer the questions.

1 What is the writer's view about whether teenagers should do housework, and whether or not they should be paid for doing it?
2 What kind of task does the writer think should be paid extra?
3 How old do you think Naomi Watkins is?
4 Who is her intended audience?

4 Match the highlighted words in the article to the meanings.

1 how useful or important something is
2 boring household tasks
3 in a way that isn't known or stated
4 an adult
5 an amount of money
6 do more than would normally be expected of you

5 Find all the questions in paragraph B. Then discuss your own answers.

THE BIG DEBATE

Chores! Yes, no, maybe?

Housework is a hot topic, with opinions divided about how much teenagers should do, and whether or not doing chores should be rewarded financially. Some of us are always being asked to help around the home and some of us aren't. Some teens are being paid for doing housework, while others have never been paid anything at all. So what should teenagers be expected to do at home, and if we have to do chores, should this be regarded as 'paid work'?

A There's the argument that we have so many essays to hand in, we have little time or energy to complete household tasks. I mean, what should our [0] *priorities* be: passing exams or clearing up the kitchen? Plus, it's [1] ________ that people are allowed to enjoy their childhood. We're supposed to look back [2] ________ this time as the best time of our lives, right? How can we enjoy ourselves if we're [3] ________ our free time wiping tables and folding towels? Having said that, each chore has to be done somehow or other. Is it fair to [4] ________ hard-working parents, who spend all day at work, to come home to cook and clean as well? There's the argument that teenagers are growing [5] ________, learning about the world and learning how to become adults. You'll have to look after yourself when you leave home, so it [6] ________ perfect sense to practise doing chores while you're [7] ________ at home. It's *your* home, after all, not a hotel, so why shouldn't you help out and be a useful [8] ________ of the household?

B There's also the question of being paid to do chores. Should we be given a small amount for every job we complete? And how much should that be? Should a teenager's allowance reflect the number of chores completed? Or should we receive a basic allowance, and then get a small sum on top of that depending on how much housework we've done? Some people are firmly in favour of teenagers being paid to do chores because it teaches people the value of money and it shows that work has benefits. On the other hand, you could argue that household chores are an essential aspect of family life. Does a teenager really need to be paid for doing what any grown-up in a family has to do?

C My opinion is that there should be a separation between a) regular allowances, b) tasks that we're expected to do for free, and c) paid tasks. Our allowance is our spending money. Parents should let us spend it as we please and we should get that regardless of anything else. Then there are standard chores that have to be performed in order for a household to function – daily tasks such as clearing up, unloading the dishwasher, washing up and putting things away. These jobs should be shared by children as soon as they're old enough, and they should do it for the family, not for cash. But I think there is a case for getting paid extra for jobs that are over and above the usual daily tasks. For example, a few months ago I gave my parents a hand repainting the living room. My parents didn't make me do it – I offered. It took us two days, about six hours a day, and it was really tiring! I was given £20 for helping, and that was brilliant for me, as it meant I could finally afford the new console I'd been saving up for!

D I've told you what I think – what's your opinion on this? Is our allowance a right or should it be earned? Should we get paid for everything or only when we 'go the extra mile'?

Naomi Watkins, Glasgow, Scotland
28 February 21:19

TALKING POINTS

Do you think that robots and machines will replace the need for people to do housework?
What are the best and worst jobs for teenagers outside the home?

GRAMMAR The passive

1 **Read the examples. Then complete the rules.**

1 Some of us **are always being asked** to help around the home.
2 Some teens **have never been paid** anything at all for doing housework .
3 What **should** teenagers **be expected** to do at home?
4 Each chore **has to be done** somehow or other.
5 I **was given** £20 **by** my parents for helping.

a We use the passive when the person or thing that causes the action is either unknown, unimportant or obvious.
b We form the passive using the appropriate form of the verb ______ and the ______ of the main verb.
c We can use ______ to say who performed the action of the verb.

» GRAMMAR REFERENCE AND PRACTICE PAGE 147

2 **Read the active sentences. Which two would be better in the passive? Why?**

1 My brother**'s cooking** dinner this evening.
2 I'm glad that someone **has cleared up** the mess.
3 The courier **hasn't delivered** the parcel yet.

3 **Complete the second sentence with the correct passive form of the verb in bold.**

1 They **installed** a new screen in our classroom.
A new screen ______ in our classroom.
2 An electrician **is fixing** the dishwasher right now.
The dishwasher ______ right now.
3 Someone **was sorting** the recycling.
The recycling ______.
4 Teachers **shouldn't give** us homework for the holidays.
We ______ homework for the holidays.
5 Someone **has put away** the plates and bowls.
The plates and bowls ______.

4 **Complete the sentences. Use the active or passive form of the verbs in brackets, adding *by* if necessary. There may be more than one possible answer.**

0 The world's first dishwasher *was designed by* (design) Josephine Cochrane in 1886.
1 Your coffees ______ (make) next.
2 The judges ______ (award) the prize to an Italian author.
3 My phone bill ______ (not pay) yet.
4 This building ______ (open) in 2013.
5 I ______ (call) my coach yesterday to check the time of the match.
6 Tickets ______ (should / collect) before 8 pm.
7 I think Bayern Munich ______ (might / beat) in the final tomorrow night.
8 This song ______ (not write) anyone famous.

5 **Complete the second sentence so that it has a similar meaning to the first sentence, using the word given. Do not change the word given. You must use between two and five words, including the word given.**

0 Tina said: 'You took my tablet!' ACCUSED
I *was accused of taking* Tina's tablet.
1 My sister made this pizza. WAS
This pizza ______ my sister.
2 They only launched Twitter in 2006. UNTIL
Twitter ______ 2006.
3 Carey Mulligan is taking the lead role in the film. IS
The lead role in the film ______ Carey Mulligan.
4 I get an allowance of about £20 a month. GIVEN
Each month, I ______ about £20.
5 They've asked me to pay back the money. BEEN
I ______ to pay back the money.
6 People are always asking me for help. AM
I ______ help.

6 **Correct the mistake in each sentence.**

1 British 16-year-olds paid an average allowance of £15 per month.
2 Cleaning are done by robots in some factories.
3 This house is built in the 1950s.
4 My bike has been stolen last year.
5 This game can be play online.
6 Read this. You can be surprised!

VOCABULARY *be allowed to, let* and *make*

1 **Read the examples. Then choose the correct meanings.**

EP

1 It's vital that people **are allowed to** enjoy their childhood.
It's important that people *can / don't* enjoy their childhood.
2 Parents should **let** teenagers spend their allowance as they please.
Teenagers *should / shouldn't* decide how to spend their allowance.
3 My parents **didn't make** me repaint the living room.
Helping to repaint the living room *was / wasn't* my choice.

2 **Compare the rules for your home in pairs. Use the ideas in the box or your own ideas. Start with *I'm (not) allowed to* or *My parents (don't) make/let me*.**

clear up after meals	eat breakfast in bed
get home before 11 pm	have friends over
use my phone in my room	miss meals
get up late at the weekend	wear whatever I like
watch what I like on TV	

I'm usually allowed to wear whatever I like.

Me too, except when we visit my grandparents.

3 » **Work in pairs. Turn to page 123.**

LISTENING

1 **Look at the photos. Then answer the questions.**

1 What do you think the devices are?
2 What do you think the Internet of Things might be?
3 How do you think the Internet of Things could change our lives?

The **Internet** of Things

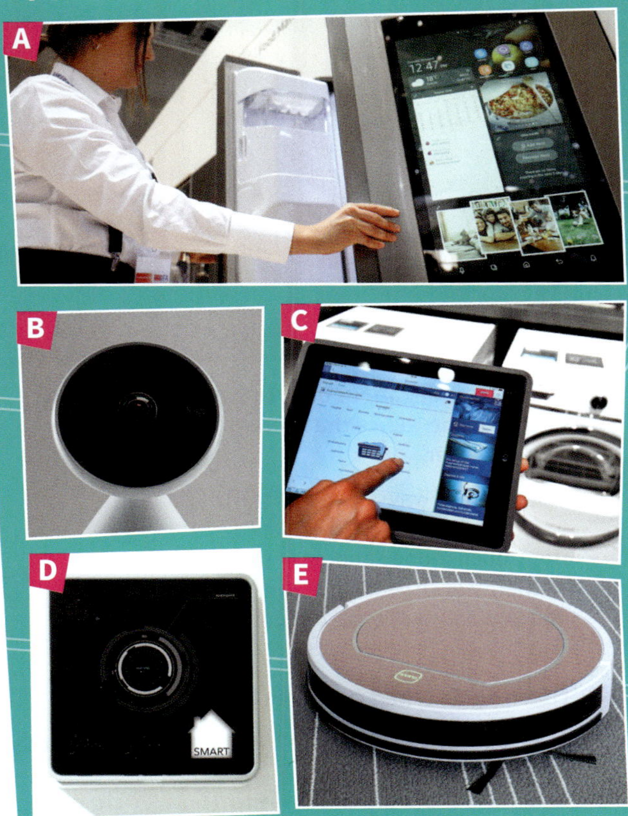

45 **2** **You will hear someone talking about how technology will change our lives. Complete the sentences with a word or short phrase.**

The Internet of Things

1 Helen works in California for a ______ firm.
2 Every home in the mid-1970s was equipped with a ______.
3 Calls to friends were usually answered by ______.
4 Helen dreamed of having a tiny machine that could reveal the ______ of friends.
5 More than ______ devices are now online.
6 The Internet of Things refers to everyday things, including ______ such as cookers and vacuum cleaners.
7 Everything in smart homes can be managed using a ______.
8 In the future, fridges will be programmed to ______.
9 Helen says people will have a device that can tell you what's going to happen and suggest that you ______.
10 People will use ______ to look for things around the house.

3 **Discuss how you could use the Internet of Things in your own home.**

SPEAKING Asking for and giving permission

46 **1** **Listen to four conversations. Then match the speakers to the people they are asking permission from in the box.**

girl in a café mother older brother teacher

46 **2** **Answer the questions. Then listen again and check.**

1 Who is given permission?
2 Who is not given permission?
3 Molly asks her brother *Do you mind if I use your tablet?* What is his response? What would he say if he was *giving* permission?

46 **3** **Read the *Prepare to speak* box. Which phrase did you hear twice? Then listen again and check.**

PREPARE TO SPEAK
Asking for and giving permission

Asking for permission
Do you mind if I … ?
Would it be OK if I … ?
Am I allowed to … ?

Giving permission
Sure, as long as you …
Go ahead.

Refusing permission
I'm sorry, but …
I'm afraid not.

4 **Look at the requests. Which would you use to: a friend, a parent, a teacher?**

use your phone
have motorcycle lessons
eat a few of their crisps
hand in homework late
borrow a tablet
have a new jacket
go shopping on Saturday
dye your hair
borrow some money
miss the last class today
have judo classes
not do PE today

5 **Work in pairs. Make conversations about some of the requests in Exercise 4.**

Is it OK if I use your phone?

Go ahead. It's on the table.

Is there a password?

Yes, I'll enter it for you.

CULTURE

ATTITUDES TO MONEY

1 Ask and answer the questions.

1 Are you more of a spender or a saver? Why?
2 Do you have any traditions in your family (or country) related to money?

2 Read the web page quickly. Then match the headings to the sections.

A Who shall we invite?
B Cash or card?
C Only one way to be 'rich'?
D Would you like to know how much I earn?
E I spent £200 on your present!
F Learning the real value of money
G Saving for a rainy day
H Ouch! Be careful, please!

3 Read the web page again. Then answer the questions.

1 What are Chinese people happy to talk about with people who they know well?
2 Who prefers paying for things in cash and why?
3 Who saves the most money?
4 Why would someone in China give you a present with the price still on it?
5 What might happen in south-western India if you accept a return invitation to a party?
6 When should the couple getting married at a Greek wedding be careful?
7 Apart from money, how else does Native American culture view wealth?
8 What are the benefits of having an allowance?

4 Match the highlighted words in the text to their meanings.

1 a large amount of money or valuable possessions
2 a small piece of paper with information on
3 using wireless technology to pay
4 money given to help a person or organisation
5 ways of paying money

TALKING POINTS

Which of the money facts or habits in the text do you find most surprising? Why?

If you were looking for a weekend job to make some money for yourself, what would you like to do?

47 **5** Listen to a talk about donating money to charity. Then put the topics that Peter talks about in the correct order.

The different ways people in the UK donate to charity ☐
How much money people in the UK donate to charity each year ☐
The world's most generous country ☐
The type of charities people in the UK donate to ☐

47 **6** Listen again. Then complete the sentences.

1 Each year, people in the UK donate approximately ________.
2 Older people prefer to give to ________ charities.
3 Every year in the UK, a total of ________ is donated using web pages, social media and apps.
4 The WGI survey asks three questions to people who are ________.
5 The second most generous country in the world is ________.

7 Complete the sentences with the words in the box.

care charity donor
fundraising support volunteer

USEFUL LANGUAGE

Talking about charities

1 How much does a typical ________ give to your charity?
2 How do they ________ for the animals they rescue?
3 It's not always easy choosing which ________ to support.
4 I would prefer to ________ for a local organisation.
5 There are lots of different ways to ________ a charity.
6 We are having our first ________ event next week.

MONEY MATTERS

48

Whether it's spending, saving, borrowing or lending, culture has a big influence on how we use and think about money.

A Greek wedding in the UK

1 ....

While people from many countries are quite secretive about how much they earn and their money habits, others are not so private. For example, the Chinese will often tell people how much they earn or how much their house cost. And it's normal for them to talk to close friends about their savings and spending habits. On the other hand, the British will also talk about their spending habits, but they rarely discuss their earnings or savings with anyone.

2 ....

Despite the availability of contactless cards and payment with mobile phone apps, there are cultures which still believe that cash is best. Germans pay for around 80% of their purchases in cash. They believe that a physical connection with money helps them be more aware of how much they are spending.

Which country uses the least cash? Well, the UK is the third most 'cashless' country. 52% of transactions are made by non-cash payment methods. But the UK is still behind Sweden, at 59%, and Canada, at 57%, the two most cashless nations.

3 ....

On average, Chinese people save around 37% of their income. That's a huge amount when we compare it to the average household in Spain, who save only 1.75% of their income. Other countries somewhere between these two are Mexico, with savings of 15%, and Russia, with nearly 8%.

4 ....

Most people make sure that they cut the price tag off a gift. But in China, for some gifts such as gold jewellery, it's common to leave the price on the gift so the receiver can see how generous you are. How would you feel about getting a gift and knowing exactly how much someone has spent?

5 ....

People in south-western India have an interesting solution for when they need money for something big like building a house. They have a party and guests are expected to make a cash donation to help raise money. However, it's not as simple as just having a party. The guest will probably return the invitation later on. And the person who organised the first party is expected to pay a larger amount than what they originally received as a donation.

6 ....

Weddings can be very expensive occasions. Guests at a Greek wedding take turns to pin banknotes onto the bride and groom's clothes … while they dance! It sounds like it could be a little painful at times! The money is to help the married couple begin their new life together.

7 ....

The idea of wealth can be a cultural matter. For example, some Native American cultures have a 'gift economy'. Instead of paying people money for something, people give things to each other. And there is no agreement that they will receive anything in return in the future. In these cultures, wealth is not just about getting and having money. It is connected to how things are distributed and shared. These things can be money, but also the time or knowledge needed to help someone.

8 ....

Parents in some countries give their kids an allowance for helping around the house and doing chores like loading the dishwasher. On average, a 15-year-old in Europe gets 20 euros a week. In the UK, it's also common for many teenagers to do paid jobs at the weekend, such as washing cars or dog walking. For many young people, this is their first financial responsibility and it teaches them how to save and make good financial choices.

PROJECT *Charitable habits*

Work in groups to research charitable habits in your country. Use these steps and the *Useful language* to help you.

1. Search online to find out how much money people donate to charity.
2. Investigate whether age and gender (or other factors) affect which organisations people donate to.
3. Research the different ways in which people donate.
4. Give examples of different ways in which people often help strangers or volunteer their time.
5. Prepare a presentation of your findings.

Present your work to the class.

08 NOW WATCH THE CULTURE VIDEO

11 THE DIGITAL AGE

A

B

C

D

E

F

G

H

I

J

ABOUT YOU

09 Watch the video. Then answer the questions.

What are the most exciting technological advances you've seen recently?

What new technologies are you interested in?

VOCABULARY Technological advances

1 Match the words to the photos.

EP

driverless car drone fitness tracker interactive whiteboard portable charger smart speaker smartwatch video game console virtual-reality headset wireless headphones

2 Choose two words/phrases in each group that go with the bold adjectives.

1 **portable** hard drive game console car
2 **smart** mouse television light bulb
3 **interactive** video headphones museum exhibition
4 **wireless** keyboard cable internet connection

3 Discuss the questions.

1 Which of the gadgets in Exercise 1 have you used?
2 Which of the technologies do you think is the
 a most useful?
 b least useful?
 c most boring?
 d most exciting?

READING

1 Read the article quickly. Then match the headings to the paragraphs.

A What about the cost?
B The technology isn't new
C What about the future?
D Negative uses of 3D printing
E A factory on your table
F How they work
G Opportunities for everyone

2 Read the article again.

Name two
1 current business uses of 3D printing.
2 reasons for the sudden popularity of 3D printing.
3 ways that 3D printing differs from 2D printing.
4 implications of 3D printers for designers.
5 potential criminal uses of 3D printers.
6 predicted developments in 3D printing.

3 Complete the sentences with the highlighted words in the article.

1 Digital technology has ________ altered our everyday lives.
2 My dad is a translator for a Chinese ________ company.
3 Schools are starting to try 3D printing because it has become ________ enough.
4 My friends have ________ arguments about who has the best phone.
5 Scientists are close to being able to print living plant and animal ________.
6 Too much ________ light makes my eyes hurt.

Want it? Need it? PRINT IT!

0 E
Buying things isn't difficult these days. You do a quick search online and within a few clicks, you're finished. You've done it hundreds of times. Within a day or two, it's delivered to your home. Could it be any easier? Well, imagine choosing something you want online, downloading a file of its design and instead of the 'buy' button, pressing 'print'. A little while later, on your desk, is … a unique case for your phone, a cool piece of original jewellery or even a musical instrument!

1 ....
Companies have been using 3D printers since the 1990s. Architects use them to make models of buildings. Companies like Adidas 'print' models of their new trainer designs with them. Over the past decade, in medicine, hospitals have been printing artificial replacements for bones in the body. However, there is another clear reason why there is a sudden interest in the machines again: price.

2 ....
When the first 2D printers went on sale, similar to those many of us have at home, they cost a fortune. Now they're cheaper than the ink that goes in them! While the 3D printer is still an expensive purchase, prices have fallen significantly and are now at the level where they are affordable for smaller businesses and schools. What's more, improvements to design mean they are easier to use than ever.

3 ....
Normal 2D printers print a thin layer of ink on a piece of paper. 3D printers are similar, except that instead of ink, they use materials such as plastic or metal. The 3D printing process involves printing layers of material on top of each other until a complete 3D object is formed. With small items, the process can take as little as 30 minutes. For more complex items, the printer will be working for several days on end. The result is a real 3D product – something you can touch, feel, hold and use! It's a unique method of manufacturing that could have a significant impact on our everyday lives.

4 ....
In product design, the possibilities for 3D printing are endless. In the past, designers spent weeks waiting for expensive models of their work. Now they can be made by anyone, professional or amateur, in an afternoon and for very little cost. In schools, there are implications across the curriculum: there are no end of applications for 3D printers in almost all subjects. A 17-year-old school student in the US designed and printed a fully functional artificial arm for just a few hundred dollars. The typical price is $10,000!

5 ....
There are many more exciting uses of 3D printers. However, there is already evidence of the misuse of these machines. As an experiment, some people have managed to print working copies of keys. They didn't even have a model of the original, they just used a photograph! And what about printing money? At the moment, it isn't economical to 3D-print metal coins, but will that change? And what about making copies of other people's work? One day, we might all be able to photograph an item we see in the shops, in a museum, at a friend's house and then produce it again at home. Is that fair?

3D printers mean artificial limbs can be printed much more cheaply.

6 ....
With the rapidly increasing interest in 3D technology, scientists have quickly developed ways of printing complex and large designs. There are now working examples of 3D-printed bikes, full-sized cars and even a five-storey office building! An American university has been developing machines that use more unusual types of 'ink'. So far, the team has successfully 'printed' real cakes and biscuits. One day, it seems likely that we will print meals at home regularly. By 2030, experts believe doctors will be able to print body parts made of real human tissue for use in operations. The ability to do this would change medicine, and the world, forever.

This building in China was printed in five days.

This bike frame was printed in metal.

TALKING POINTS

What other good and bad uses can you think of for a 3D printer?
How significant do you think the invention of the 3D printer is?

GRAMMAR Present perfect continuous

1 **Match the examples to the rules. Then complete the rules.**

1 My hands are dirty because I**'ve been putting** ink in my printer.
2 Companies **have been using** 3D printers since the 1990s.

We use the present perfect continuous to talk about an action that:
a started in the past and is still in progress. We often use it with *for/since*.
b has recently stopped and we can see the results.

We form the present perfect continuous with [1] ________ /*has* + (*not*) + [2] ________ + the [3] ________ form of a verb.

2 **Complete the sentences with the present perfect continuous form of the verbs in brackets.**

1 How long ________ you ________ (sit) outside?
2 My tablet ________ (not work) properly since it got wet.
3 Scientists ________ (dream) of wireless electricity since 1891.
4 What's all the white stuff on your T-shirt? ________ you ________ (paint)?
5 Our school ________ (use) interactive whiteboards for ages.

3 **Match the examples to the rules.**

1 You**'ve bought** stuff online hundreds of times.
2 We**'ve known** each other for ages.
3 So far, the team **has** successfully '**printed**' real cakes and biscuits.

We use the present perfect simple (not continuous):
a to talk about an action that is finished.
b to say how often an action has happened.
c with verbs that aren't used in the continuous, e.g. *like*, *know*, etc.

» GRAMMAR REFERENCE AND PRACTICE PAGE 148

4 **Choose the correct verb forms.**

1 We *have* / *'ve been having* problems with our computer for some time.
2 I *'ve worked* / *'ve been working* with children before.
3 We *'ve seen* / *'ve been seeing* all of those films.
4 He *works* / *'s been working* on that project for weeks.
5 We *'ve known* / *'ve been knowing* each other since childhood.
6 They *'ve used* / *'ve been using* interactive whiteboards many times.
7 I *was looking* / *'ve been looking* for my keys since Friday.
8 Last year, I *visited* / *'ve been visiting* many different cities.

5 **Make questions with the words. Use the present perfect simple or continuous. Then ask and answer the questions.**

0 How long / you / go / to this school?

How long have you been going to this school?

I've been going to this school for four and a half years.

1 you / ever / drive / a car?
2 Who / you / hang out / with recently?
3 What / you / watch / on TV lately?
4 How long / know / your best friend?
5 you / work / hard recently?
6 How many times / you / check / your phone today?
7 you / have / lunch today?

VOCABULARY Adjective suffixes

1 **Read the examples. What suffixes are used in the adjectives?**

EP

1 a cool piece of **original** jewellery
2 an **interactive** whiteboard
3 … the possibilities for 3D printing are **endless**.
4 … prices … are **affordable** for smaller businesses and schools.

2 **Read the table. Then make adjectives from the nouns and verbs below.**

Suffix	Adjective
-al	environment**al**
-y	fault**y**
-ous	danger**ous**
-ful/-less	use**ful**/use**less**
-able	reli**able**
-ive	creat**ive**

1 fame
2 thought
3 season
4 mystery
5 profit
6 impress
7 enjoy
8 tradition
9 innovate
10 care
11 adventure
12 spice

3 **Which of the adjectives in Exercise 2 could you use to describe these things?**

1 a lesson *enjoyable, …*
2 a piece of music
3 a meal
4 a gadget
5 someone's driving

4 » **Work in pairs. Turn to page 124.**

WRITING A persuasive email

1 **Read the task. Then answer the questions.**

1 Who is Mrs Taylor?
2 What would she like students to do?

You have received this email from the headteacher of your school.

From: Mrs Taylor
To: All students
Reply Forward

The school would like to spend some money on technology for use by students at school. What do you think the school should buy? Write to me with **one** suggestion. Explain why your suggestion is educationally useful for students and how much you would expect it to cost.

Mrs Taylor

Write your **email**.

2 **Read Anya's email. Which reasons does she give for buying tablets?**

1 They would save time in lessons.
2 They are physically tough enough for use in schools.
3 There are lots of suitable apps for students.
4 They are too expensive for students to buy themselves.
5 They would allow students to use the internet in more areas of study.

Dear Mrs Taylor,

I was pleased to read your email about new technology for our school. Young people are fascinated by this subject, so it's entirely appropriate that we've been given the opportunity to comment.

In my view, it would be incredibly useful for the school to have at least one class set of tablet computers. At the moment, we use desktop computers in the lab for very few subjects and, in reality, a lot of lesson time is wasted walking to the room and getting started. It goes without saying that tablets would be considerably easier to use in practical terms. They are portable and wireless and if they are always charged, they will always be ready to use.

Tablets will allow students to use the internet during lessons in a far wider range of subjects than at present. Furthermore, there are thousands of educational apps and games for tablets which are relevant to our studies.

In terms of cost, prices of tablets have fallen dramatically too, and no doubt there are several suitable models available for around £150 each.

I hope you will give my idea some serious consideration.

Best wishes,

Anya Noakes

3 **Read the *Prepare to write* box. Then match the highlighted phrases in Anya's email to the meanings (1–4).**

PREPARE TO WRITE

A persuasive email

When you write an email to persuade someone:

- give clear reasons and facts that support your opinions.
- use expressions to emphasise your opinions, e.g. *I was pleased that …*
- use adverbs to make adjectives and verbs stronger, e.g. *entirely appropriate.*

1 it is obvious …
2 the truth is …
3 it is very likely that …
4 it made me happy …

4 **Find five examples in Anya's email of an adverb used with an adjective or verb to make it stronger.**

5 **Replace the underlined phrases in the sentences with the phrases in the box.**

completely change	considerably longer
firmly believe	improved significantly
incredibly cheap	totally inadequate

1 3D printers are very inexpensive compared to their price a few years ago.
2 Technology can make a big difference to the way we learn.
3 Three computers are not enough for 30 students.
4 I really think that interactive whiteboards would motivate students.
5 Batteries on phones last much more time nowadays.
6 The speed of internet access has got a lot better.

6 **Read the task in Exercise 1 again. Then plan your email.**

- What new technology would you be most interested in having in your school?
- How would it be educationally useful to students?
- What would you expect it to cost?

7 **Write your email.**

- Use your answers to the questions in Exercise 6.
- Use the tips in the *Prepare to write* box to make your email persuasive.
- Write 140–190 words.
- Check your grammar and spelling.

12 MY CIRCLE OF FRIENDS

ABOUT YOU

What are your best and worst qualities?
How do you meet new friends?

VOCABULARY Personality adjectives

1 Do the quiz. Compare your answers in pairs. Then turn to page 124 and check your results. Do you agree with what the results say about you?

What are you REALLY like?

1 Your friend arrives at the cinema late and the film's started.
- a You don't mind. Everyone's late from time to time.
- b You shout at them furiously, refuse to watch the film and go home.

2 You've been asked to help some younger students with a maths problem. After 20 minutes, they're still struggling to understand.
- a You suggest a quick break and then starting again.
- b You give up. They'll never understand. It's a waste of time!

3 You're about to donate some old clothes to a charity shop when you notice a jacket you could probably sell online.
- a You still give the charity shop the jacket. It's for charity.
- b You sell the jacket online. Charity starts at home.

4 You've just got some exam results. You've done well, but your friend has done badly.
- a You offer to help your friend to revise next time.
- b You tell your friend how easy you found it.

5 You've planned a barbecue this afternoon, but the forecast says it's going to rain.
- a You go ahead with the barbecue. People will still have fun even if it's wet, and maybe the weather will improve.
- b You cancel the barbecue. If it's wet, the barbecue will be a disaster.

6 You're meant to be taking part in a school concert this evening, but you've just been invited to a party.
- a You perform at the concert as planned.
- b You make an excuse to your music teacher and you go to the party.

2 EP Match the pairs of adjectives to a and b in each question in the quiz.

generous/mean	☐	reliable/unreliable	☐
optimistic/pessimistic	☐	thoughtful/insensitive	☐
easy-going/bad-tempered	1	patient/impatient	☐

3 Which adjectives from Exercise 2 describe
- a you?
- b members of your family?
- c your close friends?

Compare your answers in pairs.

READING

1 Read the article quickly. Then choose the best title.
- A You can never have too many friends
- B Friends: What's the ideal number?
- C Too many friends, too little time

2 Read the article again. Choose the answer (A, B, C or D) which you think fits best according to the article.

1 What does *their* refer to in line 4?
- A researchers in Australia
- B 1,500 people
- C lifestyles
- D strong networks of friends

2 The writer claims that the most popular people at school
- A are also more popular at work.
- B are more likely to work in teams.
- C work harder in their careers.
- D seem to get better-paid jobs.

3 Professor Dunbar found that people with a lot of friends on social networking sites
- A live longer than people with fewer friends.
- B regularly contact no more than 150 of them.
- C tend to be from wealthier families.
- D send up to 2,000 messages per day.

4 According to Dunbar, your closest friends are
- A those with similar interests.
- B people who contact you once a week.
- C those you have known a long time.
- D people you never fall out with.

5 According to a Canadian study, young people with more than 300 friends
- A spend too much time reading updates from their friends.
- B feel more stressed than people with fewer friends.
- C are usually aged between 12 and 17.
- D are more easily influenced by their friends.

How many close friends do you have? And does the number of friends you have make a difference to your life?

Researchers in Australia, who studied 1,500 people over the age of 70 and their lifestyles, have found that people with strong networks of friends live longer than those with few friends. One of the major reasons for their findings is that good friends encourage positive behaviour that promotes good health as you get older. For instance, if you have several good friends, the report says, you're more likely to do exercise. You're also more likely to eat healthily and have a positive image of yourself.

A similar positive effect of friends on your wealth has also been found. An American study of 10,000 students, over a period of 35 years, found that if you make more friends than the average person at school, you'll earn a higher salary in later life. According to researchers, this is perfectly logical. People need good social skills at work to manage people and work in a team successfully. These are the same skills we use to make friends at school.

Through social networks, it's easy to stay in touch with people we know, wherever they live. On average, teenagers aged between 15 and 17 have 500 'friends' on their favourite social networking site. Adults have 130. So if you believe the research above, you might live for a long time and be very rich. However, according to Professor Robin Dunbar from the University of Oxford, it probably won't make any difference. Dunbar studied the number of messages between users of a popular social networking website, each of whom had between 200 and 2,000 friends. He found that they communicate with a maximum of 150 people on a regular basis. In fact, Dunbar believes this number is the limit of the number of relationships the human brain can manage.

Among this maximum number of friends, Dunbar believes that typically around five people are close friends. You've most likely been friends for a long time, and you share lots of important experiences with them. Then there are ten more friends. They aren't as close as the first five and you may not get in touch with them every week. Next, there are 35 people who you might spend time with because of a common hobby. You aren't close. And finally, there's a large group of 100. You see or speak to these people a few times every year and you always get on with them, but you don't know them well. Beyond this number, Dunbar says, it's impossible for most people to maintain relationships enough to make them meaningful.

In fact, according to research from Canada, having more than 300 social networking friends can actually be harmful for your well-being. In a study of 88 young people aged between 12 and 17 and their social media habits, the researchers observed that particularly sociable people showed the highest levels of anxiety. One reason is possibly that if you read too many posts about people's 'wonderful lives', it might actually make you feel negative about your own. Another, the researchers suggest, is that with popularity comes a social pressure that young people, in particular, might find difficult to handle.

If you have a lot of online 'friends', try this experiment: first take away all the people you can't remember. Then remove anyone you haven't been in touch with for a year and, finally, take away friends who you wouldn't care if you lost touch with. How many do you have left? Now forget about the quantity and think about the quality. How many of these people are actually *good* friends? According to the research, these are the only people that really matter.

3 **Question 6 is a global question, so you need to read the complete article to answer it. Choose the best answer (A, B, C or D).**

6 What is the main message of the article?

A It's more important to have good friends than lots of friends.
B Social networks are enabling us to live for longer.
C There is a lot of research on the effect of friends on your health.
D Maintaining worthwhile friendships with lots of people is difficult.

TALKING POINTS

What do you think of Professor Dunbar's theory that it's only possible to have 150 friends?

What are the advantages and disadvantages of having a lot of friends?

GRAMMAR Zero and first conditionals

1 **Match the examples to the rules.**

1 **If you have** several good friends, **you're** more likely to do exercise.
2 **If you make** more friends at school, **you'll earn** a higher salary in later life.
3 **If you read** too many posts about people's 'wonderful lives', **it might** actually **make** you feel negative about your own.
4 **If you have** a lot of online 'friends', **try** this experiment.

In conditional sentences, the action or situation in the main clause is a result of the *if*-clause. We:
a use conditional sentences with imperatives to give general instructions or advice.
b use the zero conditional with *if* or *when* to talk about general truths or facts.
c use the first conditional to talk about likely events in the present or future and their definite results.
d can use *may, might* or *could* instead of *will* in the first conditional.

» GRAMMAR REFERENCE AND PRACTICE PAGE 149

2 **Match the sentence halves.**

1 We could go to Jen's house
2 If you can't be more responsible,
3 Tell Jack to get in touch
4 If you go into town tomorrow,
5 I usually get an instant reply
6 If you want me to help you,
7 I'll clear up the kitchen

a don't be so bad-tempered!
b when I text my mum.
c if she has to stay in.
d if you see him.
e if you lay the table.
f we might come too.
g I won't let you sit together again.

3 **Correct the mistake in each sentence.**

1 Have you to sit at a desk all day, it's absolutely necessary to get some exercise.
2 I won't be able to help you unless if you tell me what is wrong.
3 Will it be OK if I will visit in July?
4 If you continue to be so mean, I wouldn't stay friends with you.

4 **Choose the correct verbs. Sometimes there is more than one possible answer. Explain your answers.**

Ben: Wow! You've got 456 friends! That's ridiculous!
Anna: I know. I read an article recently which said if you [1] *have / will have* over 300 friends on social networking sites, it might [2] *have / has* a negative effect on your life.
Ben: You should delete some, then.
Anna: But people [3] *might / will* get offended if I [4] *delete / 'll delete* them.
Ben: That's true. Social media is so addictive! When I [5] *start / will start* reading people's posts, I [6] *won't / can't* stop.
Anna: Well, if you don't like it, [7] *you close / close* your account.
Ben: But if I leave the site, I [8] *lose / could lose* touch with some people altogether.
Anna: Exactly. And if you [9] *don't / won't* read posts and messages, you [10] *could / may* miss an invitation to something, like a party or …
Ben: We have to leave for the film. If we [11] *'re / 'll be* late, you [12] *have / 'll have* 455 friends!
Anna: What? Oh, very funny!

VOCABULARY Adjective and noun suffixes

1 **Read the examples. Which word is a noun? Which is an adjective?**

1 Does the number of friends you have make a **difference** to your life?
2 It's easier to keep in touch with friends, even if they live in **different** places.

2 **Put the pairs of words in the correct column.**

EP
~~happiness~~ generosity patient
important organised strength
~~happy~~ generous patience
strong importance organisation

Adjectives	Nouns
happy	*happiness*

3 **Complete the sentences with a word from each pair in the box.**

fit/fitness generous/generosity
intelligent/intelligence patient/patience
qualified/qualifications strong/strength

1 Ms Woods is a good teacher, but she doesn't have much ________ with some students.
2 Isabel is one of the most ________ people in my school. She often gets the highest marks in exams.
3 You could easily improve your ________ by cycling.
4 What ________ do you need to study medicine?
5 Rosie has always had a ________ relationship with her brother. They're really close.
6 Thanks for the present. It was really ________ of you!

4 » **Work in pairs. Turn to page 124.**

LISTENING

1 **Read the short article. What do you think of Mr Hendon's unofficial ban?**

A headteacher from a British school has introduced an unofficial ban on 'best friends'. Mr Hendon, the head at Queensbridge School in Liverpool, says that having best friends can lead to difficult situations when students fall out with each other, so he is encouraging students at the school to have a wide range of friends rather than being obsessed about who their best friend is.

51 **2** **Listen to five people giving their opinion on the article in Exercise 1. Number the speakers in the order you hear them.**

A a teacher ......
B a psychologist ......
C a parent ......
D a teenager ......
E a journalist ......

51 **3** **Listen again. Choose from the list (A–H) what each speaker says. Use the letters only once. There are three extra letters which you do not need to use.**

A Some young people find it difficult to have large friendship groups.
B Friendship problems can teach young people how to deal with negative emotions.
C It's impossible to stop children from wanting to have best friends.
D Close relationships encourage young people to develop more positive aspects of their personalities.
E Young people need to be more sensitive about leaving people out of close friendship groups.
F Managing relationships with close friends is a useful skill to learn at a young age.
G Groups of three of more friends generally argue less frequently.
H Close friends are as important as family members.

4 **Read the sentences in Exercise 3 again. Which do you agree or disagree with?**

SPEAKING Describing photographs (2)

1 **Look at the two photos of friends together in different situations. Then answer the questions.**

1 What things are similar in each photo?
2 What things are different in each photo?

52 **2** **Listen to Sara talking about the photos. Which of your similarities and differences does she mention?**

52 **3** **Read the *Prepare to speak* box. Then listen again. Which phrase does Sara not use?**

PREPARE TO SPEAK | **Speculating**

I can't be sure …
It's hard to say …
It could be that …
It seems as if …
My guess is that …
Another possibility is that …
Perhaps he's/she's been …

53 **4** **Listen to Luis answering a question related to the photos. Which question does he answer?**

1 Do you think it's better for young people to have a best friend or have a wide group of friends?
2 How do you know your best friend, and what do you like most about him or her?
3 What qualities do you think are most important in a good friend?

54 **5** **Complete Sara and Luis's sentences with the phrases in the box. Then listen and check.**

look | looks | look as though | looks like

1 The girls .... they're in their late teens or early twenties.
2 They all .... friendly and easy-going.
3 The girl on the right .... upset.
4 He actually .... me, so people think we're brothers!

6 **Look at the photo. What is the situation? Make sentences using the phrases in the *Prepare to speak* box and *look*, *look as though* or *look like*.**

7 **Work in pairs. Turn to page 124 and do the task. Use phrases from the *Prepare to speak* box to speculate. Take turns to be Student A and Student B.**

LIFE SKILLS ICT LITERACY

USING SOCIAL MEDIA RESPONSIBLY

LIFE SKILLS

Using social media responsibly

Social media is a big part of everyday life for most people, from sharing our personal news to staying up to date with what is happening all over the world. However, irresponsible behaviour online can easily damage your reputation or harm other people. We should all learn how to use social media responsibly, so we can benefit from its opportunities and avoid the consequences of negative online behaviour.

1 **Ask and answer the questions.**

1 Which social media apps or sites do you use? What do you use them for?
2 Have you ever seen a post on social media which made you feel uncomfortable or angry?
3 Do you think people use social media responsibly? Why? / Why not?

2 **Read the article quickly. Which of the following topics are mentioned? There are two which you do not need.**

1 Sharing information about where you are in real time
2 How to change privacy settings on sites and apps
3 Reasons why people might post negative things about others
4 Reacting to people who intentionally try to make others angry
5 The dangers of forming personal relationships online
6 Being aware of how posts create an image of you online

3 **Read the article again and answer the questions.**

1 Which type of privacy settings should you pay particular attention to?
2 Why do some people think they can be negative to other users online?
3 What should you do about online *trolls*?
4 How can you make sure you don't spend too much time on social media?
5 How can your social media posts affect your future career?

4 **Do you agree with the advice given in the article? What other advice would you give?**

5 **Match the highlighted words in the text to the meanings.**

1 when people have a different opinion about something
2 something you definitely shouldn't do
3 understand something in a way that isn't correct
4 remove a link which identifies you on a social network

55 **6** **Listen to the introduction of a talk by an expert. Then answer the questions.**

1 What is the talk about?
2 How does the expert help the students remember the important points?

55 **7** **Listen again. Are the sentences true (T), false (F) or not mentioned (NM)?**

1 The expert wants to tell the students about the benefits of using social media.
2 You can always control how a post will be shared by using the privacy settings on an app.
3 She thinks it's a good idea for the students to post news items on social media.
4 The final question you should ask yourself is whether what you are posting is kind and respectful.
5 She encourages students to use similar memory techniques for when they use social media.

HOW RESPONSIBLE ARE YOU ONLINE?

Globally, there are around three billion active social media users, and this week's trending topic is the responsible use of social media. Social networks are a great place to share your ideas and talk about things that you like. In an ideal world, using these sites and apps should be an enjoyable experience. We'd like to offer you a few bits of advice to make sure that it is!

Staying safe online is obviously very important and your privacy is related to that. Make sure that you take the time to review any information and options in the privacy section very carefully. That's the only way you can make intelligent and informed decisions about how much personal information you want to share about yourself and with whom. Sharing too much private information is always a big no-no! This is why it's especially important to disable settings on apps which post your location automatically. Do you really want total strangers to know exactly where you are?

Some people use social media to complain and to express their frustration with things. It's really easy to get into arguments with people online. And sometimes people can be mean and write rude comments about other users just because they're jealous of the photo the other person has posted of their new computer or recent beach holiday. These people usually know that their behaviour isn't acceptable or positive, but they feel anonymous. It's easy to be a bully online, but it's much better for everyone if you're positive and don't insult other users in your posts. Also, it's important to remember that nothing you do online is 100% anonymous.

With all the discussions happening online, it's inevitable that there are some disagreements between people. This is perfectly normal and healthy if people treat each other respectfully. However, another thing which we see lots of online is *trolling*. This is when people deliberately misinterpret opinions and provoke arguments for their own enjoyment. Sometimes they make insensitive comments on purpose and that can be very harmful. The best thing you can do with people who do this is just ignore them completely or reply to their posts in a polite and respectful way.

Social media can be an addiction. Everyone knows that's not good, but more often than not, people don't realise they are addicted! Users can spend hours online each day, paying more attention to their online friends than people in real life. As a result, friendships and other personal relationships can begin to suffer. 'Do everything in moderation' is the best rule to follow here. Set yourself a daily time limit for social media. Use three hours, for example, and spend the rest of your time with friends or family or doing activities like sports.

Finally, as social media users, we should all ask ourselves: What do I want my social media to say about me? Remember that people who aren't your friends or contacts might see your posts. And that could include potential future employers. So next time you grab your phone or tablet to post something online, aim to communicate the image you want the world to see. What you post today might not feel like it matters. But remember that it will still be somewhere online in ten years' time! It's also a good habit to regularly untag yourself from other people's photos and posts which you don't want to be linked to your accounts.

On average, people aged 16–20 have nine social media apps or accounts!

8 **Complete the sentences with the words in the box.**

avoid   may   rely   remember
should   sure   wouldn't

USEFUL LANGUAGE

Giving advice

1 One thing you ________ definitely do is think very carefully before you post anything online.
2 Don't ________ on the privacy settings of an app.
3 Make ________ you don't spread any rumours or fake news!
4 Always try to ________ posting rude or offensive things.
5 ________ that when you post something online, you might never be able to delete it.
6 If you ________ say something to someone in person, don't post it online!
7 Of course, you ________ want to create your own acronym.

PROJECT

A guide to using social media responsibly

Work in groups to create a guide to using social media responsibly. Use these steps to help you.

1 Decide on the main message(s) you want to communicate.
2 Choose a specific target age group.
3 Brainstorm advice you want to give.
4 Use different ways to make your advice memorable.
5 Decide how you want to present your guide: a poster, video, blog entry, etc.
6 Divide the project into smaller individual tasks and decide who will do what.

Present your guide to the class.

REVIEW 3 UNITS 9–12

VOCABULARY

1 Complete the sentences with a noun from A and a preposition from B.

A allowance bargain cashpoint debit card savings

B of off on x2 out

1 Could you lend me some money? I'm a bit short ______ cash at the moment, and my parents don't give me my ______ until Saturday.
2 If you're going past a ______, could you take ______ some money for me?
3 If you use a credit card instead of a ______, you have to pay ______ the amount you owe at the end of the month.
4 People often waste money ______ things they don't need just because something looks like it's a ______.
5 I find it difficult to live ______ the money my parents give me, so I sometimes take a little out of my ______.

2 Complete the messages with the words in the box.

clear fold load put sorting sweeping wash water wipe

I put some clean clothes in your bedroom this morning. It took me ages to [1] ______ them all, so please [2] ______ them away carefully.

Also, please can you [3] ______ up the mess in the kitchen before I get home? The recycling needs [4] ______, so can you put the paper in one bag and glass in another?

One more thing! Can you [5] ______ the dishwasher (carefully!) and then switch it on? Don't worry about the saucepans – I'll [6] ______ those up when I get home. Then could you [7] ______ the surfaces? There's food all over them. Don't worry about [8] ______ the floor. I know it's a bit dirty, but I'll do that when I get back!

Lovely day today. If the plants in the living room are looking a bit dry, please [9] ______ them.

3 Match the words to make gadgets.

1 wireless
2 virtual reality
3 smart
4 driverless
5 fitness
6 interactive
7 portable

a headset
b tracker
c headphones
d charger
e car
f speaker
g whiteboard

4 Choose the best adjective in the box to describe each person.

bad-tempered generous impatient pessimistic reliable thoughtful

1 Jen often clears up around the house because she knows it helps her parents.
2 Sam's always on time.
3 Jack often gets annoyed easily.
4 Dan always sees the bad side of any situation.
5 Alex is always buying presents for her friends.
6 Cassie won't wait for anything or anyone. She gets bored really quickly.

5 Complete the opposites of the adjectives in Exercise 4.

1 in*sensitive*
2 un______
3 ea______
4 op______
5 me______
6 pa______

GRAMMAR

1 Choose the correct option, a or b.

1 Give me a call around 10 pm.
  a I won't do anything then.
  b I won't be doing anything then.

2 I can never remember things.
  a I'm going to forget my PIN.
  b I'll be forgetting my PIN.

3 I haven't decided yet, but I …
  a might buy a fitness tracker.
  b will buy a fitness tracker.

4 This time next week, …
  a I'll be sitting on a plane.
  b I'm going to sit on a plane.

5 I don't think I can come out on Friday.
  a I well might be short of cash by then.
  b I may well be short of cash by then.

6 I'm going away, so …
  a I might not be in touch for a few days.
  b I could not be in touch for a few days.

7 If you fix my laptop, …
  a I fold your clothes for you.
  b I'll fold your clothes for you.

8 The charger starts working only if …
  a it's connected to a phone.
  b it will be connected to a phone.

9 If you go now, …
  a you'll definitely get there in time.
  b you might definitely get there in time.

10 If you want a games console, …
  a you take some money out of your savings.
  b take some money out of your savings.

2 Rewrite the sentences in the passive.

1 They're telling us the results tomorrow.
2 Someone's fixed the dishwasher.
3 You should keep your PIN secret.
4 Someone took some money from my wallet.
5 An American engineer invented the driverless car in 1925.
6 They're giving me a prize for my project.

3 Complete the conversation with the present perfect or present perfect continuous form of the verbs.

Louis: I'm so sorry. [1] ________ you ________ (wait) a long time?
Elodie: Well, I [2] ________ (be) here since six. That's when we agreed to meet, isn't it?
Louis: Yeah. I [3] ________ (make) this journey loads of times, but I still managed to get lost!
Elodie: I [4] ________ (try) to call you too. Why didn't you answer?
Louis: My battery [5] ________ (run) out.
Elodie: Well, I can see you [6] ________ (run), so sit down and relax for a moment. The good news is that I [7] ________ already ________ (buy) the tickets.
Louis: Nice one. I think the film [8] ________ (sell) out now.

4 Choose the correct words.

1 We will *have* / *be having* more fun if we take the train.
2 How long have you *waited* / *been waiting* for your PIN?
3 Stay in touch if you *will can* / *can*.
4 The money *was* / *has been* paid into your bank account yesterday.

5 Correct the mistake in each sentence.

1 Packages will be delivering by drone soon.
2 I was using my fitness tracker a lot recently.
3 I am waiting for you tomorrow at seven, outside my house.
4 If you give me another chance, I would be more reliable.

6 Read the text and think of the word which best fits each gap. Use only one word in each gap.

THE FUTURE OF HOUSEWORK

A team of researchers at universities in the US and Canada has created a computer program which they hope will one [0] *day* make our lives a lot easier. [1] ________ the help of software that is typically used [2] ________ make computer games, they designed a virtual home with virtual robots. They then programmed the robots to understand 3,000 different household tasks. [3] ________ humans, computers don't have any common sense, and careful instructions [4] ________ needed to complete a simple household task. So the team broke each task down [5] ________ lots of different stages. For instance, making a cup of coffee begins with 'go to the kitchen', 'open a cupboard' and then 'take [6] ________ a mug'. The virtual robots are not [7] ________ able to perform almost any household task, but they can also learn to do new ones [8] ________ 'watching' other virtual robots. In the future, the researchers are aiming to use the program to train real robots to help at home.

7 Read the text. Use the word given in capitals at the end of some of the lines to form a word that fits in the gap in the same line.

What can our personalities tell us about the friends we make?

We know that we [0] *typically* make friends with	TYPICAL
people who share similar [1] ________ with us,	CHARACTER
but a recent Finnish study suggests that our	
personality can tell us a lot more about our	
friends, such as where they live, what they look	
like and how long our [2] ________ will last.	FRIEND
The researchers analysed data from 12,000	
people in the UK. They found that if you are	
open to new experiences, you tend to have a	
bigger group of friends that is more [3] ________	CULTURE
diverse. You are also more likely to have	
friends who live some [4] ________ from you and,	DISTANT
therefore, that you see [5] ________. On the other	FREQUENT
hand, if you are a more cautious person, your	
friends live closer to your home and are more	
likely to be of a similar background and culture.	
Another [6] ________ was that easy-going people	DISCOVER
are more likely to stay friends for longer. This	
means that these types of people usually	
have more [7] ________ relationships, including	TRADITION
friends from their [8] ________. And if you're	CHILD
hard-working, there's a greater chance you	
make good friends with relatives and also with	
people of the same sex.	
Are the findings true for you and your friends?	

13 SPORTS STARS

ABOUT YOU

10 Watch the video.
Then answer the questions.

Which sports do you play? How seriously do you play them?

Do you follow news stories about sports stars? Why? / Why not?

Who's your favourite sports star?

VOCABULARY Reporting nouns

57 **1** **Listen to three reports about sports personalities in the news. Then match the stories to the photos.**

2 **Read the five quotes. Which three relate to photos A–C? Check the meanings of the nouns in the quotes.**

EP

1 The fans' **response** to the signing of a new goalkeeper has been extremely negative.

2 The **threat** that the club might end the manager's contract now seems very real.

3 The player's tearful **confession** has shocked the world of racket sports.

4 The captain's injury sounded quite serious, but as yet there's no **update** on his condition.

5 The **rumours** about the runner moving look like they might actually be true.

57 **3** **Complete the sentences with the nouns in the box. Then listen again and check. Which two nouns have a related verb with the same form?**

EP

confirmation	criticism	hint	mention
prediction	proposal	statement	

1 It's probably only ________ of what you already know.
2 He made no ________ of leaving the club.
3 Maybe Carlos Silva can take a ________.
4 He's faced a lot of ________ for his decision.
5 There's been no official ________ about exactly when he'll go.
6 The current ________ is that Devlin will miss the rest of the tournaments this season.
7 There's not yet a clear ________ to punish her.

4 **Discuss the questions.**

1 Can you think of examples of confessions made by sportspeople? What happened?
2 Have you heard any interesting rumours about sports personalities recently? What are they?
3 Do you have any predictions about who might win this year's biggest sports competitions?
4 How do you think famous sportspeople deal with online threats and criticism?

READING

1 **Look at the titles of the four texts and the photos. What do you think the four girls have in common? Read the texts quickly and check your ideas.**

2 **Read questions 1 and 2 and think about the sections highlighted in green and blue. Then look at the parts of the texts in the same colour and answer the questions.**

Which girl

1 has won a record number of medals for her country?
2 was sponsored during her time at an educational institution?
3 thinks childhood dance training prepared her to compete in front of a crowd later on?
4 recalls being supplied with clothes for a particular competition?
5 had to take breaks from her sport due to a health problem?
6 experienced her sport for the first time as part of a celebration?
7 showed early talent in a new fitness activity she was doing?
8 has successfully competed with older opponents?
9 struggled initially because of the new physical demands on her?
10 was involved in a special pre-event ceremony?

A SARAH
first swimming, then cycling

Britain's highest-achieving Paralympian, Sarah Storey, has reached the top in two completely different sports. At school, she tried everything from athletics to netball and swimming: 'I just loved to compete. It didn't matter what sport I was doing.' At only 14, Sarah was selected for the ParalympicsGB female swimming squad and won six medals at her first Paralympic Games, including two golds. Her disability, a partly formed left hand, dates from birth, but has never stopped her determination to compete. 'I was brought up to always try my best and I just carried on as normal,' she says. Why did she switch from swimming to cycling? 'I started suffering severe ear infections, which meant long periods out of the water. To keep in shape, I took up cycling, and was soon spotted by British Cycling, who told me I had great potential.' And success came quickly again, when Sarah won five golds at the European Paralympic Championships. Since then, she has managed to break world records in swimming and cycling 75 times.

B KATHERINE
from field hockey to the ice rink

Katherine Gale was captain of her school field hockey team, but switched to ice hockey, where she immediately showed a lot of promise. Katherine led the Under-18 GB women's team and took part in the Winter Youth Olympic Games in Innsbruck, Austria. As a member of the Team GB squad, she has great memories of that event. 'Everyone was in GB kit from head to toe. I was shown the biggest bag of kit I have ever seen and told it was mine. Even my trainers had *Team GB* sewn on them!'

Katherine is also an ambassador athlete for TASS, the Talented Athlete Scholarship Scheme, whose financial support enabled her to attend a Canadian boarding school with academic study and ice hockey training under one roof. Katherine was an Olympic torch bearer at the 2012 London Olympics, proudly running through the town of Newbury with the torch just days before the opening of the Games.

C SOPHIE
ballet skills useful in hammer throwing

Hammer thrower Sophie Hitchon reached an Olympic final in her chosen sport, and claimed that 12 years of ballet training had helped her to aim for medal success. She argues that the time she spent on stage as a teenage dancer equipped her mentally to deal with the pressure and huge expectations of home supporters. But are there any real similarities between the two activities? Sophie said, 'At first, hammer throwing seemed impossible because it was a completely different movement, using parts of my body I had never used before, but it got easier. Ballet really helped me with my balance, too.' Sophie doesn't have the usual body shape of a hammer thrower, being slim and only 1.7 m tall, but what she lacks in size, she makes up for in strength. She broke the British record with a hammer throw of 74.5 m at the 2016 Rio Olympics.

D PAIGE
karting queen to future F1 driver?

Paige Holden showed an early talent for driving at the age of 12, when she went karting for a birthday party. Her mother says, 'After that, we started going every Sunday, and Paige became a member at the local race track. She soon got to the top of the leader board and was beating men in their late 20s! So we bought her a kart, which has a maximum speed of 60 mph.' The kart is pink and matches her racing clothes. If she is to continue to national level, and even step into motor-racing, Paige will need to be sponsored, as the cost of replacement engines is huge. However, she is confident in her ability, thanks to a family tradition – her father was a motocross champion. Perhaps once she finishes school she will end up racing bigger and faster cars – she may even end up competing in Formula 1. Who knows?

3 Look at the green and blue highlighting in texts C and D. Notice how these texts use words from questions 1 and 2 to look like correct answers.

4 Read questions 3–10 in Exercise 2 and underline the important words. Then read the texts again and answer the questions.

5 Match the highlighted words in the article to the meanings.

1 sports clothing and equipment
2 doesn't have any or enough of something that is required
3 ability to stay upright and not fall over
4 a list of who is winning a series of races at that moment
5 do something better/faster than anyone else

TALKING POINTS

What are the advantages and disadvantages of playing sport professionally?
Why do colleges and universities offer sports scholarships? Is this a good idea?

GRAMMAR Reported statements

1 Read the examples. Then complete the rules.

1 'I was brought up to always try my best.'
Sarah **explained that** she **had been brought up** to always try her best.
2 'Sarah, you have great potential!'
I was soon spotted by British Cycling, who **told me I had** great potential.
3 'We bought her a kart, which has a maximum speed of 60 mph.'
Paige's mother **said they had bought** her a kart, which **has** a maximum speed of 60 mph.

When we report a statement:
a we use a reporting verb (e.g. *say*, ... or ....) + *that*-clause. (We often omit *that*.)
b the *that*-clause verb usually moves back in the past, e.g. past simple → ....
c the tense doesn't always change with permanent or general situations, e.g. the second verb in example ....
d we also often change ...., e.g. *you* and *me*.

» GRAMMAR REFERENCE AND PRACTICE PAGE 150

2 Choose the correct words in the reported statements.

1 'We played well in the match.'
He said they *have played* / *had played* well in the match.
2 'I can't play tennis because of my leg.'
She explained that she *couldn't* / *can't* play tennis because of *my* / *her* leg.
3 'I was captain of the team at my last school.'
Jon *said* / *told* me that he'd been captain of the team at *my* / *his* last school.
4 'I didn't enjoy the game.'
Fran told me that she *didn't enjoy* / *hadn't enjoyed* the game.
5 'You aren't allowed to play ball games here.'
Someone *says* / *said* we aren't allowed to play ball games there.
6 'I've never seen Anita play, but I know she trains hard.'
Tommy said he *'s never seen* / *'d never seen* Anita play, but he *'s known* / *knows* she trains hard.

3 Finish the reported statements with a *that*-clause, making any changes necessary.

1 'I'll email confirmation of the date.'
The manager said that he ....
2 'There have been several rumours about cheating.'
The journalist claimed that ....
3 'The club has made no mention of selling our top player.'
The owner explained ....
4 'The team hasn't performed well due to the media criticism.'
The captain complained ....
5 'We can still win the league if we focus on our game.'
The captain insisted ....
6 'I don't want any mention of arguments within the team.'
She stated ....

VOCABULARY Reporting verbs

1 Read the examples. How do the different reporting verbs affect the meaning of the sentences? EP

1 Sophie **claimed** that 12 years of ballet training had helped her to aim for medal success.
2 She **argues** that the time she spent on stage was very important.
3 She **told** me not to worry.
4 The coach **encouraged** me to train harder.

2 Read the sentences. Then match the reporting verbs to the meanings. EP

1 The player **admitted** cheating during the game.
2 She **begged** the coach to let her play.
3 The coach **reminded** me to touch the side of the pool after each length.
4 The owners of the club **revealed** that they wanted to sell it.
5 Her coach **emphasised** that she must continue training.
6 The manager **declared** that she intended to retire.
7 She refused to **confirm** whether the stories about her were true.
8 The coach **proposed** that they should train twice a week.

a give information that was secret
b show that something is especially important
c ask someone very strongly to do something
d suggest a plan or action
e tell someone not to forget something
f announce something publicly or officially
g agree that something is true, often unwillingly
h say or show that something is true

3 Choose the correct verbs.

1 Kathy *reminded* / *emphasised* me not to be late for training.
2 The player has *confirmed* / *proposed* that he should move to a new club.
3 Sam *begged* / *declared* the coach to give him a place in the team.
4 It has been *emphasised* / *revealed* that the captain faces arrest for cheating.
5 The coach *declared* / *proposed* that the goalkeeper was fit to play.
6 The owner has *emphasised* / *admitted* that she still has confidence in her manager.
7 Holly has *admitted* / *reminded* that she no longer enjoys playing.
8 We can now *confirm* / *reveal* that today's match will go ahead.

4 » Work in pairs. Turn to page 125.

WRITING An informal letter

1 **Read the exam task and Stuart's reply. Find where Stuart answers each question in his letter.**

You have received this letter from your English-speaking pen friend.

> I'm doing a project about sports in various regions of the world, so I thought I'd ask about where you live. Does your country have a national sport or a sport that many people play or enjoy watching? Who is it played by? Can you describe the game and say something about its history?
>
> Write soon,
>
> Zara

Write your **letter**.

> Hi there!
>
> Thanks for your letter. It's great to hear from you. You asked about sports here in Scotland. You're asking the right person, because I'm obsessed with sports!
>
> Scottish people have a passion for football, and rugby has a massive following, too. Having said that, I'd say the national sport is golf. You weren't expecting that, were you? Golf was invented here over 600 years ago, and the world's oldest golf course is at St Andrews, in Fife. It's estimated that 50% of men and 10% of women have their own set of golf clubs. It's no surprise that there always seem to be golf tournaments on TV.
>
> There's no question that the game is simple. The aim is to hit your ball into a series of 18 holes around the course. It's rare to get a 'hole in one', which is when your ball goes into the hole on the first shot. Mostly, people take at least four shots to get the ball in. What else? Oh, yes, players spend hours wandering across the greens between holes, which means that it's a really relaxing sport.
>
> Hopefully this information is helpful.
>
> Take care,
>
> Stuart

2 **Read the *Prepare to write* box. Then read the letter again and answer the questions.**

1. What informal phrases for starting and ending a letter does Stuart use? What other features of informal language does he use?
2. Why does Stuart say, 'You weren't expecting that were you?'?
3. Why does he say, 'Having said that …'?
4. He claims that golf is always on Scottish TV. Is this a fact or an opinion?
5. Stuart argues that aim of the game is simple. Is this a fact or an opinion?

PREPARE TO WRITE An informal letter

- Use linking words to express:
  contrast: *having said that, in spite of*
  result: *this means that / which means that, consequently*
- Use questions to add interest.
- Use informal forms and expressions.
- Use phrases for:
  starting a letter:
  Thanks for your letter.; It's great to hear from you.; How have you been getting on?
  responding to a request:
  You asked about … ; You wanted to know whether …
  It sounds as if you're looking for …
  giving an opinion:
  I'd say that … ; It's no surprise that … ; It seems clear to me that …
  stating a fact:
  The fact is that … ; It's estimated that … ; There's no question that …
  ending a letter:
  Hopefully this information is helpful.
  Get in touch if you need any more information.
  Looking forward to hearing your news.

3 **Choose the correct answers.**

> [1] *There's no question that / It's no surprise that* the Murray brothers have raised the profile of tennis in Scotland: tennis is in the news in Scotland every time there's a major international tournament. [2] *Which means that / In spite of this*, more people play football (16%) than tennis (2%). [3] *I'd say that / Consequently*, there are more football pitches than tennis courts.

> I love racket sports like squash, badminton and table tennis. [4] *Having said that, / Which means that* I like swimming, too. And I live opposite a swimming pool, [5] *in spite of that / which means that* I go swimming more than I play racket sports. An article in a recent edition of a journal revealed the medical benefits of swimming, and [6] *it's estimated that / it seems clear to me that* swimming prevents 100,000 deaths every year.

4 **Make sentences giving an opinion or stating a fact about the ideas below or your own ideas. Write as many as possible in three minutes. Then compare your sentences in pairs.**

1. Basketball is better than football.
2. Female sports stars get more prize money than men.
3. Football is increasing in popularity.
4. People don't play enough sport.
5. Team sports are more fun than individual sports.
6. Playing sport regularly means that you live longer.

5 **Write your answer to the task in Exercise 1.**

- Use the tips in the *Prepare to write* box.
- Write about 140–190 words.
- Check your grammar and spelling.

14 ACCIDENT AND EMERGENCY

E

F

G
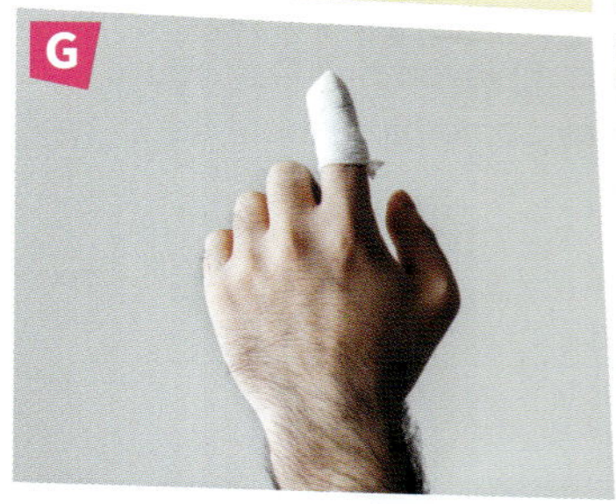

H

I

ABOUT YOU

Have you ever had an accident or been in an emergency situation? What happened? What did you do?

VOCABULARY Accidents and emergencies

59 **1** **Listen to nine short conversations. Then match the conversations to the photos.**

A

B
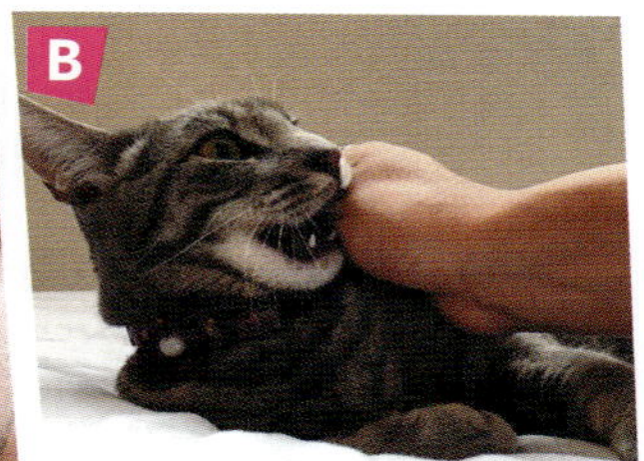

C

D

2 **Match the phrases to the pictures A–I.**

EP

be bitten by an animal bump your head
cut yourself on something sharp
have an allergic reaction to something
pass out slip on a wet floor
swallow something poisonous
trip over something twist your ankle

3 **Discuss the questions. Then check your answers on page 125.**

1 Which of these accidents do you think is the most and least common?
   A swallowing something poisonous
   B tripping over something
   C bumping into something
2 Which age group is most likely to have an accident at home?
   A 0–4 years
   B 5–15 years
   C 75+ years
3 Who have more accidents: boys or girls?
4 In which room are you most likely to have an accident at home?

READING

1 **Read the article quickly. What is the main message in the article?**

A Adults need to be more careful with their phones in case they dial 999 by accident.
B There is a need for an alternative to 999 for non-emergency situations.
C People should only call the emergency services when there is an actual emergency.
D Teenagers should be more responsible about calling the emergency services.

2 **Read the article again. What do these numbers in the text represent?**

£5,000 35 million
999 75% five

3 **Read the article again. Then answer the questions.**

1 Why did the woman in Robert's story contact the emergency services?
2 What's the main difference between 'silent calls' and 'joke calls'?
3 Why does Robert think there are fewer joke calls these days?
4 What do you think an emergency services operator would say to the woman from Italy?
5 Why are non-emergency calls a problem?

It's an EMERGENCY! ... Or is it?

60

The woman was terrified. What could she do? She dialled 999. To her, it was an emergency.

'We answered the call immediately,' said Robert Naylor, the emergency call operator who spoke to the woman. Over 95% of calls to the emergency services in the UK are answered within five seconds. Robert asked what the problem was.

'Please help me! It's in my bathroom!' the woman shouted. Her voice suddenly got louder. 'It's moving!' she screamed.

'What is moving?' Robert asked calmly.

'A spider!' the woman yelled back at him.

Robert believes that a significant number of the calls he answers are not emergencies. Of the 35 million calls made every year, the actual figure is close to 75%. That's 26 million calls!

Firstly, there are 'silent calls'. The emergency number is dialled, but when an operator answers, no one actually speaks. Often it's a small child, or even a pet, who has been playing with a phone and has accidentally rung the emergency number. More commonly, they are 'pocket calls' from mobile phones. 'The caller doesn't know we're listening, so we sometimes hear some odd conversations!' Robert says. 'But we have to stay on the line for a little while to decide whether it's a genuine emergency or not.'

Then there are 'joke calls', often from teenagers. An operator answers the phone and the caller immediately hangs up. Robert believes these are on the decline, as there are far fewer public payphones these days. 'People are less tempted to make a silly call when they're doing it from their own mobile phone and they know we have their number!'

The police always follow up both types of call and there is often no other way than visiting the address where the call came from. It's an enormous waste of money; the average cost of responding to a silent or joke call is around £250.

The vast majority of the non-emergency calls, though, are like those from the woman above. A situation like this *isn't* an emergency, at least not one that people like Robert are meant to be dealing with. But this example is far from the worst that people like Robert experience all over the world on a daily basis. What do you think of the following?

- A teenage girl in the US called the police because her parents had decorated her room and she didn't like the colour.
- A mother in Italy rang the emergency services when her 16-year-old son refused to get out of bed. The operator asked the woman what she wanted the police to do. She wanted to know if they were going to arrest him!
- A teenager in Brazil rang and asked the police to remove a video of him from YouTube. The video showed the boy falling off his bike. He told the police it was 'really embarrassing'.

There are many other examples, from complaints about the wrong pizza delivery to people who want to know today's date. And most of these are from adults. It's hard not to laugh, but these calls waste more than time and money. 'If someone makes a joke call and the police manage to find them, then they can expect a fine of up to £5,000 and, in some cases, a prison sentence,' warns Robert. 'But for people whose emergencies aren't really serious, we simply try to deal with their calls as quickly as possible,' he continues. 'The person often quickly realises their situation isn't really an emergency and ends up apologising for calling us. But if someone refuses to listen, or even starts having an argument with us, then we have to hang up. Someone with a *real* emergency is probably waiting to speak to us.'

TALKING POINTS

Have you ever phoned the emergency services by accident?

What could the emergency services do about the problem of non-emergency phone calls?

GRAMMAR Reported questions and requests

1 **Read the examples. Then match them to the direct questions. Which question is a request?**

1 Robert **asked what** the problem was.
2 A teenage boy **asked the police to** remove a video of him from YouTube.
3 The woman **wanted to know if** the police were going to arrest her son!

a Can you remove a video of me from YouTube?

b Are you going to arrest my son?

c What's the problem?

2 **Choose the correct words.**

When we report questions, we:
a *sometimes* / *always* use an object after *ask*.
b *change* / *don't change* the tenses in the same way as reported speech with statements.
c *use* / *don't use* the auxiliary verbs *do*, *does* or *did*.
d put the subject of the question *before* / *after* the verb.
e use *if* or *whether* to report *Yes/No* / *Wh-* questions.

When we report requests, we:
f use an infinitive *with* / *without* 'to'.

» GRAMMAR REFERENCE AND PRACTICE PAGE 151

3 **Choose the correct words.**

1 They asked me *I'd* / *if I'd* ever fainted before.
2 He asked *to speak* / *can he speak* to my parents.
3 The doctor asked me what *I had* / *had I* eaten that day.
4 The woman asked me *phone* / *to phone* the emergency services.
5 I asked her where *was she* / *she was* calling from.
6 The operator asked me which emergency service I *did want* / *wanted*.

61 **4** **Listen to the conversation, which is based on a real call to the emergency services in the US. Then listen again and complete the questions.**

1 **Operator:** .... the problem?
2 **Boy:** .... with my math?
3 **Operator:** .... you say?
4 **Operator:** .... are you?
5 **Operator:** .... what number this is?
6 **Woman:** .... you doing?

5 **Report the questions in Exercise 4.**

1 The operator asked the boy …
2 The boy asked the operator …
3 The operator asked the boy …
4 The operator …
5 The operator …
6 The woman …

6 **Correct the mistake in each sentence.**

1 The police officer asked me where was my mother.
2 The teacher asked me to standing up.
3 I ask her if I could take someone with me.
4 She wanted to know what she should do in an emergency?
5 He called Jack and told him if they could meet.
6 We asked the man get some help.
7 I asked him wether he had twisted his ankle.

VOCABULARY *have*, *make* and *give* + noun

1 **Read the examples. What verbs could replace the phrases?**

1 People are less tempted to **make a call** from their mobile phone.
2 If someone starts **having an argument** with us, we have to hang up.

2 **Put the phrases in the box in the correct column. Then check their meaning.**

EP

~~a promise~~ a quarrel a talk
a word (with someone) an attempt
fun of someone/something someone a hand
someone a hug the strength

give	*have*	*make*
		a promise

3 **Complete the second sentence so that it has a similar meaning to the first sentence, using the word given. Do not change the word given. You must use between two and five words, including the word given.**

1 I wasn't strong enough to lift the box. **HAVE**
I .... to lift the box.
2 'Can you speak to the whole class about your experience?' asked the head. **GIVE**
The head asked me .... to the whole class about my experience.
3 'Can you speak to Chloe about the problem?' the teacher asked me. **WORD**
The teacher asked me .... Chloe about the problem.
4 He didn't try to help us at all. **ATTEMPT**
He .... to help us.
5 'Could you help me with the suitcases, Jess?' said Dad. **HAND**
Dad asked Jess .... with the suitcases.
6 Some of Sam's friends tease him about his hair because it's so long. **FUN**
Some of Sam's friends .... his hair because it's so long.

4 **Can you think of any more nouns that can be used with the verbs *have*, *make* and *give*?**

5 » **Work in pairs. Turn to page 125.**

LISTENING

1 **Read the questions in Exercise 2. Then check the meaning of any words you do not know.**

62 **2** **You will hear people talking in eight different situations. For questions 1–8, choose the best answer (A, B or C).**

1 You hear part of a talk by a sports teacher. What is she saying to the students?
  A She's reminding them to be polite to other swimmers.
  B She's warning students to be careful around the pool.
  C She's explaining what students need to bring for swimming.

2 You hear a boy talking about an accident. Why does he think he was lucky?
  A He could have cut himself.
  B He could have injured his ankle.
  C He could have been bitten by the dog.

3 You hear two friends talking about a TV show called *Emergency!* What do they agree?
  A The TV show has put them off studying medicine.
  B The girl's performance in the TV show was impressive.
  C They won't watch the TV show in the future.

4 You hear part of a news story about an accident. Why is the story in the news?
  A because the boy hurt himself seriously
  B because the boy's actions were very unselfish
  C because the boy was charged a lot of money

5 You hear a boy talking about a nut allergy. Over the years, how has his allergy changed?
  A It's no longer something he thinks about.
  B It isn't as severe as it used to be.
  C It's become easier to manage.

6 You hear two people talking about their pet. What does the woman think about the situation?
  A She doubts that the animal is seriously unwell.
  B She proposes getting professional help for the animal.
  C She's pleased the animal is getting better.

7 You hear part of a talk by the leader of a mountain rescue team. What does she think is the biggest mistake that climbers make?
  A They lack equipment for climbing.
  B They don't think carefully enough before going climbing.
  C They are too inexperienced at climbing.

8 You hear two friends talking about a police officer who gave a talk at their school. What do they agree about?
  A It was more interesting than they expected.
  B Being a police officer must be a difficult job.
  C She wasn't a typical police officer.

SPEAKING Being polite

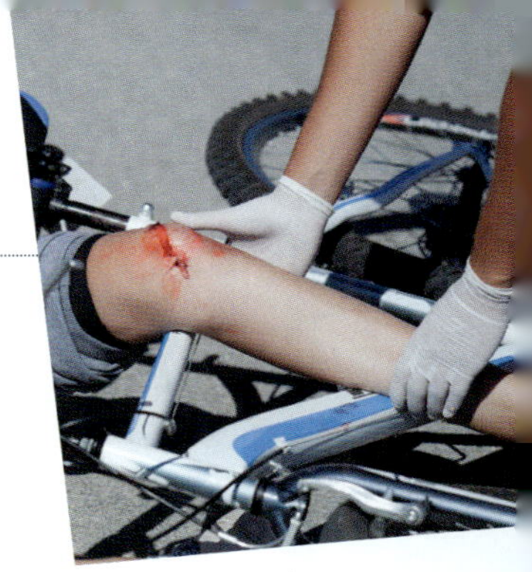

1 **Look at the photo. What would you do if you saw someone in this situation?**

63 **2** **Listen to the conversation. Then tick (✓) the correct sentences and correct the false ones.**

1 The woman saw the accident. ☐
2 The woman offers to take the boy and his bike home. ☐
3 The woman leaves a message for the boy's mum. ☐
4 The boy refuses the woman's offer. ☐
5 The woman makes two phone calls for the boy. ☐
6 The woman knew the boy before the accident. ☐

64 **3** **Listen to another version of the conversation. Who sounded more polite, the speakers in the first conversation or those in the second conversation? Why?**

4 **Read the *Prepare to speak* box. Then rewrite the indirect questions as direct questions.**

PREPARE TO SPEAK | Indirect questions

We use indirect questions to be polite. After the question phrase, they have the same word order as affirmative sentences.

Question phrases
Do you think …?
Have you any idea who/what/where … ?
Do you know if/whether … ?
Can/Could you tell me who/what/where … ?

0 Do you know if my bike is all right?
  Is my bike all right?
1 Do you think you can walk?
2 Do you think you could call my mum for me?
3 Do you know what the number is?
4 Have you any idea where she is?
5 Could you tell me where you live?

5 **Put the words in the correct order to make indirect questions.**

1 how / passed / know / you / for? / you / long / out / do
2 you / have / you? / bit / what / idea / any
3 you / home / think / get / yourself? / you / can / by / do
4 allergies? / you / you / any / do / if / from / know / suffer
5 what / me / tell / you / could / please? / is, / birth / of / date / your

6 **Practise your conversation in pairs. Then change roles.**

Student A: You're a doctor at the hospital. Student B has had an accident. Find out as much information about the accident as possible. Use indirect questions.
Student B: You've just had an accident and are at the hospital. Answer Student A's questions.

CULTURE

VOLUNTEERING FOR EMERGENCY SERVICES

1 **Ask and answer the questions.**

1. Do you know anyone who works in the emergency services? What do they do?
2. Have you ever been a volunteer for an organisation or at an event?

2 **Read the title of the article and look at the photos. What do you think the article is about? Quickly read the first paragraph to check your ideas.**

3 **Read the whole article. Are the sentences true (T), false (F) or not mentioned (NM)?**

1. The number of volunteer firefighters is similar in different countries.
2. Fire Cadets in London learn how to drive a fire engine.
3. There are 300 volunteers in the first two years of the Paris training programme.
4. In Paris, participants can be a real firefighter when they have completed the full programme.
5. The volunteer programme in Calgary trains cadets to help look for missing people.
6. All volunteers in Christchurch are trained in how to respond to fires.

4 **Match the highlighted words in the text to their meanings.**

1. movements which require skill and care
2. students training to be officers
3. fighting or dealing with
4. a feeling of satisfaction from doing something well
5. dangerous things

TALKING POINTS

Would you ever consider volunteering to help the emergency services? Why? / Why not?

How old do you think someone should be to participate in programmes like these? Why?

65 **5** **Listen to the *Helping Hands* radio show. What is the purpose of the interview? Choose the best description.**

A To inform listeners about the work of search-and-rescue volunteers

B To encourage people to volunteer in search and rescue services

C To warn volunteers about the dangers of search and rescue work

65 **6** **Listen again. Then complete the sentences.**

1. In his normal life, Michael works as a ________ instructor.
2. Michael also does volunteer work with the ________ Service.
3. Michael thinks injuries in rescue workers can be avoided if they are ________.
4. Different volunteer pilots are ________ to fly a helicopter in an emergency.
5. Janet practises rescue missions with search-and-rescue teams, and with ________ workers from hospitals.
6. According to Janet, volunteer ________ workers should always be prepared.

7 **Complete the sentences with the words and phrases in the box.**

case	helping out	incidents
missions	safety	well trained

USEFUL LANGUAGE

Talking about emergency services

1. Many emergency services depend on volunteers ________ in support roles.
2. Rescue workers and volunteers need to be ________ because people's lives are at risk.
3. Major ________ often need a large number of volunteers and rescue workers.
4. It's important to consider the ________ of both emergency workers and the people being rescued.
5. Fortunately, real emergency ________ don't happen very often.
6. We have to be prepared for any possible situation, just in ________.

YOUNG FIREFIGHTERS!

66

When most of us think of firefighters, images from the movies of fire engines and brave professionals **tackling** burning buildings come to mind. Although the numbers vary by country, you may be surprised that a lot of firefighters are in fact volunteers. Volunteer fire departments, brigades and associations can be found all over the world. And volunteering opportunities aren't only for adults. Teenagers and young people can fill important roles in these organisations. Being a volunteer firefighter can be a very rewarding experience and it's also a great way to serve your local community. Is it something you could see yourself doing? From London to Paris and Calgary to Christchurch, here are just a few such programmes from around the world.

London, UK

The London Fire Brigade runs the Fire Cadets programme for people aged 11–17. The programme lasts 12 months, and **cadets** receive an official qualification at the end. They learn practical skills like rolling out and using a fire hose, climbing ladders and giving first aid. Cadets also learn about fire safety by exploring firefighting equipment and observing **hazards** and fire risks. And they get the opportunity to become familiar with the brigade's fire engines, although they can't drive them!

Paris, France

Young Firefighters of Paris invite around 90 young people to join their programme every year in its six training centres. The Paris Firefighter Brigade asks that its young firefighters are serious and motivated. The process starts with a discovery week, where 300 young people participate, but only 90 are selected for the programme. The young firefighters who are chosen then go on to do training that takes place on 30 Saturday afternoons over two years. And for those who successfully complete these two years, the final stage is a one-year training programme to become a professional firefighter. Aged between 16 and 18 when they begin the course, the Young Firefighters also participate in military training and learn fire and rescue **manoeuvres**.

Calgary, Canada

The 18-month Calgary Fire Cadet Programme for local high-school students is open to 15- to 18-year-olds. The Calgary Fire Department asks that participants have a positive attitude and are willing to learn new things. Cadets join a class of 20 students to learn basic firefighter skills, including search-and-rescue techniques and how to use fire extinguishers. The programme, which began in 2000, emphasises key values such as **pride**, teamwork and respect.

Christchurch, New Zealand

In Christchurch, volunteers need to be at least 16 and they can help in real emergency situations or provide support, such as helping people, controlling traffic or transporting equipment. These support roles are important, because they mean that professional firefighters have more time to tackle a fire or emergency situation. Outside the city, volunteer firefighters from rural stations are specially trained in how to respond to wild fires.

PROJECT Emergency services

What emergency services should tourists know about in your area? Answer the questions. Then write an information leaflet for visitors.

1. What are the local telephone numbers for emergencies?
2. Where can tourists go to speak to a police officer?
3. Where are the most important hospitals in your area?
4. Are there any special rescue services in your area?
5. When and where should visitors be especially careful (e.g. surfing at the beach, hiking in a national park)?
6. Are there any volunteer search-and-rescue associations?

11 NOW WATCH THE CULTURE VIDEO

15 TELLING THE TRUTH

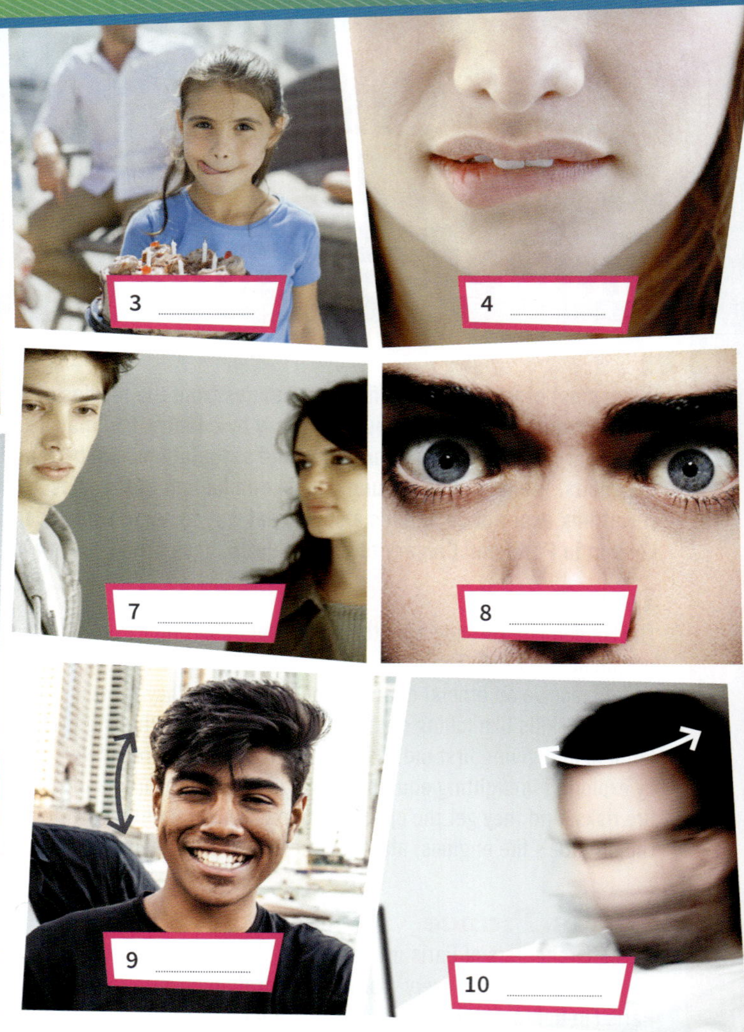

ABOUT YOU

Can you always tell how someone is feeling from their facial expression?

In what other ways can someone's body language show how they are feeling?

VOCABULARY Facial expressions

1 **Label the photos with the verbs and phrases in the box.** EP

avoid eye contact	bite your lip	blink	blush
lick your lips	nod your head	rub your eyes	
shake your head	stare	yawn	

2 **Listen and decide what the people are probably doing. Use the phrases in Exercise 1. Sometimes more than one answer is possible.** (67)

1 Jamie is ……………… .
2 Bea is ……………… .
3 Clare is ……………… .
4 Tom is ……………… .
5 Dan is ……………… .
6 Mum is ……………… .
7 Jackie is ……………… .
8 Aiden is ……………… .

3 **Work in pairs. In your country, what does it mean when you do these things?**

1 lick your lips
2 yawn
3 shake your head
4 blush
5 nod your head
6 bite your lip

READING

1 **Are you good at spotting when someone is lying? Make a list of some ways you think you can tell.**

2 **Read the article. Which of your ideas from Exercise 1 are mentioned?**

3 **Sentence A fits the first gap in the article. What does the underlined phrase refer to?**

A People who are lying might do <u>all these things</u>.

4 **Choose from the sentences B–G the one which fits each gap (2–6). Use the <u>underlined</u> words to help you decide. There is one extra sentence which you do not need to use.**

B Instead, many psychologists now believe the best <u>techniques</u> are simple things that anyone can do.
C Perhaps it's better *not* to know when someone is lying in <u>situations like these.</u>
D The theory behind <u>this</u> is that it requires more brain power to lie than to tell the truth.
E <u>It</u> works by measuring heartbeat, blood pressure and breathing patterns.
F And, as a result of <u>this</u>, they are more likely to reveal something that is obviously untrue.
G A significant difference between <u>the two</u> is a sign that the person might not be telling the truth.

The TRUTH about lying

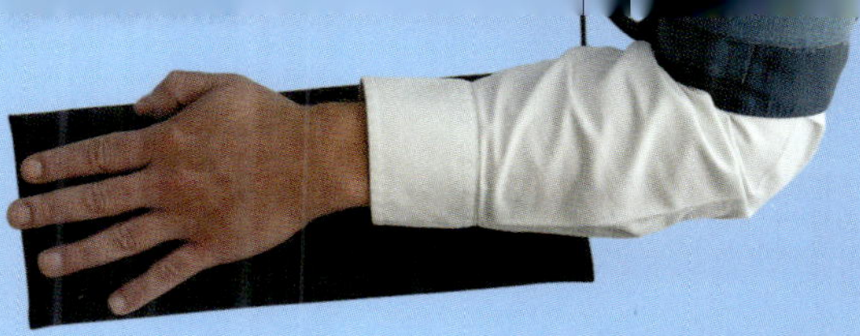

68

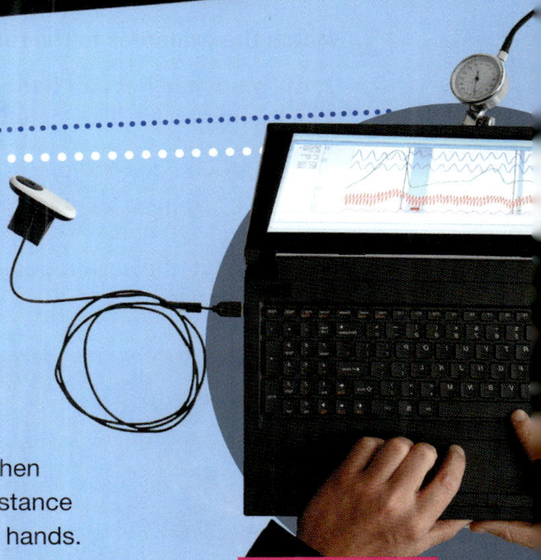

a polygraph

How can you spot when someone isn't telling the truth? This question was asked to 2,500 people in 63 countries. The top answer was that someone who is lying avoids making eye contact. Some added that liars look up and to the right. Others said they look up and to the left. Which is it? The answer is neither, of course.

As a matter of fact, people who are lying and people who are telling the truth make eye contact for a similar amount of time. They look up, down, left and right. Therefore, none of this proves whether someone is telling the truth or not. Other answers in the survey were related to facial expressions and body language. Liars blush and look nervous. Liars scratch their nose or ear. Again, these are myths. (1) ______. However, so does anyone who is telling the truth – especially if they are feeling genuinely anxious.

In criminal matters, some countries use a polygraph, or lie detector, when they interview suspects. (2) ______. The machine was first produced in 1921 using research by a psychologist, William Marston. Marston didn't invent the polygraph himself – a medical student, John Larson, came up with the idea. But the invention inspired Marston in later life when he did some work for a comic-book publisher and created the superhero Wonder Woman. Her 'lasso of truth' was a piece of rope which forced criminals to tell the truth. Many experts believe the science behind the polygraph is no better than Wonder Woman's magic lasso.

More recently, scientists have used computers to analyse people's eyes, voices and even brains in order to discover if someone is lying. However, the fact of the matter is that there is little proof that any of these methods actually work. (3) ______

One example of a successful strategy is the 'Baseline Method'. It involves knowing how someone typically acts when they *are* telling the truth, for instance perhaps someone waves their hands. Compare this to how they are acting now. (4) ______ However, according to tests, the Baseline Method only increases your chances of spotting a liar from 50% to around 60%.

Another method is useful when someone is telling a story, for example about where they were yesterday and what they did. This is a popular method used by the police when interviewing suspects. First, the police get the person to tell their story in detail. Then they ask them to repeat their story, but backwards, starting at the end and going back to the beginning. (5) ______ And, therefore, it's much more difficult to do this task if you're making things up. A liar will typically make mistakes in the order in which they retell their story.

But how useful is being able to spot a liar, really? Research shows that, on average, people tell between one and two lies every day. However, the vast majority are trivial. We tell small lies, also called 'white lies', to be polite, to avoid upsetting someone or to make someone feel better. Examples from one study included 'My mum had her hair done for a party and I didn't like it. But I told her it looked great.' 'A friend had his bike stolen and I told him the same thing had happened to me recently. It actually happened years ago.' (6) ______ If we did, then soon we might not want to speak to anyone!

TALKING POINTS

What are the benefits of being honest?

What might happen if we were all completely honest with each other all the time?

Is looking up and left a sign of lying?
Or is it up and right?

GRAMMAR *have something done*

1 **Match the examples to the rules.**

1 My mum **had** her hair **done** for a party.
2 A friend **had** his bike **stolen**.

We use *have* + object + past participle to:
a say we arranged for someone to do something for us.
b talk about unpleasant things that have happened to us.

2 **Write the questions and add two more. Then ask and answer them.**

Have you ever had
1 eyes / test?
2 photo / take / professionally?
3 anything / publish / online?
4 anything / steal?

get someone to do something

3 **Read the example. Then complete the rule.**

The police **get** the person **to tell** their story in detail.

We use *get* + object (person) + ________ for things we ask or persuade someone to do.

» GRAMMAR REFERENCE AND PRACTICE PAGE 152

4 **Read the questions and add two more. Then ask and answer them.**

Have you ever got anyone to
1 do your homework for you?
2 admit they were wrong about something?
3 bring something you'd forgotten to school?
4 pick you up late after a party?

5 **Choose the correct words.**

1 Are you having your hair *cut* / *to cut* tomorrow?
2 My mum had her bag *taken* / *took* from a café last week.
3 I got one of my brother's friends *repaired* / *to repair* my computer.
4 My sister has her nails *to do* / *done* regularly.
5 Mum *got* / *had* us to tidy the whole house at the weekend!
6 After the party, my parents had to have the carpet *clean* / *cleaned*.

6 **Rewrite the sentences using the phrases in brackets.**

0 Someone repaired my phone after I dropped it. (had my phone)
I had my phone repaired after I dropped it.
1 I asked my dad and he took us to the station. (got my dad)
2 Someone is making my brother a suit for his wedding. (having a suit)
3 Our neighbour looked after our cat while we were away. (got our neighbour)
4 Someone spilled a drink over Tomas. (had a drink)

7 **Correct the mistake in each sentence.**

1 On Saturday morning, I went to cut my hair.
2 Can you get them to changed their minds?
3 We've all had stolen something at some point.
4 I got my brother clear up the mess in the kitchen.

8 **Imagine you could have/get anything done for you or get anyone to do anything for you. Make a list in pairs.**

I'd have my meals cooked by a chef.
I'd get someone to drive me to school every day.

VOCABULARY *-self, -selves* for emphasis

1 **Read the example. Then answer the questions.**

EP Marston didn't invent the polygraph **himself** – a medical student, John Larson, came up with the idea.

1 Who invented the polygraph?
2 The word *himself* is optional. Can you explain why it is used?

2 **Complete the sentences with the correct words.**

1 I'm not doing your homework for you. Do it ________!
2 My brother repaired our computer ________. He's only 12!
3 After the concert, we met the band members ________ backstage.
4 The city centre ________ is very small.
5 He definitely knew about the party. I told him ________.
6 I didn't make the cake ________. My mum helped me.

3 » **Work in pairs.** **Turn to page 125.**

WRITING A story (2)

1 **Read the beginnings and endings of three stories. Then match them to the titles.**

1 Honesty pays!
2 An honest mistake
3 A little lie cost me a friend

A

When I picked up my phone and saw who was calling, my heart sank. It was Jenny. 'Oh, no,' I thought. I didn't want to listen to her problems again. Anyway, I was going out soon. I didn't answer the phone, but I sent her a message. 'Can't talk. Not feeling well.' …

… Leaving the cinema, I suddenly heard my name. I turned around and saw Jenny. I felt myself blushing and opened my mouth to explain. But Jenny didn't want to listen and she hasn't spoken to me since that night. That was a month ago.

B

As I was hurrying into the café, I walked straight into a young woman on her way out. We both apologised and I joined the queue to get a coffee. A few minutes later, I needed to pay and reached for my purse in my bag. It wasn't there! I must have had it stolen, I thought. But how? Suddenly I realised and ran out of the café. …

… I went straight home after that. I was desperate to tell my brother the story of the woman who took my purse, and how I had chased her and got it back from her! But before I could speak, my brother gave me something. 'You left your purse at home this morning.' I stared at him. 'I think I've just stolen someone's purse,' I said.

C

While I was walking across the park, I saw something shiny in the grass. At first, I thought it was just a piece of glass. But as I looked closer, I could see it was made of metal. I bent down and saw that it was a ring. …

… Then the woman suddenly grabbed her bag and quickly took out a €50 note. I shook my head and tried to refuse, but she insisted. She said I deserved it and that she was going to write to my school!

2 **Read the *Prepare to write* box. Then read the first part of story A again and think of answers to the questions.**

1 Where is the person going?
2 Why doesn't the person want to listen to Jenny's problems?

PREPARE TO WRITE

Getting ideas for a story

We can get ideas to continue stories by thinking of questions a reader might ask. For example:

Simon looked at the woman's face and suddenly stopped speaking.

- Who was the woman?
- Why did Simon stop speaking?
- What was the woman's expression?

3 **Read the first part of stories B and C again. Write two questions a reader might ask for each of them.**

4 **In pairs, compare your questions and discuss possible answers.**

5 **In pairs or small groups read the beginnings and ends of the stories B and C and discuss what you think happened in the middle of them. Use your answers from Exercise 4 to help you.**

6 **You see this announcement on an international website for teenagers. Plan your story, following the instructions below.**

> **Stories wanted**
> Would you like to have your story published on our website? Enter our competition! Your story must begin with this sentence:
> *Jess and Ruby had a choice – they could give the money back or keep it themselves.*
> Your story must include:
> - a reward
> - a surprise

1 Read the first line of the story and write questions to get ideas.
2 Plan ideas for how to include a reward and a surprise in your story.
3 Plan a good ending for your story.
4 Think of a title for your story.

7 **Write your story.**

- Use the plan you wrote in Exercise 6.
- Use the tips in the *Prepare to write* box on page 45.
- Write 140–190 words.
- Check your grammar and spelling.

16 WHO CARES?

ABOUT YOU

▶ 12 **Watch the video. Then answer the questions.**

What do you know about climate change? What problems does it cause?

What's the greenest form of transport that you use?

What materials do you and your family recycle?

VOCABULARY Climate change

1 **Look at the photos. Then discuss how they are related to environmental issues. Use some of the vocabulary in the box.**

EP

carbon dioxide emissions	carbon footprint
energy efficient	greenhouse gases
environmentally friendly	fossil fuels
exhaust fumes	global warming
renewable energy sources	solar power
wind power	

69 **2** **Discuss the questions. Then listen and check.**

1 What are rising global temperatures causing?
droughts, …
2 What is surprising about the continued growth of global warming?
3 What do greenhouse gases do?
4 Which is the worst greenhouse gas, and where does it come from?
5 What three things can we do to reduce our carbon footprint?
6 What are the greenest forms of transport?

3 **Complete the fact file using the vocabulary in Exercise 1. Use each expression once only.**

CLIMATE CHANGE ▶ FACT FILE

THE PROBLEM …

[1] ________, mainly carbon dioxide, occur naturally in the atmosphere, but when there's too much greenhouse gas, [2] ________ occurs. Recently, carbon dioxide levels have gone up, mainly due to [3] ________ from human activity such as generating electricity from [4] ________ and [5] ________ from vehicles.

THE SOLUTIONS?

We can reduce our [6] ________ by switching to [7] ________ such as solar power and [8] ________. Buildings need to be much more [9] ________, and we need to travel in [10] ________ ways.

4 **Discuss the questions.**

1 Has climate change affected where you live? How?
2 How environmentally friendly is your lifestyle?

READING

1 **Read the article quickly, ignoring the gaps. Then look at the posters. Which film poster is not mentioned?**

2 **Read the article again. Then choose the best summary.**

A People have enjoyed disaster movies for the past 100 years. A lot of them are about our greatest hopes and fears. Recent disaster movies all tend to deal with climate change.

B Movies explain a lot about the society that makes them. A number of disaster movies are about climate change. Unlike other disasters, climate disaster is one that humans can prevent.

C Disaster movies used to be about spies and space travel Nowadays, they are about natural disasters such as extreme weather. Climate change is a disaster that no one can control.

3 **Read paragraphs 1 and 2 again and decide which answer (A, B, C or D) best fits each gap.**

0	A emphasising	(B) featuring	C promoting	D starring
1	A arranging	B creating	C designing	D planning
2	A comedies	B documentaries	C musicals	D thrillers
3	A broke	B came	C died	D sold
4	A destruction	B exhaustion	C explosion	D extinction
5	A lacked	B lost	C omitted	D missed
6	A off	B out	C up	D away
7	A psychologically	B consequently	C irrationally	D traditionally

FACT OR FICTION?

Popular movies are a mirror on society, reflecting back at audiences their dreams, as well as their inner fears. Films [0]*featuring* space travel and creatures from outer space were popular in the 1950s, an era when mankind was [1] ________ the first space flights. From the 1960s until the 80s, concern about international espionage dominated the news, and some of the biggest movies of the day were [2] ________ about spies like James Bond.

The first disaster movie [3] ________ out over 100 years ago, not long after the invention of film itself. *The Last Days of Pompeii* (1913) showed the [4] ________ of the Roman city of Pompeii after Mount Vesuvius erupted. But it was a silent movie filmed in black and white, and it [5] ________ the pace and excitement we expect from modern movies. Disaster movies really took [6] ________ after the introduction of special effects. One of the first big hits was *Airport* (1970), filmed at a time when air travel was becoming popular. Although air travel was relatively safe, people were [7] ________ scared of flying, and *Airport* exploited people's worries about crashes.

Continuing the transport theme, *The Poseidon Adventure* (1972) is set on a huge cruise ship that is sunk by a tsunami. In *Earthquake* (1974), most of Los Angeles is in ruins, and perhaps the best of the 70s disaster films was *The Towering Inferno* (1974), about a deadly fire in a 138-**storey** office tower. Other films saw asteroid impacts, survival after a nuclear war, or the spread of a terrible disease, as in *Outbreak* (1995), and attacks by monsters or killer animals, most famously the shark in *Jaws* (1975).

Today, many people believe that climate change is the most serious **threat** to our existence on Earth, and there is increasing **concern** about its extreme consequences, such as the polar ice caps melting.

Scientists believe that if the ice caps melted, sea levels would rise and the climate would change very significantly. So it comes as no surprise that there are plenty of films about extreme weather events like floods and thunderstorms, or changes to the climate that would make the world impossible for people to live in. *The Day after Tomorrow* (2004) is a classic story about a future world in which the climate has become so extreme that our present way of life is no longer possible. In the film, a climate specialist sets out on a **trek** across North America to save his son in New York, which has been buried under a frozen sea of ice after a giant snowstorm, triggered by the **collapse** of the ice sheets in Antarctica.

Traditional disaster movies explore people's anxieties about things beyond their control, but climate disaster films are different because we could actually control climate change if we wanted to. Solar power and wind farms are affordable, environmentally friendly alternatives to oil and gas. Assuming we wanted to stop global warming getting worse, we would switch to renewable energy sources right now. Scientists have set targets for carbon reduction and, if we all worked hard to meet them, we might prevent some of the worst consequences of climate change.

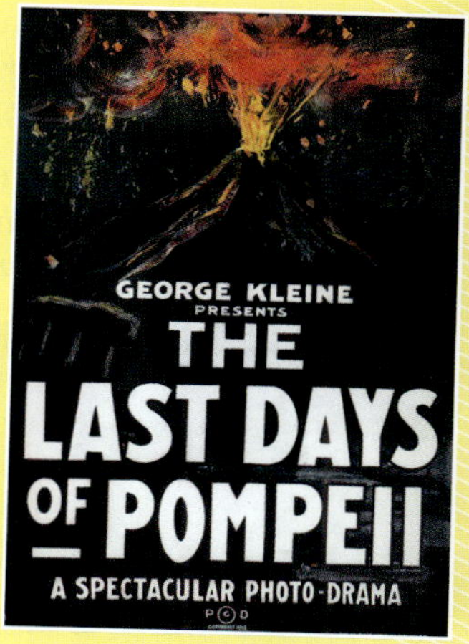

Obviously, disaster movies are made mainly for entertainment. If they weren't entertaining, people wouldn't go and watch them. But perhaps movies such as *The Day after Tomorrow* can also be helpful, by encouraging us to focus on the issue of climate change and take it more seriously.

4 **Read the article again. Then answer the questions.**

1 What did the first disaster film lack?
2 What changed about disaster films in the 1970s?
3 How do climate disaster movies differ from other disaster movies?
4 How can humans avoid a disaster caused by climate change?

5 **Match the highlighted nouns in the article to the meanings.**

1 something that could cause damage
2 a long, sometimes hard, journey on foot
3 a level of a building
4 when something suddenly falls over or fails to work
5 when people feel nervous or worried about something

6 **Discuss the questions.**

1 What can you guess about the plots of *Airport* and *Earthquake*?
2 Do you agree that popular movies are a mirror on society? Give examples that agree or disagree with this theory.

TALKING POINTS

Why do you think disaster movies are so popular? How could movies change people's attitudes to global issues?

GRAMMAR Second conditional: *would, could* and *might*

1 **Match the examples to the rules.**

1 **If** the ice caps **melted**, the climate **would change** very significantly.
2 We **could** actually control climate change **if** we **wanted** to.
3 **If** we all **worked** hard to meet these targets, we **might prevent** some of the worst consequences of climate change.
4 **If** they **weren't** entertaining, people **wouldn't watch** them.

We use *if* + past simple, *would* + infinitive to talk about:
a an unlikely situation in the future and its results.
b an imaginary situation in the present.

Instead of *would,* we can use:
c *could* to talk about ability.
d *might* for things that are uncertain or unlikely.

» GRAMMAR REFERENCE AND PRACTICE PAGE 153

2 **Choose the correct verbs to complete the second conditional sentences.**

1 You could afford to go out if you *save / saved* some money.
2 If you *would ask / asked* your sister, she might help us.
3 I *wouldn't / won't* say anything if I wasn't sure.
4 She *might / could* buy some trainers if she wanted to join the running club.
5 What *will / would* you do if there was a bad storm?
6 If you came for a bike ride, you *might / could* like it.

3 **Complete the text with the verbs in brackets in the second conditional. Sometimes more than one modal verb (*could*, *would* or *might*) is possible.**

The planet's average temperature is gradually rising. If we [1] ___ (use) less petrol and oil, climate change [2] ___ (slow down). We should re-use materials more, too: for example we [3] ___ (not need) to produce so much new plastic if we [4] ___ (recycle) more of our used plastic. I'm really worried about it. If I [5] ___ (be) in charge of this country, I [6] ___ (not waste) any more time just *talking* about climate change, I [7] ___ (do) something about it now!

if only and *wish*

4 **Read the examples. Then answer the questions.**

1 *I* ***wish*** *I* ***spoke*** *Spanish.*
Does the person speak Spanish?
2 ***If only*** *Marc* ***wouldn't tell*** *lies.*
What does Marc do? What does the person wish?
3 *They* ***wish*** *they* ***could meet*** *more often.*
Do they meet often enough?

5 **Complete the rules.**

We use *if only* or *wish* with:
a the ___ tense to express a present desire.
b *would* or ___ to express a present or future desire.

» GRAMMAR REFERENCE AND PRACTICE PAGE 153

6 **Complete the sentences with the correct form of the verbs in brackets.**

1 It's freezing! I wish it ___ (be) warmer.
2 I can't concentrate! I wish you ___ (be) quiet!
3 It's so sunny! If only we ___ (hang out). I wish it ___ (not be) a school day.
4 I wish I ___ (go out) tonight, but I can't get a lift. If only I ___ (drive).
5 I hate this weather. If only the rain ___ (stop).

7 **What would you say in these situations? Write sentences starting *I wish …* or *If only …***

1 A friend always uses your phone without asking.
2 It's very sunny, but you haven't got sunglasses.
3 Your best friend isn't free this evening.
4 You can't afford lunch today.

VOCABULARY Alternatives to *if*

1 **Read the examples. Which two phrases have the same meaning?**

1 **Assuming** we wanted to stop global warming, we would switch to renewable energy sources right now.
2 The Earth would eventually get too hot, **even if** we completely stopped producing greenhouse gases.
3 We'd be fine **as long as** we cut vehicle emissions.
4 We'd meet our carbon reduction targets **provided that** we made changes to our lifestyle.

2 **Match the sentence halves.**

1 I'd watch a film in a foreign language …
2 Sam's happy to sell you her old phone …
3 I'd love to have some new trainers …
4 I'd go to university in a foreign country …

a as long as I could speak the language there.
b even if it didn't have subtitles.
c assuming you still want it.
d provided that I didn't have to pay for them.

3 » **Work in pairs.** **Turn to page 125.**

LISTENING

1 **Look at the photo. Then discuss what you think an eco-house might be.**

71 **2** **You will hear an interview with Lara Baum about her family's year in an eco-house. Were your guesses in Exercise 1 correct?**

3 **Read the questions and possible answers. Then underline the key words.**

1 How did Lara Baum feel about her family being selected for the 'One-Tonne, One-Year' experiment?
A fortunate to be chosen
B nervous about how to contribute
C uncertain about the value of taking part

2 What did Lara and her family think of their experience?
A It was fairly straightforward.
B It wasn't that much fun.
C It was quite challenging.

3 Which country has the lowest annual carbon dioxide emissions per person?
A Australia
B India
C Switzerland

4 What is the largest source of Swiss families' annual carbon dioxide production?
A domestic energy needs
B car journeys
C international flights

5 What did Lara consider the least attractive aspect of living in the eco-house?
A uncomfortable furniture
B a lack of space
C an inefficient heating system

6 Why did Lara's family become vegetarian?
A because the meat and dairy industries aren't environmentally friendly
B because avoiding meat and dairy was a healthier option
C because fresh food has to be transported a long way

7 What is Lara's conclusion about the experiment?
A She thought the family had to give up too much.
B She found the constant day-to-day choices made it too hard.
C She felt her whole family enjoyed the green way of life.

71 **4** **Listen to the interview again. For questions 1–7 in Exercise 3, choose the best answer (A, B or C). Remember that the answers will not contain exactly the same words as the recording.**

5 **Discuss the questions.**

1 What would you enjoy about living in an eco-house? Why?
2 What would you find it most difficult to give up if you lived in an eco-house? Why?

SPEAKING Arguing for and against something

72 **1** **Listen to Millie and Toby taking part in a class debate. Who argues in favour of plans to build an airport?**

72 **2** **Read the sentences. Then listen again and decide which factors are pros (*P*) and which are cons (*C*).**

1 the environmental impact of planes ☐
2 the ease of foreign travel ☐
3 the fact that trains and buses can't cross oceans ☐
4 the noise from a new airport ☐

72 **3** **Read the *Prepare to speak* box. Then listen again. Which two expressions do Toby and Millie both use?**

PREPARE TO SPEAK | Arguing for and against

There are (various) pros and cons …
The main advantage/disadvantage is that …
To start with …
Another factor is …
It's also worth bearing in mind the advantages/disadvantages …
Overall …

4 **In pairs, choose a topic and make notes about its pros and cons.**

1 living in an eco-house
2 only allowing electric cars
3 being vegetarian
4 having bike lanes next to every road
5 banning planes
6 making recycling compulsory

5 **Decide who is for and who is against the topic you chose in Exercise 4. Then prepare a conversation about the pros and cons. Use phrases from the *Prepare to speak* box.**

6 **Practise your conversation. Then present it to the class.**

LIFE SKILLS SOCIAL RESPONSIBILITY

REDUCING YOUR CARBON FOOTPRINT

1 **Ask and answer the questions.**

1 What do you think are the main activities which contribute to your carbon footprint?
2 Are you doing anything to reduce your carbon footprint?

2 **Read the text quickly. Then match the headings to the sections.**

a Just a question of style?
b What's on your plate?
c Much more than a destination

3 **Read the text again. Then answer the questions.**

1 What does the writer suggest as an alternative to Planet B?
2 Why shouldn't we make quick trips in a car?
3 How can planting trees help compensate for our carbon footprint?
4 Why does buying food from far away increase our carbon footprint?
5 How have our habits with buying clothes changed since the start of the millennium?

4 **Match the highlighted words in the text to the meanings.**

1 obtained from a particular place
2 pay for things that will reduce carbon dioxide in order to reduce the negative effect of your activities
3 avoiding unnecessary use of natural materials and resources
4 substances that prevent heat from Earth's atmosphere escaping into space and cause the planet to become warmer
5 reduces in size or quantity

LIFE SKILLS

Reducing your carbon footprint

Carbon dioxide (CO_2) is a gas produced when fossil fuels are burned for electricity, heat and transport and is the leading cause of global warming. Your carbon footprint is the total of all the CO_2 emissions which are caused by your activity over a period of time. This not only includes the electricity and fuel you use directly in your daily life, but also the energy used to produce and transport the food you eat, the clothes you wear, and other products you use. Reducing your carbon footprint is a critical part of the fight against climate change.

73 **5** **Listen to Mark and Lucy finding out how to measure a carbon footprint. Which three areas do they calculate for Mark's footprint?**

1 the amount his household recycles
2 his food and eating habits
3 how often he buys new clothes
4 his typical travel habits
5 ways to offset his carbon footprint

73 **6** **Listen again. Who said these things: Lucy, Mark or both?**

1 On average, a person from the UK has a carbon footprint of approximately 10 tonnes.
2 Animals in a household aren't included in the calculations.
3 Meals eaten in restaurants need to be included.
4 I travel by car, but not by motorbike.
5 Mark's footprint is relatively high compared to international averages.

7 **Complete the sentences with the words in the box.**

account	approximately	closest
enough	measure	rough

USEFUL LANGUAGE

Estimating

1 That's close ________ to what I found, too.
2 I'm not really sure how to ________ that.
3 Just find the ________ option and choose that.
4 Do I need to take eating out into ________?
5 Don't worry, you only need a ________ estimate.
6 I guess it's ________ two hours a week by car.

The human factor

Ask yourself this question: If we were given a new planet, would we treat it better than this one? Hopefully, your answer would be 'yes'. But there is no Planet B. So what's the next best thing? Well, probably to take a long, hard look at how human activity has affected the Earth. We urgently need to look for ways to avoid the negative impact of our activity and to make conservation and sustainability a priority. Reducing our carbon footprint is a crucial part of that. Let's start by taking a look at some of the main factors involved.

1 Around 15% of man-made CO_2 emissions come from road travel and lots can be done to reduce this impact. For example, we can all avoid making short journeys by car – a cold engine uses almost double the amount of fuel. If you can, cycle, walk or use public transport instead. However, compared to other modes of transport, including driving, air travel has a bigger environmental impact. To help the environment, you're faced with two choices here: fly less and take the train, which produces less CO_2, or you can offset the greenhouse gases you emit as a result of your flight. An example of this could be giving money to initiatives that replant trees, which will then absorb CO_2 from the atmosphere.

2 Intensive food production not only contributes to climate change, but it also depletes our planet's biodiversity. We should avoid buying food that's been grown on the other side of the world and has travelled many miles to reach us. Buying food which has been grown and sourced locally creates a much smaller carbon footprint, because less transport is needed to get it to us. Similarly, eating more vegetables and less meat will mean that less CO_2 is released into the atmosphere.

3 We now buy on average 60% more clothes than we did in the year 2000. This can largely be attributed to so-called 'fast fashion', where clothes are made as quickly and cheaply as possible. People buy more clothes because they are cheaper and they don't expect to wear them as long. So what's the problem? How can having lots of clothes be a bad thing?! Well, overall, global textile production produces 1.2 billion tonnes of CO_2 every year. That's actually more emissions than shipping and international flights! So next time you see some jeans you really want, ask yourself: should I buy a more expensive pair that will last longer and help to keep my carbon footprint down?

There are currently around four billion air passengers every year. This figure is predicted to reach nearly eight billion by 2036!

PROJECT

A plan to reduce your carbon footprint

Work in groups to create a plan to reduce your carbon footprint. Use these steps and the *Useful language* to help you.

1. Look up the average carbon footprint for someone in your country.
2. Find a good online carbon footprint calculator in English and use it to calculate your carbon footprint.
3. Use the calculations and results to identify ways in which you can reduce your carbon footprint. Think about food, travel, fashion, recycling, etc.
4. Create a plan of how your group members can reduce their carbon footprints.
5. Decide how you want to present your plan: a presentation, poster, etc.

Present your plan to the class.

REVIEW 4 UNITS 13–16

VOCABULARY

1 Complete the sentences with the correct pairs of nouns in the box. The words can be used in either order.

confirmation/statement criticism/mention prediction/hint response/proposal rumour/update

1 There's a .... the concert has been called off. We're waiting for an .... online.
2 We've written a .... for the school to buy some tablet computers, but we haven't had a .... yet.
3 The player gave reporters a .... about the club he might move to, but the most popular .... was wrong.
4 There was a lot of .... of the boring plot, but the review made no .... of the terrible acting!
5 The actor's released a short ...., but there's still no .... of whether he will be appearing in the next film in the series.

2 Match the sentence halves.

1 I sometimes have an allergic reaction
2 'I'm not interested in going,' I said, shaking
3 There's a cupboard door open above you, so don't bump
4 I've been scared of dogs ever since I was bitten
5 It's not very polite to stare
6 If you've been cutting up chillies, never rub
7 You are deliberately avoiding making
8 The floor's still a bit wet, so be careful you don't slip

a your head on it.
b on it.
c your eyes afterwards!
d at people.
e to cats.
f eye contact with me.
g my head.
h by one as a kid.

3 Match the words. Then write them next to the meanings.

renewable	friendly
carbon	power
fossil	warming
solar	energy
global	fuels
carbon	dioxide
environmentally	footprint

0 a type of power that can be used again and again and never runs out: *renewable energy*
1 energy sources produced under the ground over millions of years, e.g. oil and gas: ....
2 a gradual increase in world temperatures caused by polluting gases: ....
3 the amount of carbon dioxide that someone produces from using energy: ....
4 a gas that humans breathe out: ....
5 in a way that doesn't damage the air, land or water: ....
6 energy produced from sunshine: ....

GRAMMAR

1 Complete the reported statements.

1 'As long as you're on time, I won't leave without you,' James promised Ruth.
James promised Ruth that ....
2 'I'm blinking because there's something in my eye,' Robert replied.
Robert replied that ....
3 'You have to take out the recycling,' Mum told me.
Mum told me that ....
4 'In India, shaking your head can mean that you agree,' the teacher said.
The teacher told us ....
5 'I've had an allergic reaction to something I've eaten,' Abbie said.
Abbie explained that she ....

2 Rewrite the questions and requests as reported speech.

1 'Do you want anything else?' the waiter asked us.
2 'Can you lend me a few pounds?' my brother asked me.
3 'Please don't walk on the grass,' the police officer said to the boys.
4 'Do you know what time the match starts?' Dad asked me.
5 'Are you listening?' Mrs Grayson asked Jack.
6 'Please don't say anything,' we begged our uncle.

3 Match the sentence halves. Then complete them with the correct form of the verbs in the box.

cut deliver drive repair search test

1 I had my luggage ....
2 I'll get my dad to ....
3 My sister's had her hair ....
4 Can you get the package ....
5 You should get your eyes ....
6 Are you getting your phone ....

a really short.
b or are you going to get a new one?
c at the airport!
d to a neighbour's house?
e if you can't read that sign from here!
f you to the station.

4 Complete the second conditional sentences. Use *would*, *could* or *might* and the verbs in brackets. Sometimes more than one modal verb is possible.

1 You ________ (learn) something if you ________ (listen) more carefully.
2 If you ________ (have) a car, you ________ (go out) whenever you wanted to.
3 I ________ (not understand) this website if I ________ (not speak) Italian.
4 If you ________ (help) me, I ________ (finish) twice as quickly.
5 If you ________ (lose) your phone, you ________ (not be able to) contact us.
6 What ________ (you / do) if you ________ (win) a lot of money?

5 Rewrite the <u>underlined</u> sections in the conversation. Use sentences with *I wish* or *if only*.

0 I wish / If only I didn't live in this village!

Tom: [0] <u>I hate living in this village.</u>
Leo: Me too. [1] <u>I'd love to live somewhere exciting.</u>
Tom: My parents were thinking of moving. [2] <u>It would be great if we could move to the city.</u>
Leo: Or go to university! [3] <u>I can't wait to be at university.</u>
Tom: I don't know if I'll get the grades to get in. [4] <u>Why don't they make the exams a bit easier?</u>
Leo: Yeah. [5] <u>It'd be great if the exams weren't so tough.</u>

6 Choose the correct words.

1 They told me that I *have* / *had* just missed the plane.
2 I asked Alex *to give* / *give* me her notes from the lesson.
3 I had *stolen my phone* / *my phone stolen,* so I couldn't call the police.
4 It *could* / *would* be good if you suggested an alternative.

7 Correct the mistake in each sentence.

1 She explained him that she had not broken the glass.
2 You asked me what did I do to get the prize.
3 I got my parents lent me the money in advance.
4 I would understand if they would stay at home.

8 Read the text and decide which answer (A, B, C or D) best fits each gap.

CLIMBER SURVIVES 300M FALL

Keen climber Adam Potter had just [0] *reached* the top of one of steepest mountain ridges in Scotland when he slipped on the ice and fell over the edge. In seconds, he fell about 300 metres, gathering speed all the time until he hit a rock. Potter thinks he briefly [1] ________ out, but then he remembers getting to his feet and wondering what had happened. He got out his map and [2] ________ an attempt to work out where he was. He then [3] ________ a rescue helicopter above him, but within minutes it had flown off. [4] ________ falling down a rocky mountain a distance similar to the height of the Eiffel Tower, Potter had suffered very few injuries. He had cut himself on some rocks and injured his back and shoulders, but he was [5] ________ fine. Soon the helicopter rescue team returned and lifted him to safety. They had initially thought the man couldn't have been Potter, as he had been walking around, collecting his equipment. From his hospital bed, Potter [6] ________ feeling very lucky, but said that the incident would not put him off climbing. [7] ________ that he is well enough, he has [8] ________ himself the goal of climbing Everest later in the year.

	A	B	C	D
0	got	(B) reached	landed	struck
1	passed	fainted	lost	dropped
2	made	took	gave	tried
3	stared	blinked	spotted	glanced
4	However	Whereas	Although	Despite
5	alternatively	otherwise	besides	instead
6	revealed	admitted	claimed	accepted
7	Conditioned	Supposed	Provided	Assumed
8	emphasised	instructed	set	specified

9 Complete the second sentence so that it has a similar meaning to the first sentence, using the word given. Do not change the word given. You must use between two and five words, including the word given.

0 Jo asked me if the film had started. **IF**
'Do you *know if the film has* started?' asked Jo.

1 Somebody stole Kay's phone in the café. **HAD**
Kay ________ in the café.

2 'Please give me another chance,' said Mark. **BEGGED**
Mark ________ given another chance.

3 The film wasn't as good as we'd hoped it would be. **LIVE**
The film ________ our expectations.

4 'Don't yawn when you're talking to me,' said Rob's teacher. **TOLD**
Rob's teacher ________ yawn when he was talking to her.

5 I'd prefer not to cancel the party. **CALL**
I'd rather we ________ the party.

6 I'll lend you my laptop, provided you bring it back tomorrow. **AS**
You can borrow my laptop ________ it back tomorrow.

17 ART IS FUN!

ABOUT YOU

13 **Watch the video. Then answer the questions.**

What works of art have you seen in museums or galleries?

Are there any outdoor pieces of art in your town or city?

VOCABULARY Adjectives describing art

1 **Look at the photos. Then describe what you can see. Which looks the most interesting? Why?**

75 **2** **Listen to people talking about three of the works of art. Which of the photos do they describe?**

75 **3** **Complete the descriptions with the words in the boxes. Then listen again and check.**

EP

bizarre	controversial
remarkable	stunning

This work of art was quite [1] ______ at the time – some people liked it, but others didn't, or they just found it [2] ______. But I actually thought it looked beautiful – [3] ______, in fact. It really made people stop and look. It's a [4] ______ sight the first time you see it.

conventional	dramatic
humorous	unique

I think some people prefer works of art to be more [5] ______ – you know, like the sort of traditional paintings and sculptures you get in an art gallery – so they didn't like it. But I love this particular work because it's [6] ______: I've never seen anything else like it. It looks quite [7] ______, too – these massive eggs just lying in the street. And it's [8] ______, it makes everyone smile when they see it as they walk through the market square.

abstract	classic	contemporary	powerful

This definitely isn't a [9] ______ or 'normal' work. I mean, it doesn't really represent anything real. It's quite [10] ______. It's just this long line of them, all half-buried in the sand. I like it because it's very [11] ______ – you know, modern – because it uses this symbol of the modern age: the car. And although it's quite a simple idea in some ways, it's getting across a [12] ______ message about how we design and use things, then just throw them away.

4 **Describe the other two photos in Exercise 1. Use adjectives from Exercise 3.**

A

B

C

D

E

READING

1 **Describe the two works of art on page 99. Which one looks the most interesting? Why?**

2 **Read the introduction to the article, ignoring the gaps. Then choose the best title.**

A Art is always fun!
B Does art have to be serious?
C We need more art!

3 **Read the introduction again and think of the word which best fits each gap. Use only one word in each gap.**

4 **Read the sentences. Which work of art on page 99 do you think they refer to? Then read the article quickly and check.**

1 It's made of an unusual material.
2 People saw it in many different countries.
3 It is intended to make people feel happy.
4 It was destroyed after a few weeks.

5 **Read the article again. Then decide if the sentences are true for Anna, Alexei or both.**

1 I saw this work of art twice.
2 It made me think about my childhood.
3 It looked strange because of the contrast with its surroundings.
4 It made me feel closer to home.
5 I think it's a work of art because it encourages people to think.
6 It made me more aware of my senses.

For centuries, sculptures by artists [0] *like* Michelangelo tended to be human figures or people sitting [1] ________ a horse. Their works were stunning – perfect, sometimes – but contemporary artists have [2] ________ evolving these classic forms. They've moved [3] ________ of galleries and museums too, and they [4] ________ now exhibiting their art in outdoor urban settings all over the world. Their works are often abstract: [5] ________ look at life in humorous and original ways. Take Yayoi Kusama's yellow pumpkin with black spots. This work is entertaining and fun, but is it really 'art'? What should art be like, and what is [6] ________ function? Should 'good art' be beautiful or is 'good art' supposed [7] ________ be challenging, controversial and unique? Two young people give us their opinions and talk about unusual works [8] ________ art they've seen.

76

ALEXEI, 15

Last year, I went to see this amazing chocolate room in a gallery near my home in Minsk, in Belarus. Everything in it was chocolate – the furniture, the cups and saucers, even the flowers. It was weird to see all those familiar things made out of chocolate. My first thought was: 'Wow! There must be a lot of chocolate in here!' In fact, the artist, Elena Kliment, used over 600 kilos of chocolate. The smell reminded me of weighing sugar on the scales and melting chocolate in a pan when my grandmother and I used to make cakes when I was younger. The temptation to touch it or taste it was incredibly strong. I went back on the last day of the exhibition and they were giving people pieces of it to eat. It made me think about our senses. We live in a very visual world, but this work made me appreciate how powerful our senses of smell, taste and touch are, but we don't rely on them as much. I think this might well be what the artist was trying to get across. Or it could be that she wanted us to appreciate chocolate! Would I call it art? Definitely! For me, anything that takes you away from everyday life and makes you think is art.

ANNA, 16

I saw this massive rubber duck when I was in Hong Kong last year. It was over 30 metres high, so I guess it could well be the biggest rubber duck ever made! In the business-like environment of the city centre, this huge kids' toy floating on the water was a pretty bizarre sight. It was by a Dutch artist called Florentijn Hofman, and it had travelled all over the world, from China and Japan to Brazil and the US. The tour was entitled 'Spreading joy around the world' and I think it definitely did that. When I saw it, I instantly remembered being a little kid again. But it also made me think about the scale of the world we live in. Before I saw it, Hong Kong had seemed a long way from my home in London. But thinking that this rubber duck could travel all that way made the world feel a bit smaller and friendlier. Some people would say that something like this can't possibly be art because it's not serious enough. But I don't agree. I think art is about getting people to look at the world in a new way. Is it a great work of art? I don't think it was awarded any prizes, but I loved it. On a scale of one to ten, I'd definitely give it a ten!

TALKING POINTS

What do you think big outdoor works of art can bring to a town or city?
Do you agree that anything can be art if it makes you think?

GRAMMAR Modals of deduction: present

1 **Read the examples. Then complete the rules with the modal verbs. What is the opposite of *must be*?**

1 It **could be** that she wanted us to appreciate chocolate.
2 This **might well be** what the artist was trying to get across.
3 It **could well be** the biggest rubber duck ever made.
4 Some people would say this **can't** possibly **be** art.
5 There **must be** a lot of chocolate in here!

We can use modal verbs to indicate how sure or unsure we are about something.

a We use ______ *be* if we are sure that something is true.
b We use ______ *be* if we are sure that something isn't true.
c We can use ______ *be* or ______ *be* if we are unsure about something.
d We use ______ after *might* or *could* to confirm that we are fairly sure about something.

» GRAMMAR REFERENCE AND PRACTICE PAGE 154

2 **Choose the correct modal verbs.**

1 That painting *mustn't* / *can't* be genuine. It's very cheap.
2 The style of the picture over there's identical, so it *must* / *might* be by the same artist.
3 The art teacher isn't here. I think she *could* / *can* be ill.
4 The two buildings *can* / *could* be the same height, but I'm not sure.
5 I've phoned the gallery a few times, but no one's answered, so the exhibition *might* / *must* well be closed.
6 That paintbrush *can't* / *mustn't* be mine. It's black, but mine are all orange.

3 **Read A's statements. Then complete B's replies with *must be*, *might be* or *can't be* and the words/phrases in brackets.**

0 A: I'm studying art history. (fascinating)
B: You love art! It *must be fascinating*!
1 A: That massive sculpture is made of iron. (easy to lift)
B: It ______.
2 A: Her gold ring has three huge diamonds. (very valuable)
B: It ______.
3 A: Our art homework is just learning a few dates. (very interesting)
B: That ______.
4 A: My brother's just sold his first painting! (so satisfying)
B: That ______.
5 A: Helen's thinking of changing schools. (serious)
B: But why? She'd miss all her friends! She ______!
6 A: The jewels in this necklace look like glass, but I'm not certain. (a fake)
B: Do you think it ______?

4 **Use *might* or *could* to describe what you think you can see behind each keyhole. Add *well* if you are fairly sure.**

I think it could well be …

VOCABULARY Verbs often used in the passive

1 **Read the examples. Can you think of any other verbs that are often used in the passive?**

1 The tour **was entitled** 'Spreading joy around the world'.
2 I don't think it **was awarded** any prizes.

2 **Choose the correct passive verbs.**

1 The art gallery *is set* / *is influenced* in a beautiful forest.
2 Josie *was devoted* / *was elected* as our student representative yesterday.
3 The art gallery *was regarded* / *was established* in 1977.
4 The sculpture *is composed* / *is prohibited* of five moving parts.
5 The artist Kandinsky *was influenced* / *was set* by Malevich.
6 Photography *is elected* / *is prohibited* throughout the gallery.
7 Last spring, the ground floor *was devoted* / *was composed* to an exhibition of modern art.
8 Jackson Pollock *is influenced* / *is regarded* as a very important artist.

3 » **Work in pairs. Turn to page 125.**

Park and Slide work of art, Bristol (UK)

WRITING An essay (2)

1 Look at the photo of the Park and Slide work of art in Bristol. What do you think is happening? Do you think this is art?

2 Read the essay question. Then make notes on ideas 1 and 2 and your own ideas.

> 'Public works of art are good for cities.'
> Do you agree?
>
> Notes
> Write about:
> 1 the popularity of classic public works of art
> 2 the effect of controversial works of art
> 3 .... (your own idea)

3 Read the essay. Does it mention any of your ideas from Exercise 2?

1 A lot of cities around the world have large public works of art. **However**, is this kind of art good for the cities that have it?

2 Popular works of art can bring a lot of benefits to a city. **For example**, they add cultural richness and make it more interesting for the people who live and work there. **Furthermore**, they might have specific historical or political significance, **such as** celebrating a victory or independence.

3 **On the other hand**, contemporary works of art are sometimes criticised for being abstract or ugly. People who are conservative would argue that only conventional, classic art is 'real' art. **What's more**, some people don't like art at all, of course.

4 In my view, even though public works of art might be expensive to buy, they can be good for the local economy if they attract visitors from the region or internationally.

5 To sum up, **while** it is true that we can't please everyone all of the time, I believe that a good range of traditional and contemporary art is good for a city.

4 Read the *Prepare to write* box. Then match the paragraphs in the essay to the functions (a–e).

PREPARE TO WRITE An essay

In an essay:
- everything you write should be relevant to the question.
- you must use the two ideas given and your own idea to answer the question.
- give your opinions – include examples of what you mean and use linking words to join your ideas.
- organise your ideas into five paragraphs.
- include a conclusion with your own opinion.

a Discussion of the second idea in the essay question
b Conclusion
c Introduction
d Discussion of the first idea in the essay question
e The writer's own opinion

5 Look at the **highlighted** expressions in the essay. Then answer the questions.

1 Which three expressions introduce a contrasting idea?
2 Which two expressions introduce a similar idea?
3 Which two expressions introduce examples?

6 Look at the essay again.

Find
1 an expression which introduces other people's opinions.
2 two expressions which introduce the writer's opinion.
3 an expression which introduces the writer's conclusion.

7 Read the task in Exercise 2 again. Then plan your own essay.

8 Write your essay.
- Use the tips in the *Prepare to write* box.
- Write 140–190 words.
- Check your grammar and spelling.

18 CHALLENGING FATE

A B C

ABOUT YOU

What major decisions have you had to make in your life?
What do you consider to be your main qualities and strengths?
How have these qualities helped you?

VOCABULARY Personal qualities: nouns

1 (77) **Listen to three people talking about impressive personal qualities. Then match the speakers to the photos.**

2 (77) EP **Listen again. Then complete the sentences with the words in the box. One word is not needed. What does this word mean?**

ambition	bravery	commitment	courage
determination	drive	inspiration	kindness
passion	sense	spirit	strength

1 Climber Joe Simpson showed great ________ in making the decision he made.
2 With a broken leg, Joe had the ________ to know he would never manage to climb back up.
3 His story is an ________ to climbers everywhere.
4 The mental ________ and ________ shown by three Samoan teenagers during their 50 days lost at sea is breathtaking.
5 Their joint ________ had kept them alive, along with some rainwater, a few coconuts and one seabird.
6 Their story is a perfect example of the ________ humans have to stay alive under any circumstances.
7 Sabrina's first ________ was to graduate from high school with the rest of her class.
8 Since then, Sabrina has shown an endless ________ to improving the lives of disabled people.
9 Her ________ and ________ for the rights of disabled people have changed lives everywhere.

3 (77) **In groups of three, tell each other the stories you have just heard, using the sentences in Exercise 2 to help you. Then listen again to check you remembered everything.**

4 **Discuss the questions.**

1 Do you know anyone who has shown great bravery and courage? What happened?
2 Who is an inspiration to you? Why?
3 What ambitions do you have for the future?
4 Do you have any interesting passions?
5 Have you shown determination in doing something difficult? What was it?
6 How important to you is the quality of kindness?

READING

1 **Read the title and the first sentence of each text on page 103. What do you think these people's stories might be about? Then match the texts to the possible topics.**

1 leaving hardship behind
2 moving to another country
3 coping with a serious problem
4 surviving a difficult childhood

2 **Read the texts quickly to check.**

3 **Read the questions. Then underline the important words.**

Which person …
1 has had a book published about their life?
2 adopted a new nationality?
3 had to make a major decision for the sake of their health?
4 took up a new interest in order to eat?
5 often achieved high marks?
6 used their own experience to assist others?
7 did a degree related to languages?
8 represented their country in competitions?
9 received financial support thanks to a physical talent?
10 achieved second place in an international tournament?

4 **For questions 1–10 in Exercise 3, choose from the texts (A–D). The texts may be chosen more than once.**

TALES of COURAGE

Four stories of incredible passion, strength and determination

A Dawn

Dawn Loggins had a tough upbringing in North Carolina, USA, due to her parents' problems. There was never enough money for food and rent, so the family often lived in buildings without electricity or running water. Dawn really wanted to learn, but even reading at home was difficult with no electric lights. As she got older, Dawn realised that education was the only way she could escape her troubled background. When her parents suddenly moved away to Tennessee, she was left behind and moved in with the woman who drove her school bus. She was finally in a normal home environment, where she could eat, sleep and study normally. To earn money, she took a job as a school cleaner and worked every day before classes began. Showing great courage and incredible drive, she maintained a straight-A average in her studies and aimed high, hoping to get into Harvard University. Out of 36,000 candidates, Dawn was selected for a full scholarship and studied linguistics there. It was a fantastic achievement for a teenager whose life had been far from easy.

B Ahmed

The challenge Ahmed Dini faced on his arrival in Australia was adjusting from a survival lifestyle to one of opportunities and freedom. Ahmed was three when his parents left Somalia and went to a refugee camp in Kenya. Ahmed remembers his mother's sadness in the camp. She always wished she hadn't had to leave her home, but she had had no choice. If the family had stayed in Somalia, they could never have lived in safety. The family spent over five years in the refugee camp, but were finally given the chance to become Australian citizens. When they eventually boarded their flight to Australia, he noticed the smile on his mother's face. At last, her kids would get a real education and fresh opportunities. Although Ahmed learned English quickly, he experienced difficulties in finding his place in Australian society. However, with determination, he got through his schooling and is now a social worker in his local community, helping Somali teenagers to achieve their ambitions. He also manages a Somali-Australian football team, Unite, and got them to the final of the Madrid Youth Cup in Spain, though sadly they didn't win.

C Phiona

As a child, Phiona Mutesi grew up in poverty in Uganda, unable to read or write. Her father died when she was very young and she had to find food for herself and her brother. It was that basic need that decided her fate, because it led her to Robert Katende's chess programme. For any child that came to his centre to learn chess, Katende was offering meals. Phiona wouldn't have gone there if she hadn't been desperate, and her life changed with that one decision. Her potential at chess was obvious from the start and she enjoyed playing, so she began to practise more and more. She walked four miles a day to attend training, and within six months she was beating the older girls and boys in the programme. Since then, she has played for Uganda in several international tournaments, with trips to Russia, Turkey and the USA. On one of these trips, she was offered a scholarship to an American university, where she now studies sociology. Phiona has brought hope to her family and is becoming an inspiration worldwide, with the appearance of her biography and recently an international film about her success.

D Koni

Koni Dole's bravery and fighting spirit are remarkable. Koni comes from Montana in the USA and his passion is American football. He regularly represented his high school in competitions until, in the final game of the season, he suffered a horrific break to his leg. Despite several operations, the leg became infected and Koni was eventually told that without removing the leg, he risked further problems. Koni accepted the doctors' recommendations and he had to face up to the fact that he might never play football again. However, immediately after the surgery, he began training again, lifting weights to build his muscles up and, with the help of an artificial leg, he also started running to improve his fitness. Despite being in great pain at times, he returned to the football field just a year after his injury. He even got back his place on the school team! On graduating from high school, Koni was given a football scholarship by Montana State University, where he played for their team while studying for a degree in business.

TALKING POINTS

How important is it to get a good start in life?
Which person in the texts do you admire the most?

GRAMMAR Third conditional

1 **Read the examples. Then answer the questions.**

1 Phiona **wouldn't have gone** there if she **hadn't been** desperate.
2 If the family **had stayed** in Somalia, they **could** never **have lived** in safety.

a Did Phiona go to the chess club?
b Was she desperate?
c Did Ahmed's family stay in Somalia?
d Was it safe in Somalia?

2 **Complete the rules with the words in the box.**

could	*have*	past perfect	*would*

We use the third conditional to talk about imaginary results of situations in the past that didn't happen.
a We use *if* + ________, + ________ + *have* + past participle.
b We can also use the modal verbs ________ or *might* + ________ + past participle.

» GRAMMAR REFERENCE AND PRACTICE PAGE 155

3 **Match the sentence halves.**

1 If I hadn't lost my phone, I
2 If you had stayed for a coffee, you
3 If everyone had come to the beach party, there
4 If you'd revised for the test, you
5 If we'd moved to another town, we

a would have had to make new friends.
b might have got higher marks.
c would have missed the bus.
d wouldn't have missed your call.
e could have been over 100 people.

4 **Complete the third conditional sentences with the correct form of the verbs in brackets.**

1 If I ________ (know) how difficult the course was, I ________ (would / choose) an easier one.
2 If Paul ________ (not go) surfing at the weekend, he ________ (could / finish) his homework.
3 You ________ (might / enjoy) the film more if you ________ (not fall) asleep!
4 The team ________ (could / win) their match if they ________ (not have) so many injuries.
5 If Jenny ________ (get) in touch earlier, I ________ (might / be) able to meet her.
6 Simon's sister ________ (would not / meet) her husband if she ________ (not move) to London.

wish + past perfect

5 **Read the examples. What tense follows *wish* and *If only*?**

1 She always **wished she hadn't had** to leave home.
2 **I wish I had listened** to you more carefully.

» GRAMMAR REFERENCE AND PRACTICE PAGE 155

6 **Rewrite the sentences using *wish* and a suitable tense. Then write a third conditional sentence for each one.**

0 I left my jacket at the party and I lost it.
I wish I hadn't left my jacket at the party. If I hadn't left my jacket at the party, I wouldn't have lost it.
1 You forgot to check the time of the train, so we missed it.
2 The organisers didn't advertise the concert, so we didn't know about it.
3 My guitar got broken when my cousin dropped it.
4 James didn't wear gloves on the mountain and his hands froze.

7 **Correct the mistake in each sentence.**

1 If you have been there last night, you would have enjoyed yourself.
2 I wish you were there. It was amazing!
3 We might not lose the game if I hadn't made that mistake.
4 If you hadn't helped them, what would happened?
5 We would have missed the train if it wouldn't have been late.
6 We wish we'd knew you were going to be there.

VOCABULARY Phrasal verbs with *get*

1 **Read the examples. Then explain the meaning of the phrasal verbs.**

EP

1 Dawn aimed high, hoping to **get into** Harvard University.
2 He **got through** his schooling and is now a social worker.
3 He even **got back** his place on the school team!

2 **Some phrasal verbs with *get* have three parts. Choose the correct phrasal verbs to complete the definitions.**

EP

1 If you **get on with** / **get out of** something, you continue doing it.
2 If you **get on with** / **get away with** something, you avoid being punished for it.
3 If you **get out of** / **get round to** something, you avoid doing it.
4 If you **get away with** / **get round to** something, you finally do it, after intending to for a long time.

3 **Complete the sentences with the correct form of a phrasal verb from Exercises 1 and 2.**

1 Our band ________ the first round of the tournament, but we lost in the second.
2 I need to stay in and ________ with my homework.
3 Matt plays for the second team, but he'd like to ________ the first team.
4 We finally ________ watching that film you recommended.
5 I never ________ the money that I lent my brother.
6 If the police hadn't searched the man, he'd have ________ the theft.
7 I ________ doing the washing-up, as I was feeling ill.

4 » **Work in pairs.** **Turn to page 126.**

LISTENING

1 **You will hear people talking in eight different situations. Read the context sentence for each question. Which recordings will only have one speaker?**

1 You hear two friends talking about a school trip. What is the girl doing?
- **A** persuading her friend to sign up for the trip
- **B** checking what she has to prepare before the trip
- **C** complaining about the lack of information on the trip

2 You hear a teacher talking to her class at the end of term. What is she doing?
- **A** praising the students for their exam results
- **B** encouraging the whole class to work harder
- **C** indicating what the class could achieve

3 You hear an interview with a musician. Why does he think he has been successful?
- **A** He won a talent competition.
- **B** He got a lot of fans through social media.
- **C** He met a record producer at the right time.

4 You hear two classmates discussing a careers day they have attended. What do they disagree about?
- **A** how the event was different from their expectations
- **B** which speaker they enjoyed the most at the event
- **C** whether they would go to a similar event in the future

5 You hear a woman leaving a phone message. Why is she leaving the message?
- **A** to confirm a decision
- **B** to apologise for a mistake
- **C** to change an arrangement

6 You hear two girls talking about their ideal university. What do they agree is a priority for them both?
- **A** the size of the campus
- **B** the quality of the classes
- **C** the choice of social activities

7 You overhear a boy leaving a phone message. Why is he calling?
- **A** to ask a favour
- **B** to apologise for being late
- **C** to arrange a time to meet

8 You hear two friends talking about a film. What is the girl's opinion of it?
- **A** It was impossible to watch without being moved.
- **B** She felt motivated by the main character's commitment.
- **C** The plot was too predictable.

2 **Read the question that follows each context sentence in Exercise 1. Then answer these questions.**

1 Which four questions are asking about the speaker's purpose?

2 For the four remaining questions, which one focuses on
- **a** an explanation?
- **b** one person's opinion?
- **c** a shared opinion?
- **d** a disagreement?

79 **3** **For questions 1–8 in Exercise 1, listen and choose the best answer (A, B or C). Then listen again and check.**

SPEAKING Discussing ideas

80 **1** **Look at the task. Then listen to Polina and Konstantin's conversation. In what order do they discuss the things in the diagram?**

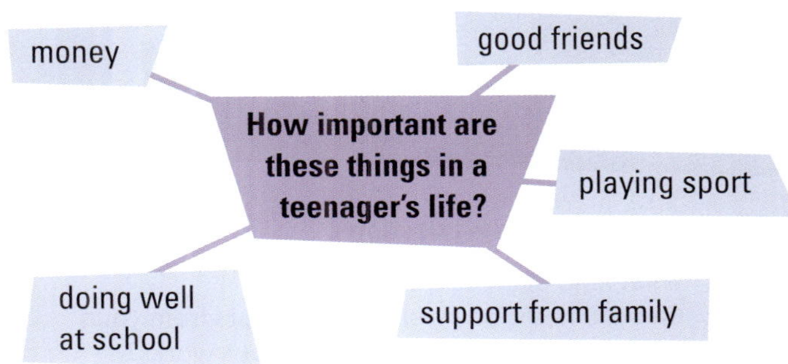

80 **2** **Read the *Prepare to speak* box. Then listen again. Which phrases do Polina and Konstantin *not* use?**

PREPARE TO SPEAK | Reacting to ideas

Agreeing
Absolutely!
Yes, that makes sense.
I'd agree (with you) up to a point.

Disagreeing politely
I'm not so sure.
I think that's only true for …

Adding another idea
The thing is …
In actual fact, …
But on the other hand, …

3 **Discuss which *two* of the ideas are the most important in a teenager's life. Remember to use the phrases in the *Prepare to speak* box.**

81 **4** **Listen to Polina and Konstantin deciding the same thing. Did you agree on the same two ideas?**

5 **Discuss the questions. Use the phrases in the *Prepare to speak* box and remember to ask your partner's opinion.**

1 What makes you feel really happy?
2 If you could change one thing about your life, what would you change?
3 What's the most important thing for a happy school life?
4 Do you think schools should teach students how to be happy?
5 What will life be like in 50 years from now?

CULTURE

MODERN AND CONTEMPORARY ART

1

2

3
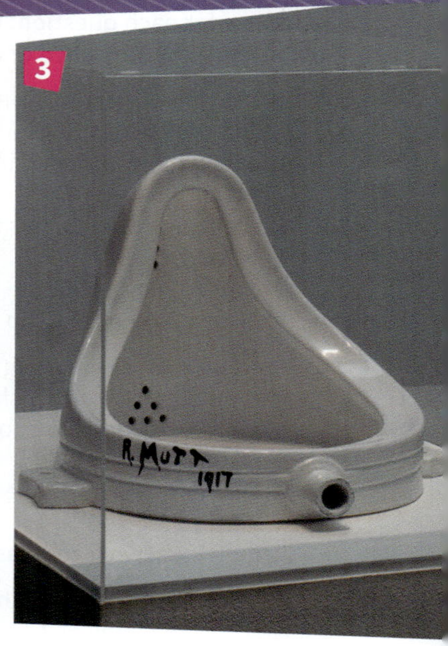

1 **Ask and answer the questions.**

1 What kind of art do you like?
2 Can you name any well-known artists from your country? What are their most famous works?
3 Can you think of any examples of art that express the 'culture' of your region or country?

2 **Look at the photos of three art galleries on page 107. Read the article quickly. Then match photos A–C to the galleries.**

3 **Read the article again. Then complete the sentences with information from the article.**

1 Visitors to the Turbine Hall couldn't ______ the whole *Marsyas* installation because it was so big.
2 You don't need to pay to visit Tate Modern, but the museum does ask visitors to make a ______.
3 MoMA has a total of ______ to display its collection and to hold exhibitions.
4 Aside from holding exhibitions, MoMA also runs ______ programmes for visitors.
5 The exterior of the Guggenheim Museum Bilbao building is made of ______ pieces of shiny metal.
6 At the Guggenheim, all of the galleries can be accessed from ______.

TALKING POINTS

Have you ever seen any large-scale art installations? What did you think of them?
Which of the three places mentioned in the article would you most like to visit? Why?

4 **Look at photos 1–3. Are they art? Why? / Why not?**

82 **5** **Listen to a tour of Tate Modern in London. Which pieces of art are mentioned? Which are shown above?**

82 **6** **Listen again. Are the sentences true (T), false (F) or not mentioned (NM)?**

1 The boy has seen something similar to Duchamp's *Fountain* recently.
2 The guide wants visitors to remember what the work of art is used for.
3 The guide thinks that the perspective in Robert Delaunay's painting is amazing.
4 The girl couldn't look at Delaunay's painting for very long.
5 The Robert Delaunay painting is titled *Endless Movement*.

7 **Complete the sentences with the words in the box.**

concept	hidden	offended
point	simplistic	statement

USEFUL LANGUAGE

Talking about modern and contemporary art

1 People sometimes feel ______ by unpleasant content in modern art.
2 There isn't always a ______ message in a work of art.
3 When I look at this, I ask myself, what's the ______?
4 Artists are often trying to make a ______ about an issue that's important to them.
5 We need to understand the central ______ which this work of art is based on.
6 This artist's work is ______ but powerful.

MODeRN aRt at iTs BeST

83

Are you a fan of modern and contemporary art? Well, if you are, sit back and let us take you on a journey to three of the best places to see it. Viewing works of art in a gallery is so much better than looking at them online. And just like travelling, looking at art that's not from our own culture helps us to think in different and new ways.

A

B

C

Tate Modern, London, UK

The gallery's home is a huge old power station on the River Thames. Its incredible Turbine Hall, which is 35 metres high and 155 metres long, is the entrance area to the museum. Not surprisingly, it's also where the Tate Modern displays large art installations, such as Anish Kapoor's enormous red *Marsyas* sculpture, exhibited in 2002. It was impossible to see the entire sculpture from one place because of its size, so visitors needed to move around the Hall to explore it. More recently, in 2017, the Hall was transformed into a huge playground for adults! *One Two Three Swing!* encouraged visitors to play on swings and have fun together and to make new friends. Although the gallery asks for a voluntary donation from visitors, entry to the main displays is free. Tate Modern has welcomed over 40 million visitors since it opened in 2000, making it one of the top three UK tourist attractions.

Museum of Modern Art, New York, USA

One of the biggest institutions in the United States and dedicated only to contemporary art, the Museum of Modern Art (MoMA) is located in midtown Manhattan. Originally opened in 1929 as an educational institution, MoMA now has 38,000 square metres of gallery space, including galleries for media, prints, architecture and design, drawings, and paintings and sculpture. The museum presents world-class exhibitions and educational programmes to its many visitors from around the world. Well-known pieces in the MoMA collection include Salvador Dalí's surrealist painting *The Persistence of Memory* and Frida Kahlo's symbolic *Self-Portrait with Cropped Hair*.

Guggenheim Museum Bilbao, Basque Country, Spain

Guggenheim Museum Bilbao was built between 1993 and 1997 on a former industrial site in the Basque Country in northern Spain. Many people feel that the building itself is just as important as the works of art inside it. The building is like a giant sculpture and has a complex mathematical design. It was created by the American architect Frank Gehry and is a magnificent example of 20th-century architecture. It is covered by around 33,000 extremely thin sheets of titanium. Guggenheim Museum Bilbao is best known for artwork on a large scale, which is often created especially for the space inside the museum. For example, for the museum's inauguration, a 104-metre-long steel snake was made by the American Minimalist artist, Richard Serra. From inside the Museum Hall, the heart of the museum, the 20 gallery spaces extend out, providing 11,000 square metres of exhibition space for visitors to enjoy.

PROJECT

Finding out about contemporary art

Work in groups. Choose a local or national modern art museum or gallery. Then make a poster about it.

1. Research the galleries and different spaces at the museum.
2. Choose a selection of works of art from different artists in its collection.
3. Write a summary to describe each work.
4. Include your own opinions about the works of art.

Present your poster to the class.

14 NOW WATCH THE CULTURE VIDEO

19 AGAINST THE LAW

ABOUT YOU

Which crime shows do you watch on TV?
Why do you think people enjoy books, films and TV shows about crime?

VOCABULARY Crime and criminals

1 Listen and match five stories to the headlines. (84)

a Actor speaks about experience of **burglary**
b **Prisoner** escapes during accident
c **Hacker** latest: police **make an arrest**
d Police find **burglar** asleep in car
e Police **release suspect** in stolen painting mystery

2 Complete the stories with the words in the boxes. Then listen again and check. (84)

charged	committed a crime	court	
denies the charge	sentenced	theft	witness

1 David Rentham, who was arrested on Tuesday for the recent [1] ________ of a Picasso from a New York museum, was freed today. As he left the police station, Rentham said, 'I have not [2] ________. Please leave me alone now.'

2 Inspector Ian Payne of the Online Investigations Unit said that they had [3] ________ James Wallgrove, 27, at Central Manchester Police Station with recent attempts to hack government computers. Wallgrove [4] ________.

3 A [5] ________ explained yesterday how she watched from her car as Robert Thomas, due to be [6] ________ in [7] ________ today, escaped from the back of a prison van during a road accident.

burgled	investigating	judge	jury
statement	suspect	victim	

4 Police [8] ________ a series of break-ins woke a man in his car to ask him if he had seen anything. They started to [9] ________ his involvement when they spotted gloves and a mask on the back seat of his vehicle.

5 Soap star Carrie Anderson, whose home was [10] ________ last October, gave a [11] ________ in a packed London court yesterday. Before she spoke and described what she had seen, the [12] ________ warned the [13] ________ they should treat the [14] ________ in this case as they would any normal person.

3 Look at the **words** in the headlines in Exercise 1 and the words in the boxes in Exercise 2.

Find
1 six words for people who might be seen in a court room.
2 four things the police do to someone.
3 three things a criminal does.
4 two types of criminal.
5 one thing a judge does.

READING

1 Imagine you saw someone you know doing one of these things. Would you tell anyone? Why? / Why not?

1 dropping litter
2 downloading a film or music illegally
3 shoplifting
4 making a joke emergency call

2 Read the article quickly. Then put the events in the order they happened.

a The Griffin family's house was burgled. ☐
b Martin Griffin came home. ☐
c Mr and Mrs Griffin told the police about their son. ☐
d The police arrived at the Griffin family's home. ☐
e Stuart Tiller persuaded Martin to burgle his parents' house. ☐
f Martin's parents told him about the burglary. ☐
g Nikki Griffin arrived home. ☐
h Mr and Mrs Griffin realised who the burglar was. ☐

3 Read the article again. Then answer the questions.

1 What do you think led the Griffins to suspect their son had burgled their home?
2 What circumstances helped Martin to get a less serious sentence from the judge?
3 What do you think you would have done in Martin's parents' situation?
4 How would you have felt if you were Martin?

The DECISION:

WE ASKED THE POLICE TO ARREST OUR SON

By Sally Fenton | Saturday 3 May

85

Nikki Griffin remembers the events as clearly as if they had happened yesterday.

'It was a normal Friday afternoon back in January. I was looking forward to doing very little for a couple of days.'

She unlocked her front door and turned off the burglar alarm – which meant no one else was at home. Nikki wasn't surprised. She guessed her husband, Phil, must still have been at work and their son, Martin, could have been anywhere. She went straight upstairs to change.

When Nikki entered her bedroom, she stepped back in shock. Their possessions were lying all over the floor. She ran to her jewellery drawer. It was completely empty except for an inexpensive ring her son had once bought her. Nikki immediately phoned her husband and then the police.

The first thing the police spotted was that a window in the kitchen was open. But why hadn't the alarm gone off? It was switched on when Nikki returned home, so someone must have set it when they left the house in the morning. When the police checked, they found that the alarm *had* been set, but someone had actually turned it off temporarily, using the correct code. Something only a handful of people knew. Then, when Phil returned home, they found that some money was missing – £50 that they kept hidden in a box of cereal for emergencies. A burglar couldn't have known about that money. It was almost impossible.

The police suspected that someone in the family was involved in the burglary. They started asking questions about the Griffins' son. At first, Nikki and Phil refused to believe Martin could be involved. He'd never done anything dishonest or illegal in the past.

Do you think the Griffins made the right decision? YES NO SEE RESULTS

'It was the hardest thing we'd ever done, but we're glad we did it.'

Later, when Martin arrived home, his parents explained what had happened. They didn't accuse him directly, but they asked him if he knew anything about it.

'It was obvious as soon as Martin spoke,' said Nikki. 'He denied it, of course, but we knew.'

The next step must have been a hard decision for the Griffins. In fact, Nikki said that she and her husband spent most of the night talking about what to do. However, the next morning they rang the police and told them what they suspected had happened.

Martin was arrested the same day and charged with burglary. He admitted everything immediately. According to the Griffins, he seemed relieved to confess. It turns out the whole thing had been someone else's idea. At first, Martin had been unwilling to take part, but his friend, Stuart Tiller, 20, had eventually persuaded him. Tiller, who had a criminal record dating back several years, had already spent time in prison for car theft. He was sentenced to eight months for his part in the Griffins' burglary. Everything stolen from the Griffins was found at his home.

Martin was more fortunate. As it was the first time he had committed a crime, and because of Tiller's influence, he avoided a prison sentence. Instead, he received 200 hours of community service – unpaid work such as picking up litter or cleaning graffiti off walls. The judge was also impressed by Martin's statement in court. He strongly regretted what he had done and fully understood his parents' actions.

And how do the Griffins feel six months on from that Friday afternoon?

'We know we made the right decision to call the police,' says Nikki, and Martin agrees. 'I made a stupid mistake that day, and luckily my parents did the right thing. Without that, I might have carried on and got involved in more serious crimes. But it's all behind me now, and I can look forward to the future. I just want to get my normal life back again.'

TALKING POINTS

When you see someone do something wrong, is it important to tell someone?

How can friends influence each other to do things?

GRAMMAR Modals of deduction: past

1 Read the examples. Then complete the rules with *must*, *might*/*could* or *can't*/*couldn't*.

1 Someone **must have set** the alarm when they left the house.
2 A burglar **couldn't have known** about that money.
3 I **might have got** involved in more serious crimes.

We use modal verbs + *have* + past participle to talk about possibility in the past.
We use:
a ______ + *have* + past participle when we think something possibly happened.
b ______ + *have* + past participle when we are certain something happened.
c ______ + *have* + past participle when we are certain something didn't happen.

» GRAMMAR REFERENCE AND PRACTICE PAGE 156

2 Choose the correct words.

1 He's late. Something must *have happened* / *happened* / *happen* to him.
2 We wondered if you *must* / *might* / *can* have seen anything suspicious yesterday.
3 Jack wasn't here last week. It *can't been* / *couldn't have be* / *couldn't have been* him.
4 I had my phone when I left home and I didn't have it when I got here, so I *could* / *might* / *must* have lost it on the way.
5 I'm not sure, but I think I *couldn't* / *might* / *must* have had my wallet stolen.
6 Do you think *might you* / *must you* / *you could* have left your keys at home?

3 Complete the sentences with *must*, *might/could* or *can't/couldn't* + *have* and the correct form of the verb in brackets.

1 The police haven't found the thieves yet. They think they ______ (leave) the country, but they aren't sure.
2 The witness is very short-sighted and wasn't wearing her glasses, so she ______ (see) the suspect clearly.
3 When the men entered the bank, the police were waiting for them. Someone ______ (tell) them about the thieves' plan.
4 The burglar ______ (come) in through the window. It was locked and it still is.
5 Police think someone ______ (start) the fire on purpose, but it's possible it was an accident.
6 The robbery happened on a busy street in the middle of the day. There ______ (be) some witnesses!

4 Look at the photos. What must/might/could/can't/couldn't have happened in each photo?

1 He might/could have witnessed a crime.

5 Read the puzzle. What do you think the answer is? Write sentences with *must/might/can't have* + past participle. Compare your ideas. Then check the answer on page 126.

The police suspected a man of murder. They only knew his name – John – and his address. They went to the house and found four people: a builder, a lorry driver, a mechanic and a fireman. All four of them were playing cards. They immediately arrested the fireman. How did they know he was the murderer?

VOCABULARY Negative prefixes

1 Make these words into their opposites by adding a prefix. Use *un-*, *in-*, *im-*, *dis-* or *il-*. Then check in the article on page 109.

1 expensive
2 possible
3 honest
4 willing
5 legal

2 Complete the sentences with the opposite of the adjectives in the box.

EP

accurate	clear	fair	organised
patient	polite	safe	visible

1 I wouldn't trust that website. It's full of ______ information.
2 The lawyer was so ______ that he brought the wrong papers to the court.
3 Dressed in black, the burglar was almost ______ in the dark.
4 In many countries, it's considered ______ to point at people.
5 The woman's ______ behaviour at the crime scene made the police suspicious.
6 I wouldn't walk through that area alone at night. It's ______.
7 It's ______ why the police are investigating Mr Thomas, but a statement is expected soon.
8 It's ______ to blame Mike for losing his phone. He had it stolen!

3 » Work in pairs. Turn to page 126.

WRITING A news article

1 **Discuss the questions.**

1 What interesting crime-related news stories have you read or heard recently?
2 Why did you find them interesting?

2 **You see this announcement on the website of an international magazine for teenagers. Read the announcement. Then answer the questions.**

1 Who are you writing for?
2 Where might the article be published?

> Articles wanted
> Tell us an interesting crime-related news story you've read or heard about recently. Who was involved and what crime was committed? Were the criminals caught and punished? How?
> The best articles will appear in the next issue of our magazine and on our website.

3 **Read the article below. Then answer the questions.**

1 Who is the main person the story is about?
2 What did this person do?
3 Where did the event take place?
4 When did it happen?
5 Why did it happen?
6 How was her crime discovered?

4 **Read the *Prepare to write* box. Then match the tips to the five sections of the article.**

> **PREPARE TO WRITE** | A news article
>
> A good news article:
> **a** includes a quote from someone.
> **b** explains the detail of the story in the middle paragraphs.
> **c** might end by talking about the situation now.
> **d** gives the main points of the story in a short first paragraph.
> **e** uses an interesting headline to catch readers' attention.

5 **Read the task in Exercise 2 again. Then plan your news article.**

- Think of an interesting news article you have read or heard recently. If you prefer, invent one yourself.
- Find a report online to get details and suitable quotations. You could also invent these.

6 **Write your news article.**

- Use the tips in the *Prepare to write* box.
- Don't forget to include a headline.
- Write 140–190 words.
- Check your grammar and spelling.

1 **MOTHER DISGUISES HERSELF TO SIT DAUGHTER'S EXAM**

2 **A 52-year-old mother was arrested in Paris, France, last week for attempting to sit her 19-year-old daughter's English exam.**

3 The woman, who has not been named, turned up at the examination centre wearing jeans, trainers and heavy make-up. She quickly showed her ID card and was allowed to take a seat. Since the exam centre was not the daughter's school and adult students regularly take the exam, no one suspected the woman of any dishonest behaviour.

During the exam, one of the supervisors glanced at the ID card. He recognised the photograph because he had met the student at an exam a week earlier. But clearly the woman at the desk was not the same person. The police were called and someone quietly asked the woman to come outside.

4 'Thankfully, she left with no difficulties,' a representative from the centre commented.

5 The woman admitted what she had done. She said she wanted to help as she was better at English than her daughter. She now faces a fine of up to €8,000 and her daughter could be banned from public examinations for five years.

20 PLACES TO HANG OUT

A

B

C

ABOUT YOU

15 Watch the video. Then answer the questions.

Where do you hang out with your friends?
What would be your ideal place to hang out?
Are there enough places for teenagers to hang out in your town/city?

VOCABULARY Places

86 **1** **Listen to three teenagers talking about their favourite place to hang out. Then match the speakers to the photos.**

87 **2** **Complete the paragraphs with the words in the boxes. Then listen and check.**

EP

barriers basement complex
concrete surface

The Southbank Centre is a massive arts [1] ________ where people go to see concerts, shows and exhibitions. And in a [2] ________ area underneath, there's one of the best skateboarding parks in the country. It's all [3] ________ down there, which is a great [4] ________ for skateboarding, and there are metal [5] ________ and hand rails that you can slide along as well.

chimney community centre hut steps

Before, this was just a dirty old wooden [6] ________. I heard it used to be some sort of [7] ________ in the 1960s. Now it's been done up, we can play music here and there's even a [8] ________ so we can light a fire and keep warm in winter. On Friday nights and Saturdays, you can't even get up the [9] ________ to get into the place.

bench frame ladder
rug shed shelter

The tree house started with a wooden [10] ________, just long bits of wood, and then we filled in the sides with old wooden floorboards to form walls. We made a roof too, to act as a kind of [11] ________ from the rain. It looks a bit like the sort of [12] ________ you might keep your tools in in a garden, but it's up a tree! There's a long [13] ________ for climbing up to it and we've done it up really nicely inside. There's an old wooden [14] ________ for sitting on and there's a [15] ________ on the floor.

3 **Categorise the words in the boxes in Exercise 2.**

1 Which are buildings? Of those that aren't buildings, how do we use them?
2 What types of complex are there (as well as arts complexes)?
3 What do people use community centres for?
4 What is the difference between a hut, a shed and a shelter?

4 **Describe three places that you use. Use some of the words in Exercise 2.**

READING

1 **Read the first line of each text. Then answer the questions.**

1 What is going to happen to the tree house? Why?
2 What is Celina Dill building? Why?
3 What do you think the differences and similarities between the two projects may be?

2 **Read both texts quickly to check your ideas for question 3 in Exercise 1.**

A PLACE OF YOUR OWN

Have you ever wished you had your own space where no one could bother you? Here are two different stories of people who did just that …

An award-winning tree house, which a group of boys spent three years building, will be pulled down over health and safety fears.

The group built their magical hangout, hiding 28 metres up a tree, at the edge of a farmer's field. The five main builders estimate that 1,000 hours of work went into building the tree house. The friends hunted for old construction materials and built up from an existing shelter that was 15 metres up the tree, using only nails and a hammer. It has a front door, windows, a circular staircase and a viewing platform. To complete the relaxed atmosphere, they even carried up a sofa to chill out on. The astonishing palace in the sky was entered into a competition on Facebook to find the nation's best tree house. Praising the tree house as 'ludicrously high up', the judges awarded them the top prize.

But the farmer who owns the field has said it must come down because he could be taken to court if someone fell off it and did themselves harm. Apparently, the construction is now so wrapped in branches that the whole tree will have to be cut down. On learning the tree house's fate, the group said they were very upset, but understood why it had to happen. Dougie Haynes was 16 when he started work on the project, and hopes to study architecture at university. He said, 'I put so much time into it. In October, we started building the top half, which was when the leaves were falling off the trees – that's when people started to notice it. It's sad – this summer could have been pretty awesome. You'd have to be pretty crazy to ever fall or hurt yourself. We are always very careful with new people. Standing on a nail was the worst injury I ever had there, and that was when I was building it. I wouldn't say it's dangerous at all.'

88

It was the 'Small House Movement' that inspired Celina Dill's project of building a tiny home on wheels for herself. She's only 16 but is making serious plans for her future.

'I decided that I'll probably want to move out in a couple of years and I don't know where I want to live, so it needs to be able to go anywhere. So a house on wheels makes sense.'

Although Celina Dill was an excellent student, she decided after three semesters at South Whidbey High School that she had learned what she needed and wanted to move on with her life. She came away from her metalwork class with some useful practical skills. She added these skills to those her carpenter dad had shown her.

Celina enjoys working on her project enormously and isn't even considering a pre-planned design. Everything is going to be individual to her. Celina is capable of building every part of the house herself and is determined to do so. She has learned about how the sun moves through a house so that it warms its inhabitants and lights spaces, and how to build her home so the sun doesn't wake a sleeper too early in the morning.

She has found a stylish 1950s cooking stove, which will be great for cooking on, and an eco-friendly toilet. She's spent most of her savings on the heavy-duty truck that will pull her tiny house behind her on a wheeled trailer.

3 **Read the texts again and find the parts that provide these answers. Then suggest possible questions for the answers.**

Said by one of the boys:

0 'We took some furniture up to the tree house.'
To complete the relaxed atmosphere, they even carried up a sofa to chill out on.
Did you take anything up to the tree house?
1 'They chose us because they were impressed by its extreme height.'
2 'It's impossible to remove it because of how the tree has grown.'
3 'We're not happy about it, but we can see his point of view.'
4 'It was autumn in Britain, so it got spotted!'
5 'There's no danger if people behave sensibly.'

Said by Celina:

6 'I left because I didn't think there was anything more they could teach me.'
7 'Well, how to work with metals – you know, welding, that kind of thing.'
8 'My dad's a carpenter so he taught me how to work with wood.'
9 'Nothing. I want the design to be all mine.'
10 'It may be about 70 years old, but it works well and looks great.'

TALKING POINTS

What kind of hangouts do young people need? Do you have any cool hangouts locally?
What would be the advantages of having a place on wheels to hang out in?

GRAMMAR -ing forms

1 **Read the examples. Then match them to the rules.**

1 **On learning** the tree house's fate, they said they were very upset.
2 **Standing on a nail** was the worst injury I ever had there.
3 Celina **enjoys working** on her project enormously.
4 She has found a stylish 1950s stove, which will be **great for cooking** on.

We can use *-ing* forms:
a as the subject or object of a clause, or to talk about an activity.
b after verbs and phrases that express likes and dislikes.
c after prepositions.
d after adjective + preposition combinations.

» GRAMMAR REFERENCE AND PRACTICE PAGE 157

2 **Complete the sentences with the *-ing* form of the verbs in the box. Then match them to the rules in Exercise 1.**

have observe ride take travel win

1 I really love ________ a place to hang out in.
2 Maya gets anxious about ________ by plane.
3 Steve learned metalwork from ________ his uncle.
4 ________ horses is popular around here.
5 By ________ more exercise, Holly soon got fitter.
6 ________ a gold medal made all Jimi's training worthwhile.

3 **Correct the mistake in each sentence.**

1 Design your own home must be so satisfying.
2 We enjoyed to sleep in the new house.
3 We're excited about visit your new place.
4 I'm looking forward to see your plans.
5 The architect suggested add a viewing platform.
6 The idea of build my own home before finishing college is very attractive!

Participle clauses

4 **Read the examples. Then match them to the rules.**

1 **Praising** the tree house as 'ludicrously high up', the judges awarded them the top prize.
2 The group built their magical hangout, **hiding** 28 metres up a tree, at the edge of a farmer's field.

We can use *-ing* forms to introduce a participle clause. We use participle clauses:
a to talk about an action that happens at the same time as the action in the main clause.
b to add more information about something that is mentioned in the main clause.

» GRAMMAR REFERENCE AND PRACTICE PAGE 157

5 **Complete the sentences with the participle clauses in the box. Then match them to the rules in Exercise 4 (a or b).**

consisting of metalwork and woodwork
having no heating
not wanting to disturb anyone
realising his mistake
shining in the darkness
talking to John

1 ________, I whispered into my phone.
2 The old wooden hut, ________, was freezing cold.
3 ________, Tim went bright red and apologised.
4 Among the trees, they saw lights ________.
5 The classes, ________, lasted three terms.
6 ________, I realised what I had missed.

6 **Join the pairs of sentences using a participle clause. Start each sentence with the *-ing* form of the verb in bold.**

0 She **smiled** at the judges. She accepted her prize.
Smiling at the judges, she accepted her prize.
1 I **grew** more confident. I started to add more details to my tree house.
2 We **had** no idea about how to build a tree house. We looked online for ideas.
3 The shelter was useless. It **had** no roof.
4 The hut is very quiet. It'**s** miles away from the nearest house.

VOCABULARY Compound adjectives ending in -ing

1 **Read the example. What parts of speech can you use to form some compound adjectives?**

*an **award-winning** tree house*

2 EP **Try to work out the meaning of the compound adjectives in the box. Then use them to complete the sentences.**

cost-cutting eye-catching heartwarming life-threatening mouth-watering record-breaking time-consuming

1 Building a tree house can be a very ________ project if it's done properly.
2 My aunt has recently recovered from a ________ illness.
3 Their advert combines ________ images of surfers with a clever slogan.
4 The athlete's ________ run ended badly, as she injured herself.
5 It was such a ________ menu that it was hard to choose what to eat.
6 The company is in serious debt and has had to take ________ measures.
7 This ________ tale is about four friends who do everything to stay together.

3 » **Work in pairs.** Turn to page 126.

LISTENING

1 **You are going to listen to three people talking about the places in the photos. Where do you think these places are, and why might they be significant to the speakers?**

89 **2** **Listen and match the speakers to the places in Exercise 1.**

3 **Which place do you think sounds the most interesting? Why?**

89 **4** **Listen again.**

Which speaker

A emphasises that their town is small?
B praises the extraordinary design of the place they love?
C accepts that tourists are naturally attracted to this well-known site?
D suggests that there is a good view from the place?
E approves of the link between the design and local history?
F explains that the place was constructed many centuries ago?

SPEAKING Talking about yourself

1 **Read the questions. Which ones ask about places? Which ask about activities?**

1. Tell us about your favourite building. (Why do you like it?)
2. Do you enjoy doing watersports? (Why? / Why not?)
3. What do you like about your school? (Is there anything you'd change about it?)
4. What kind of exercise do you like doing? (Why?)
5. Where do you like hanging out in your neighbourhood? (Why? What's it like?)
6. What game did you use to enjoy playing when you were younger? (Why did you like it?)
7. What do you like about your town or city? (Why?)
8. Tell us something about a sport you enjoy watching or playing.

90 **2** **Listen to Marta. Which questions from Exercise 1 does she answer?**

91 **3** **Read the** ***Prepare to speak*** **box. Then listen to Marta's last answer again. Which phrases does she use to make her answers longer?**

PREPARE TO SPEAK | Giving long answers

Adding more information
also   and now   too

Contrasting
but   except
yet   … either
(but) on the other hand

Giving examples
like   such as
for instance

Giving reasons
because

Giving your opinion
I think   in my opinion

4 **Read Marta's answer to the last question. Then underline the adjectives that she uses. How do they improve her answer?**

I don't take part in much sport myself, except at school, but I love watching football with my brothers. We have some really strong clubs in Spain, like Real Madrid, Atlético de Madrid, Barça … My city's team, Valencia FC, are in the Spanish league, which is called *La Liga*. I think it can sometimes be more exciting to watch a match on TV because then you appreciate the skilful way they pass the ball to each other. But on the other hand, being in the stadium when your team scores a goal is the best – there's such a fantastic atmosphere!

91 **5** **Listen again and notice how Marta adds emphasis to these positive adjectives, to sound enthusiastic.**

6 **Ask and answer the other questions from Exercise 1.**

- Use phrases from the *Prepare to speak* box to give longer answers.
- Use adjectives to make your answers more interesting.
- Add emphasis to positive words to sound enthusiastic.

LIFE SKILLS EMOTIONAL SKILLS

BUILDING SELF-CONFIDENCE

1 **Ask and answer the questions.**

1 How does a self-confident person look and act?
2 Who is the most self-confident person you know?
3 How do you think someone could build and improve their self-confidence?

2 **Read the text quickly. Then match the headings to sections 2, 4, 5 and 6.**

a It's OK to feel the way you feel
b Look after your body
c Focus on the things you're good at
d Express yourself clearly

3 **Read the text again. Are the sentences true (T), false (F) or not mentioned (NM)?**

1 How self-confident people feel is something that rarely changes.
2 Not giving an answer, even when you know what it is, can be a sign of low self-confidence.
3 Self-acceptance can turn not succeeding at something into a positive.
4 Social media profiles usually reflect how confident a person is.
5 Negative emotions can help to make us stronger.

4 **Match the highlighted words in the text to the meanings.**

1 improve or increase something
2 say you are pleased about someone's special achievement
3 feel unsure or that something is uncertain
4 accept that something is true or exists
5 the way something is done

93 **5** **Listen to a counsellor giving a group of teenagers some advice on building their self-confidence. Then choose the best summary.**

A We all have the same negative messages in our heads and can use the same phrases to stop them.
B We shouldn't let people talk to us in a negative way.
C Turning negative self-talk into positive self-talk has various benefits.
D Negative self-talk is the truth and we should all learn how to react to it.

LIFE SKILLS

Building self-confidence
Self-confidence is the belief in your own ideas and ability to be successful in a specific situation. Lots of people suffer from low self-confidence. Fortunately, there are many ways to become more self-confident. This will help you to feel happier and be more successful.

92

Ready for a self-confidence boost?

Do you ever doubt or question yourself? And do you often feel insecure? If so, you might be suffering from low self-confidence. But don't worry, that's perfectly normal! After all, growing up is tough – you have to deal with difficult situations on a daily basis at school, at home and online.

However, that doesn't mean that you should do nothing about it. Self-confidence is really important as it gives you the power to be yourself, do what's right for you and achieve your goals in life. So if you think you need a self-confidence boost, read on for some tips.

1 Self-acceptance and self-improvement

Don't make decisions about yourself just because you haven't done something well. Getting a bad mark for an art project doesn't mean that you're not artistic. Or not qualifying to play in the volleyball team doesn't mean that you'll never be good at sports. Try to accept your failures and remember that we learn through our mistakes and they help us become better.

2 ....

When you don't like how someone is treating you, tell them in a direct manner. And asking for help when you don't understand something at school will help you to avoid the loss of confidence which often results from not understanding.

3 Social media isn't everything

Don't make judgments about your popularity based on how many likes you get or the number of friends you have online. Feeling confident on social media doesn't necessarily mean you'll feel confident in your daily life.

6 Listen again. Then choose the best options.

93

1 Self-talk
   A only takes place occasionally.
   B doesn't affect our confidence.
   C is often not a good representation of reality.
2 Self-talk mechanisms help us to
   A stop irrational thoughts.
   B accept the truth.
   C create a positive voice in our minds.
3 What does the writer suggest?
   A Trying to remember negative messages.
   B Keeping a record of negative self-talk.
   C Accepting that sometimes there isn't a positive message.
4 When should we listen to our self-talk?
   A throughout the day
   B when it doesn't feel silly to do so
   C until we feel in control again

7 Complete the sentences with the words in the box.

accept	becoming	best
exist	know	right

USEFUL LANGUAGE

Positivity

1 I ________ my mistake and I'm learning from this situation.
2 I'm learning from my mistakes and ________ a better person.
3 I ________ I can pass this exam.
4 I'm doing the ________ I can.
5 Does any real evidence ________ for what I'm thinking?
6 Is there anything I can do ________ now which will help me do this?

4 ________

Exercise produces endorphins, natural chemicals in the brain which make you feel good. Taking care of your body by eating well and sleeping enough will also make you feel great. All of these things will help boost your confidence.

5 ________

Whether it's fear, anger or feeling impatient, we often think that some emotions are 'wrong'. But it's never wrong to feel a negative emotion – it's what makes us human and everyone experiences emotions like these. If you pretend to be or feel something that's not true to yourself, you might think that you're not good enough and your confidence will suffer. Notice how you feel, pause for a moment and tell yourself that it's fine to feel that way.

6 ________

Spending too much time thinking about your weaknesses isn't good for anyone. Congratulate yourself on your strengths and acknowledge when you use them.

7 Do something that scares you

Being scared by something doesn't mean that you should avoid it! Doing something that makes you feel afraid and then succeeding will be a huge confidence builder. You can do it!

PROJECT

Building self-confidence

Work in groups. Choose one of these topics related to building self-confidence or use your own idea. Then prepare a presentation about it using the steps below and the *Useful language* to help you.

- Becoming more independent and responsible
- Developing positive self-talk
- Building on your strengths

1 Research your chosen topic on the internet. Find an interesting short video about it.
2 Write a summary about your topic, including any useful advice and techniques.
3 Prepare some questions about the topic for classmates to discuss in small groups.
4 Decide how you want to present your summary, video and questions to the class.

Present your work to the class.

REVIEW 5 UNITS 17–20

VOCABULARY

1 Match the adjectives in the box to the meanings. There are two adjectives you do not need.

abstract	bizarre	contemporary
controversial	conventional	
powerful	stunning	unique

1 very strange
2 causing disagreement or discussion
3 the only one of its kind
4 traditional and ordinary
5 modern; existing or happening now
6 very beautiful

2 Complete the sentences with the nouns in the box.

bravery	commitment	inspiration
passion	sense	spirit

1 Our players always show great team ________ , even when they lose a match.
2 The teenager was awarded a medal for his ________ in rescuing the child.
3 Talented musicians usually have a ________ for music from an early age.
4 Many 19th-century artists found ________ for their paintings in nature.
5 The coach had the ________ to realise that the team needed a rest.
6 Everyone who was in the play showed huge ________ to making it a success.

3 Put the sentences in the correct order.

a an arrest. The man, a US national aged 52, was charged ☐
b and in a statement, police said they had released ☐
c any crime. Mr X claimed he was an innocent victim, ☐
d charge, and late last night, a judge found that ☐
e Last week, police in Austin, Texas, who were investigating *1*
f him while they widen their search for the hacker. ☐
g the theft of military secrets at Fort Worth, made ☐
h there was insufficient evidence that Mr X had committed ☐
i with hacking. The suspect, known only as Mr X, denied the ☐

4 Complete the sentences with suitable words related to places. The first letter of each word is given.

1 A: There's a party at the c________ c________ this afternoon. Are you coming?
B: Sorry, I promised my mum I'd go with her to the new arts c________ to see an exhibition.
2 There are concrete s________ down into the b________ underneath my block of flats. Be careful in case they're slippery.
3 We've built a tree house with old wooden doors attached to a f________. It has a roof, big windows, there's a b________ to sit on and a r________ on the floor. There's a l________ to climb up to it.

GRAMMAR

1 Choose the correct modal verbs.

1 Jude *could* / *must* well be away this week. I haven't seen him at all.
2 That answer *mustn't* / *can't* be correct. The numbers don't add up.
3 Our flight was delayed, so it *can* / *might* be possible to get a refund.
4 Why did you walk all the way home? *Couldn't* / *Can't* you have caught a bus?
5 The boys' tree house is fairly basic. They *can* / *must* have built it themselves.
6 It *can't* / *might* have taken you long to do this! It's really simple.

2 Rewrite the sentences using the third conditional.

1 The window was open, so the burglar got into the apartment. If the window hadn't …
2 Sally spent too much time on the first question, so she didn't finish the test. If Sally had spent less …
3 I bought a leather jacket last month, so I haven't got any money now. If I hadn't …
4 Ben forgot his sports bag, so he couldn't play football. If Ben hadn't …
5 It was raining, so we couldn't hang out in the park. If it hadn't …
6 I didn't know about the competition, so I didn't enter. If I'd …

3 Complete the sentences with the correct form of the verbs in brackets.

1 I wish I ________ (know) you were going into town.
2 If only you ________ (tell) me you were free yesterday.
3 Pete wished he ________ (not leave) the party.
4 If only we ________ (talk) about this problem earlier!
5 Do you ever wish you ________ (be born) in a different time?
6 I missed my station last night – if only I ________ (not fall) asleep!

4 Complete the sentences with the *-ing* form of the verbs in the box.

find	keep	make	miss	visit	win

1 I hate __________ art galleries and places like that.
2 After __________ out the truth, Ella blamed her sister.
3 __________ the prize was the best thing that had ever happened to Dan.
4 I don't mind __________ the gig tonight. The band aren't that remarkable.
5 __________ her news secret was difficult for Jo.
6 Freya is interested in __________ her own documentary.

5 Choose the correct words.

1 It *could* / *can* be mine. I have a cap just like that.
2 If you'd come with us, you'd *had* / *have had* fun.
3 I wish you *were* / *'d been* there. It was so dramatic.
4 Sometimes, *going* / *go* to school is difficult because of the traffic.

6 Correct the mistake in each sentence.

1 They mustn't be friends. They hardly know each other.
2 We would have got there quicker if we had took the train.
3 He must had a good time because he looks happy.
4 Thank you for call me yesterday.

7 Read the text. Use the word given in capitals at the end of some of the lines to form a word that fits in the gap in the same line.

The world's worst robber

In Louisiana, USA, a thief went into a bank with	
the [0]*intention* of stealing a couple of thousand	INTEND
dollars in cash. He walked [1]__________ over to the	CONFIDENT
counter and gave a handwritten note to a bank	
[2]__________, informing her that this was a bank	EMPLOY
robbery. The note warned her not to raise the	
alarm and demanded that she hand over rolls	
of used $100 notes. But [3]__________ for him, the	FORTUNE
robber didn't have a gun or any other weapon,	
and so she refused to give him anything. They	
argued, but after a few minutes the [4]__________	LUCKY
would-be robber was forced to leave the bank	
empty-handed.	
This useless robber had also been [5]__________.	CARE
He'd [6]__________ left behind his note, which	ACCIDENT
provided clues as to his identity. It was written	
on the back of a job [7]__________ containing all his	APPLY
personal details! Police quickly located their	
suspect using CCTV cameras, and [8]__________	INSTANT
arrested him. His fingerprints matched those on	
the note, and despite denying all responsibility,	
he was charged with attempted robbery.	

8 Read the text and decide which answer (A, B, C or D) best fits each gap.

The Shard

Designed by the architect Renzo Piano, the Shard became the tallest building in Europe when [0]*construction* was completed in 2012. There are 87 storeys in [1]__________, and three viewing areas high above the City of London are [2]__________ to the public for an entry fee.
The [3]__________ building materials are concrete and 11,000 individual sheets of glass, each one [4]__________ in the best position to reflect sunlight and the sky. This clever use of glass [5]__________ the appearance of the Shard to vary according to the weather and the season.
Several people have [6]__________ attempts to climb the Shard, including six female Greenpeace volunteers, all of them very [7]__________ climbers. After completing their 16-hour climb, the women were arrested by police, who claimed they had [8]__________ a crime in being on the property without permission.

0 (A) construction B development C finishing D manufacturing
1 A amount B sum C total D quantity
2 A accessible B achievable C attainable D visible
3 A dominant B principal C major D vital
4 A balanced B distributed C placed D planted
5 A creates B produces C causes D happens
6 A taken B done C kept D made
7 A capable B mature C precise D sophisticated
8 A committed B done C performed D engaged

EXTRA ACTIVITIES

UNIT 1 VOCABULARY, PAGE 10

2 **Circle your score for each answer and work out your total.**

1a	0	2a	2	3a	1	4a	0	5a	0	6a	2
1b	2	2b	1	3b	2	4b	2	5b	2	6b	1

Results

3–5 Oh, dear. This year at school could be tough! Maybe you need to be more willing to join in and get involved.

6–9 You're an all-rounder who tends to get on quite well at school without having to try too hard.

10–12 You're always looking for fresh challenges and you're keen to experience as much as you can – and fast. Life's an adventure!

UNIT 1 VOCABULARY, PAGE 12

3 **Take turns to ask each other the questions. Try to use the noun form of the bold verbs in your replies.**

0 Do you **collect** anything?
Yes. I have a massive collection of trainers! I've been collecting them since I was little.
1 Can you **suggest** anything cool to do after school?
2 Have you **applied** to do any extra-curricular activities this term?
3 Can you **describe** your best friend?
4 Who or what really **inspires** you?
5 How do you **motivate** yourself to study?
6 How do you **react** if people are late to meet you?

UNIT 2 VOCABULARY, PAGE 16

3 Student A

Read the example. Then tell your partner …

1 something you will always remember doing.
I will always remember going to my first concert.
2 something you stopped to do on your way to school this morning.
3 someone you will never forget meeting.
4 something you should try to do at home more often.

UNIT 3 VOCABULARY, PAGE 22

3 **Discuss the questions.**

1 Who do you feel you identify with the most in your family? Why?
2 Do you take after anyone in your family? Or does anyone take after you?
3 Who do you fall out the most with? What's the most common reason?
4 What was the last thing you talked your parents into allowing you to do?
5 What do you do when you feel you're being picked on?
6 Who would you depend on most in your family if you needed help?

UNIT 4 GRAMMAR, PAGE 26

5 1 The River Amazon is about 6,400 km long and the River Thames is only 346 km long, so the Amazon is far longer than the Thames.

2 The Red Sea covers 438,000 square kilometres and the Pacific Ocean covers 165 million square kilometres, so the Red Sea is a great deal smaller than the Pacific Ocean.

3 The Tokyo metropolitan area has a population of 38,140,000; New York metropolitan area's population is only 18,604,000 and the São Paulo metropolitan area has a population of 21,297,000, so Tokyo is easily the biggest city.

4 The Sahara Desert gets rain every few years. In parts of the Atacama Desert in Chile, until 2015 it hadn't rained for 500 years, but it isn't as dry as the Dry Valleys in Antarctica, which have had no measureable rain for millions of years.

Student B

Read the example. Then tell your partner …

1 something you must remember to do regularly.
I must remember to charge my phone every night.
2 something you are going to stop doing soon.
3 someone you often forget to keep in touch with.
4 something you would like to try doing.

Tell the class about your partner.

UNIT 4 VOCABULARY, PAGE 26

3 Student A

1 Look at photos A and B and complete the sentences. Student B will suggest some possible answers.
2 Look at photos C and D and listen to Student B's suggestions. Then share the possible answers.

A
There are too many people to …
There are so many people that …
It's such a busy train that …

B
The stage is too far away to …
There's such a big crowd that …
It's so hot that … / It's so wet that …

C
It's so cold that *the ice sculpture isn't melting.*
It's such a huge sculpture that *the artists need to use ladders.*
The sculpture is too big to *be made by a single person.*

D
The basket is too heavy to *be carried by one person.*
It's so warm that *no one is wearing a jacket / some people are holding umbrellas.*
It's such fresh fish that *everyone wants to buy some.*

UNIT 5 VOCABULARY, PAGE 34

5'

Student A

3 **Make nouns from the adjectives and verbs in the box. Then write a sentence with each word. You have five minutes!**

agree	careless	commit	disagree
eager	judge	lazy	manage
sick	unhappy		

Read your sentences aloud, but leave out the noun. Can Student B guess the noun?

Listen to Student B's sentences and guess the missing nouns from the box.

assessment	attachment	illness
involvement	kindness	movement
politeness	sadness	statement
willingness		

UNIT 6 VOCABULARY, PAGE 38

3 **Take turns to talk about the subjects. Use the adverb form of the adjectives in brackets. Try to talk for 30 seconds for each subject.**

- a food you could (happy) live on
- a food you've tried that was (absolute) disgusting
- how (easy) you think you could cut out sugar from your diet
- how (enthusiastic) you clear up after a meal
- how many fast-food restaurants you (typical) visit in a month
- how (confident) you can cook

EXTRA ACTIVITIES

UNIT 6 SPEAKING, PAGE 39

6 **The photos show people eating together in different situations. Follow the instructions.**

Student A: Compare the photos and say what the people are enjoying about eating together in each situation.
(*Try to speak for one minute*)
Student B: Which of these situations do you think would be more enjoyable? Why?
(*Try to speak for about 30 seconds*)

What are the people enjoying about eating together in each situation?

UNIT 7 VOCABULARY, PAGE 44

4 **Complete the sentences by adding a suitable preposition from the box and your own ideas. Then compare your sentences in pairs.**

about	at	by	for	of	to	with

1 I'm most motivated …
2 I used to be frightened …
3 I sometimes feel sorry …
4 I'm absolutely mad …
5 I think I'm quite good …
6 My interests are similar …
7 I get completely bored …

UNIT 8 VOCABULARY, PAGE 46

3 **Circle your score for each answer and work out your total.**

1a 3	2a 1	3a 3	4a 1	5a 2
1b 2	2b 3	3b 1	4b 2	5b 3
1c 1	2c 2	3c 2	4c 3	5c 1

Results

5–7 When you get away, you just want to relax. You don't want to do anything energetic, like sightseeing or water sports. For you, the best thing about a holiday is being able to do as little as possible!

8–12 You like a mixture of relaxation and being active while you're on holiday. You enjoy culture, learning and seeing new things, and you're a relatively adventurous holiday companion.

13–15 Life is for living. You can't sit still and you love a bit of danger in your life. You have to be sensible during term-time, so holidays are the perfect opportunity to go wild.

UNIT 8 VOCABULARY, PAGE 48

3 **Match the question halves.**

1 What's the difference between checking
2 Which three world cities would you most like to look
3 What's your favourite way of getting
4 Where would you go if you really wanted to get
5 If you had a visitor and you wanted to take them
6 How often do you stay
7 Who saw you
8 Have you ever stopped

a around? Who would be your perfect sightseeing partner?
b around your city, where would you go? Why?
c around when you're on holiday? Why?
d over at friends' houses? When was the last time?
e off the last time you travelled?
f over on the way to another destination?
g away from everything?
h in and checking out?

Ask and answer the questions.

UNIT 9 VOCABULARY, PAGE 56

4 **Complete the sentences with your own ideas.**

0 These days, where I live, there's a reduced number of … (*noun*)
These days, where I live, there's a reduced number of bus services.
1 Amongst my friends, there's a growing number of people who are/want/hate/love …
2 I have a limited number of … (*noun*)
3 I could spend an unlimited number of hours playing/doing/going …
4 I know a considerable number of places where you can / they sell / there are …

Compare your answers in pairs.

UNIT 10 VOCABULARY, PAGE 60

3 **Invent ten imaginary rules for your parents. Use *be allowed to*, *let* or *make*.**

Don't make us do our homework every day.
We're allowed to go out anywhere and at any time.

Compare your ideas in pairs.

EXTRA ACTIVITIES

UNIT 11 VOCABULARY, PAGE 66

4 **Complete the questions with an adjective from the word in brackets. Then ask and answer the questions.**

1 Do you think .... (interact) whiteboards help you to learn things? How?
2 Do you think any wireless technology might be .... (harm) to our health?
3 Which of your favourite possessions would be completely .... (use) without electricity?
4 Does technology like robots make you .... (nerve)?
5 Do you think it is .... (accept) to 3D print a copy of something you've seen in a shop?
6 Do you think playing computer games can be .... (education)?

UNIT 12 VOCABULARY, PAGE 68

1 **Read your answers for each question.**

1 a You're obviously quite a relaxed person, which is always a positive quality.
  b Are you always on time for everything? Perhaps your friend had a reason. Try to be a little calmer!
2 a Well done! You sound like you would make a good teacher one day.
  b You should probably avoid teaching as a future profession!
3 a That's very kind of you. Kindness is a great quality.
  b Do you really need the money? And do you really have time?
4 a It's good of you to think about your friend's needs.
  b Is that the kind of reaction that's going to make your friend feel better? Probably not!
5 a It's good to see the positive side of situations.
  b Are you really going to let a bit of rain stop you from having fun? Why?
6 a Good! Without you, the concert wouldn't be the same!
  b What would happen if everyone did this? Think of the hard work others have put in and how they are relying on you to be there too.

UNIT 12 VOCABULARY, PAGE 70

4 **Look at the adjectives in the box and answer the questions. Use the noun forms of the adjectives.**

confident	generous	intelligent	kind	organised
patient	polite	popular	sensitive	thoughtful

1 Which are your three best qualities?
2 Which quality would you like to improve in yourself?
3 What are the top three qualities you look for in a friend?

UNIT 12 SPEAKING, PAGE 71

7 **The photos show two different groups of friends.**

Student A: Compare the photos and say what you think the people are enjoying about being with their friends.
Student B: Do you spend more time with a best friend or a wide group of friends?

What are the people enjoying about being with their friends?

UNIT 13 VOCABULARY, PAGE 78

4 **Working on your own, write as many sentences as you can for each sentence beginning. You have a time limit of five minutes!**

1 I've never/always argued that …
I've always argued that doing exercise reduces your lifespan.
2 Once I admitted that …
3 I'd never beg anyone to …
4 I've never/always claimed that I …
5 I'd never reveal that …
6 Why would anyone declare that they …?
7 I wouldn't emphasise the fact that …
8 Has anyone ever encouraged you to …?
9 I'd like to propose that …
10 I'd never admit that …

Compare your sentences in pairs.

UNIT 14 VOCABULARY, PAGE 80

3 **Accidents in the home**

1 Over 50% of accidents at home involve falls, most often as a result of (b) tripping over something or slipping on a wet floor. Next is (c) bumping into something, such as furniture. Swallowing something poisonous (a) is less frequent than most other accidents, but can result in the most serious harm.
2 The most likely age group to have an accident at home is (a) 0–4-year-olds. The next most likely is (b) 5–15-year-olds and then (c) people aged over 75.
3 Boys are twice as likely as girls to have an accident at home.
4 The most common place to have an accident is in the living room, followed by the kitchen.

UNIT 14 VOCABULARY, PAGE 82

5 **Ask and answer questions using the table.**

When was the last time you	had made gave	an attempt at not using your phone for a few days? anyone a hug? a promise that you didn't keep? a talk to more than 50 people? a quarrel with your best friend? your parents a hand with the cooking?

UNIT 15 VOCABULARY, PAGE 88

3 **Read the questions. Add two more questions using *yourself*. Then ask and answer.**

Have you ever cut your hair yourself?

Yes, I did. I cut my hair myself when I was about ten. It was a disaster!

Have you ever …
1 cut your hair yourself?
2 fixed a flat tyre on a bike yourself?
3 painted your room yourself?
4 repaired something yourself?

UNIT 16 VOCABULARY, PAGE 92

3 **Read the questions and complete the sentences for you. Then ask and answer the questions.**

1 What would you buy or do, assuming you had unlimited cash?
Provided that I had enough money, I'd …
I wouldn't … even if I was/were a millionaire.
2 If you were able to do anything for a week, what would you do?
Assuming I didn't have to go to school, I'd love to spend my time …
I'd definitely … provided that my family wasn't/weren't there.
3 What would you refuse to do, even if someone offered you £10,000?
I'd never … even if you paid me £10,000!
I might … assuming it didn't seem too dangerous.
4 What would be your dream car?
Assuming I could drive any car, I'd choose …
Even if I could drive, I'd rather …
5 Is there anything you're not allowed to do that you'd really like to do?
As long as no one could see me, I'd …
I might … assuming I'd never get caught!

UNIT 17 VOCABULARY, PAGE 100

3 **Discuss the questions.**

1 What things are prohibited in your school?
2 How much time is devoted to art in your school?
3 When was your school established?
4 Who do you think you are influenced by?
5 Who is regarded as a great singer in your country?
6 What's your favourite song, and who is it sung by?
7 What's your favourite book, and who was it written by?
8 What's your favourite film, and who stars in it? Where is it set? Who was it directed by?

EXTRA ACTIVITIES

UNIT 18 VOCABULARY, PAGE 104

4 **Discuss the questions.**

1 What homework are you waiting to get back from your teachers? Do you think you'll get a good mark for it?
2 Have you ever got away with something? What did you do?
3 What should you get round to doing soon? Why?
4 What chores do you try to get out of doing at home?
5 Are you hoping to get into college or university one day?
6 What are the most difficult exams you've ever had to get through?

UNIT 19 GRAMMAR, PAGE 110

5 The police knew the fireman was the murderer because he was the only man. The builder, the lorry driver and the mechanic were all women.

UNIT 19 VOCABULARY, PAGE 110

3 **Add a suitable prefix to the adjectives. Then discuss the questions.**

1 Which areas of your town do you think are ____safe at night?
2 Do you think it is ____appropriate for children to watch crime films?
3 Is it ____honest to keep something you find in a public place?
4 What things are legal that you personally think should be ____legal?
5 Is it always ____moral to tell a lie?
6 Can you think of any ____solved crimes?

UNIT 20 VOCABULARY, PAGE 114

3 **Discuss the meaning of the compound adjectives in bold.**

0 Spain is an **olive-producing** country.
somewhere that produces olives
1 Getting a new passport can be very **time-consuming**.
2 California isn't a **coffee-growing** region.
3 Toni's shed has a **water-heating** system.
4 My room is small, but it has some cool **space-saving** features, like a fold-down desk.
5 That's a **self-driving** car. It even has **rear-facing** seats.

4 **Write as many sentences as you can in four minutes! Use the compound adjectives above or the ones in the box. Some of them have obvious meanings and some are idiomatic.**

award-winning	breathtaking	eye-catching
heartwarming	life-threatening	outstanding
record-breaking	time-consuming	

UNIT 4 VOCABULARY, PAGE 26

3 Student B

1 Look at photos A and B and listen to Student A's suggestions. Then share the possible answers.
2 Look at photos C and D and complete the sentences. Student A will suggest some possible answers.

A
There are too many people to *fit on the train*.
There are so many people that *it must be very crowded and uncomfortable on the train.*
It's such a busy train that *no one can move*.

C
It's so cold that …
It's such a huge sculpture that …
The sculpture is too big to …

B
The stage is too far away to *see anything*.
There's such a big crowd that *the stage looks tiny*.
It's so hot that *people are using umbrellas as sunshades.*

D
The basket is too heavy to …
It's so warm that …
It's such fresh fish that …

UNIT 5 VOCABULARY, PAGE 34

5'

Student B

3 **Make nouns from the adjectives and verbs in the box. Then write a sentence with each word. You have five minutes!**

assess	attach	ill	involve	kind
move	polite	sad	state	willing

Listen to Student A's sentences and guess the missing nouns from the box.

agreement carelessness commitment
disagreement eagerness judgment
laziness management sickness
unhappiness

Read your sentences from above, but leave out the noun. Can Student A guess the nouns?

EP VOCABULARY LIST

adj = adjective *adv* = adverb *conj* = conjunction
n = noun *v* = verb *pv* = phrasal verb
prep = preposition *phr* = phrase

UNIT 1

EDUCATION: PHRASAL VERBS

break up /breɪk 'ʌp/ *pv* When schools or colleges break up, the classes end and the holidays begin.

figure (sth) out /fɪgə 'aʊt/ *pv* to find the answer to something by thinking about it

get in /get 'ɪn/ *pv* to succeed in being chosen or elected

get on /get 'ɒn/ *pv* to manage or deal with a situation, especially successfully

give (sth) out /gɪv 'aʊt/ *pv* to give something to each of a number of people

go for (sth) /'gəʊ fɔː/ *pv* to try to get or achieve something

hand (sth) in /hænd 'ɪn/ *pv* to give a piece of written work or a document to someone to read, judge or deal with

join in (sth) /dʒɔɪn 'ɪn/ *pv* to become involved in an activity with other people

note (sth) down /nəʊt 'daʊn/ *pv* to write something so that you do not forget it

put (sth) off /pʊt 'ɒf/ *pv* to decide or arrange to delay an event or activity until a later time or date

read (sth) out /riːd 'aʊt/ *pv* to read something and say the words aloud so that other people can hear

stay behind /steɪ bɪ'haɪnd/ *pv* to not leave a place when other people leave it

try (sth) out /traɪ 'aʊt/ *pv* to use or do something to discover if it works or if you like it

EDUCATION: *-ION* NOUNS

action /'ækʃən/ *n* something that you do

concentration /ˌkɒnsən'treɪʃən/ *n* the ability to think carefully about something you are doing and nothing else

connection /kə'nekʃən/ *n* something that joins things together

decision /dɪ'sɪʒən/ *n* a choice that you make about something after thinking about several possibilities

definition /ˌdefɪ'nɪʃən/ *n* the meaning of a word or phrase

discussion /dɪ'skʌʃən/ *n* when people talk about something and tell each other their ideas or opinions

education /edʒʊ'keɪʃən/ *n* the process of teaching or learning in a school or college, or the knowledge that you get from this

explanation /ˌeksplə'neɪʃən/ *n* the details or reasons that someone gives to make something clear or easy to understand

expression /ɪk'spreʃən/ *n* a word or group of words having a particular meaning

introduction /ˌɪntrə'dʌkʃən/ *n* the first part of a book or speech

invention /ɪn'venʃən/ *n* something which has been designed or created for the first time

motivation /ˌməʊtɪ'veɪʃən/ *n* enthusiasm for doing something

permission /pə'mɪʃən/ *n* when you allow someone to do something

preparation /prepə'reɪʃən/ *n* the things that you do or the time that you spend preparing for something

recommendation /ˌrekəmen'deɪʃən/ *n* a piece of advice about what to do in a particular situation

registration /redʒɪ'streɪʃən/ *n* when a name or information is recorded on an official list

selection /sɪ'lekʃən/ *n* a group of people or things that has been chosen

UNIT 2

MUSIC PHRASES

background music /'bækgraʊnd ˌmjuːzɪk/ *n* music that you can hear in films and TV programmes that are not the main sounds that you are listening to

the charts /ðə 'tʃɑːts/ *n* the lists produced each week of the songs and albums with the highest sales and streams

concert venue /'kɒnsət ˌvenjuː/ *n* the place where a concert happens

debut album /'deɪbjuː ˌælbəm/ *n* the first album that an artist releases

devoted fans /dɪˌvəʊtɪd 'fænz/ *n* extremely loving or loyal admirers of a person, sport, team, etc.

give a performance /gɪv ə pə'fɔːməns/ *phr* to act, dance, sing or play music to entertain people

go solo /gəʊ 'səʊləʊ/ *phr* to leave a band to follow a music career by yourself

lead singer /ˌliːd 'sɪŋə/ *n* the main singer in a band or musical group

massive hit /ˌmæsɪv 'hɪt/ *n* a song, film, TV programme, etc. that is extremely popular or successful

musical talent /ˌmjuːzɪkəl 'tælənt/ *n* a natural ability to play an instrument, sing or write music

release a track /rɪˌliːs ə 'træk/ *phr* to make a song available to buy or stream

tour the world /tʊə ðə 'wɜːld/ *phr* to visit several different places around the world to give concerts

VERBS + INFINITIVE/*-ING* WITH A CHANGE IN MEANING

forget /fə'get/ *v* [+ infinitive] to not remember to do something

forget /fə'get/ *v* [+ *-ing*] to not remember something that happened

remember /rɪ'membə/ *v* [+ infinitive] to not forget to do something

remember /rɪ'membə/ *v* [+ *-ing*] to not forget something that happened

stop /stɒp/ *v* [+ infinitive] to interrupt an activity for a short time in order to do something else

stop /stɒp/ *v* [+ *-ing*] to finish doing something

try /traɪ/ *v* [+ infinitive] to attempt to do something

try /traɪ/ *v* [+ *-ing*] to do, test, taste, etc. something to discover if it works or if you like it

UNIT 3

VERBS OF COMMUNICATION

accuse /ə'kjuːz/ *v* to say that someone has done something bad
claim /kleɪm/ *v* to say that something is true or is a fact, although you cannot prove it and other people might not believe it
confess /kən'fes/ *v* to admit that you have done something wrong or something that you feel guilty or bad about
deny /dɪ'naɪ/ *v* to say that something is not true
order /'ɔːdə/ *v* to give someone an instruction that they must obey
suggest /sə'dʒest/ *v* to express an idea or plan for someone to consider
threaten /'θretən/ *v* to tell someone that you will cause problems for them if they do not do what you want
warn /wɔːn/ *v* to make someone realise a possible danger or problem, especially one in the future

PHRASAL VERBS: RELATIONSHIPS

depend on (sb) /dɪ'pend ɒn/ *pv* to be able to trust someone or something to help, or to do what you expect
fall out with (sb) /fɔːl 'aʊt wɪð/ *pv* to argue with someone and stop being friendly with them
identify with (sb) /aɪ'dentɪfaɪ wɪð/ *pv* to feel that you are similar to someone in some way and that you can understand that person or their situation because of this
pick on (sb) /'pɪk ɒn/ *pv* to criticise, punish or be unkind to the same person often and unfairly
take after (sb) /teɪk 'ɑːftə/ *pv* to be similar to an older member of your family
talk (sb) into /tɔːk 'ɪntu/ *pv* to persuade someone to do something

UNIT 4

NATURAL DISASTERS: VERBS

collapse /kə'læps/ *v* to fall down suddenly because of pressure or having no strength or support
crack /kræk/ *v* to break in a way that very thin lines appear on its surface but it does not separate
drag /dræg/ *v* to pull someone or something along the ground, usually with difficulty
erupt /ɪ'rʌpt/ *v* If a volcano erupts, it suddenly throws out smoke, fire and melted rocks.
float /fləʊt/ *v* to stay in the air or water, or move gently through the air or water
knock over /nɒk 'əʊvə/ *pv* to hit something or someone so that they fall down
run /rʌn/ *v* If liquid runs somewhere, it flows.
shake /ʃeɪk/ *v* to move backwards and forwards or up and down in quick, short movements
smash /smæʃ/ *v* to break into a lot of pieces with a loud noise, or to make something break into a lot of pieces with a loud noise

TOO ... TO, SO ... THAT, SUCH ... THAT

far too ... to /fɑː tuː ... tə/ *adv It's far too hot to go running today.*
so ... that /səʊ ... ðæt/ *adv The concert tickets were so expensive that few fans could afford them.*
such ... that /sʌtʃ ... ðæt/ *adv It was such a good film that we watched it three times.*

UNIT 5

VIDEO GAMING: VERBS

balance /'bæləns/ *v* to be or put yourself in a position where you will not fall to either side
brake /breɪk/ *v* to make a vehicle stop or move more slowly
chase /tʃeɪs/ *v* to run after someone or something in order to catch them
construct /kən'strʌkt/ *v* to build something from several parts
dive /daɪv/ *v* to move somewhere quickly often downwards or into or behind something
exchange /ɪks'tʃeɪndʒ/ *v* to give something to someone and receive something similar from them
gather /'gæðə/ *v* to collect several things, often from different places or people
interact /ˌɪntə'rækt/ *v* to talk and do things with other people
overtake /əʊvə'teɪk/ *v* to go past a vehicle or person that is going in the same direction
reverse /rɪ'vɜːs/ *v* to drive a vehicle backwards
roll /rəʊl/ *v* to move somewhere by turning in a circular direction
slide /slaɪd/ *v* to move smoothly over a surface, or to make something move smoothly over a surface
steer /stɪə/ *v* to control the direction of a vehicle

NOUNS: *-NESS* AND *-MENT*

argument /'ɑːgjʊmənt/ *n* an angry discussion with someone in which you both disagree
arrangement /ə'reɪndʒmənt/ *n* plans for how something will happen
darkness /'dɑːknəs/ *n* when there is little or no light
embarrassment /ɪm'bærəsmənt/ *n* when you feel embarrassed
encouragement /ɪn'kʌrɪdʒmənt/ *n* when someone talks or behaves in a way that gives you confidence to do something
fitness /'fɪtnəs/ *n* the condition of being physically strong and healthy
friendliness /'frendlinəs/ *n* the quality of being friendly
tiredness /'taɪədnəs/ *n* the feeling that you want to rest or sleep
treatment /'triːtmənt/ *n* medical care
weakness /'wiːknəs/ *n* when someone or something is not strong or powerful

VOCABULARY LIST

UNIT 6

FOOD AND DRINK: PHRASAL VERBS

cool down /kuːl 'daʊn/ *pv* to become less hot, or to make someone or something become less hot

cut (sth) out /kʌt 'aʊt/ *pv* to stop eating or drinking something, usually to improve your health

eat out /iːt 'aʊt/ *pv* to eat in a restaurant

eat (sth) up /iːt 'ʌp/ *pv* to eat all the food that you have been given

fill up on (sth) /fɪl 'ʌp ɒn/ *pv* to eat something to make yourself feel full

go off /gəʊ 'ɒf/ *pv* If food goes off, it stops being good to eat because it is too old.

heat (sth) up /hiːt 'ʌp/ *pv* to make food hot so that it can be eaten

live on (sth) /'lɪv ɒn/ *pv* to only eat a particular type of food

FORMING ADVERBS WITH *-LY*

accidentally /æksɪ'dentəli/ *adv* by chance or by mistake

basically /'beɪsɪkli/ *adv* used to introduce a short explanation about something

completely /kəm'pliːtli/ *adv* in every way or as much as possible

deeply /'diːpli/ *adv* very much

dramatically /drə'mætɪkli/ *adv* very sudden or noticeable

extremely /ɪk'striːmli/ *adv* very, or much more than usual

happily /'hæpəli/ *adv* in a way that is very willing

incredibly /ɪn'kredəbli/ *adv* very, or much more than usual

merely /'mɪəli/ *adv* used to emphasise that you mean exactly what you are saying and nothing more

necessarily /nesə'serɪli/ *adv* used in negatives to mean 'in every case' or 'therefore'

physically /'fɪzɪkli/ *adv* in a way that relates to the body

sensibly /'sensɪbli/ *adv* showing good judgment

terribly /'terəbli/ *adv* very, or much more than usual

typically /'tɪpɪkli/ *adv* used for saying what usually happens

UNIT 7

FICTION: ADJECTIVES AND NOUNS

complex issue /ˌkɒmpleks 'ɪʃuː/ *n* a subject or problem which people are thinking and talking about that is difficult to solve or understand

major role /ˌmeɪdʒə 'rəʊl/ *n* If a character has a major role in a book, film, etc. they have an important purpose in its story.

minor character /ˌmaɪnə 'kærɪktə/ *n* a person in a book, film, etc. that is not one of the main people in the story

moving novel /ˌmuːvɪŋ 'nɒvəl/ *n* a sad story about imaginary characters and events

opening chapter /ˌəʊpənɪŋ 'tʃæptə/ *n* the first part of a book

predictable plot /prɪˌdɪktəbl 'plɒt/ *n* If a book, play or film has a predictable plot, its story happens in a way that you expect and that isn't unusual or interesting.

stunning illustration /ˌstʌnɪŋ ɪlə'streɪʃən/ *n* a very beautiful drawing in a book, magazine, etc.

ADJECTIVE + PREPOSITION

addicted (to) /ə'dɪktɪd (tə)/ *adj* liking something very much and doing or having it too often

annoyed (by) /ə'nɔɪd (baɪ)/ *adj* slightly angry (with sth)

disappointed (with) /dɪsə'pɔɪntɪd (wɪð)/ *adj* unhappy because something was not as good as you hoped or expected

furious (with) /'fjʊəriəs (wɪð)/ *adj* extremely angry (with sb)

keen (on) /kiːn (ɒn)/ *adj* very interested in or enthusiastic about

nervous (about) /'nɜːvəs (əˌbaʊt)/ *adj* worried or anxious

suitable (for) /'suːtəbl (fə)/ *adj* acceptable or right for someone or something

surprised (at) /sə'praɪzd (ət)/ *adj* feeling surprise because something has happened that you did not expect

UNIT 8

HOLIDAY ACTIVITIES

chill out /tʃɪl 'aʊt/ *pv* to relax completely, or not allow things to upset you

cool down /kuːl 'daʊn/ *pv* to become less hot

cruise /kruːz/ *v* to go on a cruise or boat trip

get a tan /get ə 'tæn/ *phr* when your skin is brown from being in the sun

go trekking /gəʊ 'trekɪŋ/ *phr* to go on a long, difficult journey on foot

hire /haɪə/ *v* to pay to use something for a short time

photograph /'fəʊtəgrɑːf/ *v* to take a picture or pictures using a camera

sign up (for sth) /saɪn 'ʌp/ *pv* to arrange to do an organised activity

socialise /'səʊʃəlaɪz/ *v* to spend time enjoying yourself with other people

stay up /steɪ 'ʌp/ *pv* to go to bed later than usual

take a selfie /teɪk ə 'selfi/ *phr* to take a photograph of yourself, usually with a mobile phone

wander around /ˌwɒndər ə'raʊnd/ *pv* to walk slowly in a relaxed way or without any clear purpose or direction

PHRASAL VERBS: TRAVEL

check in /tʃek 'ɪn/ *pv* to say who you are when you arrive at a hotel so that you can be given a key for your room
check out /tʃek 'aʊt/ *pv* to leave a hotel after paying and returning your room key
get around /get ə'raʊnd/ *pv* to travel or move from place to place
get away /get ə'weɪ/ *pv* to go somewhere to have a holiday, often because you need to rest
look around /lʊk ə'raʊnd/ *pv* to visit a place and look at the things in it
see (sb) off /siː 'ɒf/ *pv* to go to the place that someone is leaving from in order to say goodbye to them
stay over /steɪ 'əʊvə/ *pv* to spend the night somewhere instead of returning to your home or continuing your journey
stop over /stɒp 'əʊvə/ *pv* to stop somewhere for a short period of time when you are on a long journey
take (sb) around /teɪk ə'raʊnd/ *pv* to visit a place with someone, showing them the most interesting or important parts

UNIT 9

MONEY

allowance /ə'laʊəns/ *n* money that you are given regularly, especially to pay for a particular thing
balance /'bæləns/ *n* the amount of money that you still have to pay, or that you have left to use
bargain /'bɑːgɪn/ *n* something that is on sale for less than its usual price or its real value
budget /'bʌdʒɪt/ *n* the amount of money a person or organisation has available to spend
cashpoint /'kæʃpɔɪnt/ *n* a machine, usually in a wall outside a bank, that you can get money from using a plastic card
debit card /'debɪt kɑːd/ *n* a plastic card used to pay for things directly from your bank account
financially independent /faɪˌnænʃəli ɪndɪ'pendənt/ *adj* not needing money from other people
live on /'lɪv ɒn/ *pv* If you live on an amount of money, that is the money that you use to buy all the things that you need.
pay off /peɪ 'ɒf/ *pv* to finish paying back money that you owe
PIN /pɪn/ *n* personal identification number: a short series of letters or numbers that allows you to use a bank card
savings /'seɪvɪŋz/ *n* money that you have saved, usually in a bank
short of cash /ʃɔːt əv 'kæʃ/ *adj* not having enough money
take out /teɪk 'aʊt/ *pv* to get money from a bank
wealthy /'welθi/ *adj* rich

A/THE NUMBER OF

a number of /ə 'nʌmbər əv/ *phr* several
the number of /ðə 'nʌmbər əv/ *phr* the quantity of
a/the considerable number of /ə/ðə kənˌsɪdərəbl 'nʌmbər əv/ *phr* a/the large quantity of
a/the growing number of /ə/ðə ˌgrəʊɪŋ 'nʌmbər əv/ *phr* a/the quantity that is getting bigger
a/the increasing number of /ə/ði ɪnˌkriːsɪŋ 'nʌmbər əv/ *phr* a/the quantity that is getting bigger
a/the limited number of /ə/ðə ˌlɪmɪtɪd 'nʌmbər əv/ *phr* a/the small quantity of
a/the maximum number of /ə/ðə ˌmæksɪməm 'nʌmbər əv/ *phr* a/the largest quantity of
a/the minimum number of /ə/ðə ˌmɪnɪməm 'nʌmbər əv/ *phr* a/the smallest quantity of
a/the record number of /ə/ðə ˌrekɔːd 'nʌmbər əv/ *phr* a/the largest quantity there has ever been
a/the reduced number of /ə/ðə ˌrɪ'djuːst 'nʌmbər əv/ *phr* a/the quantity that is smaller than it was before
a/the unlimited number of /ə/ði ʌnˌlɪmɪtɪd 'nʌmbər əv/ *phr* a/the quantity that has no limit

UNIT 10

HOUSEHOLD TASKS

clear up /klɪər 'ʌp/ *pv* to make a place tidy by removing things from it or putting them where they should be
fix /fɪks/ *v* to repair something
fold /fəʊld/ *v* If you fold paper, cloth, etc., you bend it so that one part of it lies flat on top of another part.
load /ləʊd/ *v* to put a lot of things into a vehicle or machine
put (sth) away /pʊt ə'weɪ/ *pv* to put something in the place or container where it is usually kept
sort /sɔːt/ *v* to arrange things into different groups or types or into an order
sweep /swiːp/ *v* to clean the floor using a brush
wash (sth) up /wɒʃ 'ʌp/ *pv* to wash plates, bowls, knives, etc. after a meal
water /'wɔːtə/ *v* to pour water on to plants or the soil that they are growing in
wipe /waɪp/ *v* to clean or dry something by moving a cloth across it

BE ALLOWED TO, LET AND *MAKE*

be allowed to /biː ə'laʊd tə/ *phr* to have permission to do something
let (sb do sth) /let/ *v* to allow someone to do something, or to allow something to happen
make (sb do sth) /meɪk/ *v* to force someone to do something

VOCABULARY LIST

UNIT 11

TECHNOLOGICAL ADVANCES

driverless car /ˌdraɪvələs ˈkɑː/ *n* a car that does not have a person as a driver

drone /drəʊn/ *n* a small aircraft without a pilot that is controlled by someone on the ground

fitness tracker /ˈfɪtnəs ˌtrækə/ *n* an electronic device, usually worn on the wrist, that is designed to record information about your physical fitness and activity, for example your heart rate and how many steps you have walked

interactive whiteboard /ɪntəˌræktɪv ˈwaɪtbɔːd/ *n* a white surface that can be written on in class and which can display the contents of a computer screen

portable charger /ˌpɔːtəbl ˈtʃɑːdʒə/ *n* a device that can charge the battery of a mobile phone or tablet computer without using the main power supply of a building

smart speaker /ˈsmɑːt ˌspiːkə/ *n* a voice-controlled speaker that is connected to the internet and can answer simple questions and control other devices

smartwatch /ˈsmɑːt wɒtʃ/ *n* a watch that has many of the features of a smartphone or a computer

video game console /ˈvɪdiəʊ geɪm ˌkɒnsəʊl/ *n* a piece of electronic equipment for playing games on

virtual-reality headset /ˌvɜːtʃuəl riˈæləti ˌhedset/ *n* a piece of equipment that you wear over your eyes and ears so that you can see and hear computer images and sounds that make you feel an imagined situation is real

wireless headphones /ˌwaɪələs ˈhedfəʊnz/ *n* a piece of equipment used to listen to music that connects to your mobile phone, tablet or computer using radio signals rather than wires

ADJECTIVE SUFFIXES

affordable /əˈfɔːdəbl/ *adj* cheap enough for most people

careful /ˈkeəfəl/ *adj* giving a lot of attention to what you are doing so that you do not have an accident, make a mistake or damage something

careless /ˈkeələs/ *adj* not giving enough attention to what you are doing

creative /kriːˈeɪtɪv/ *adj* producing or using original and unusual ideas

dangerous /ˈdeɪndʒərəs/ *adj* If someone or something is dangerous, they could harm you.

endless /ˈendləs/ *adj* continuing for a long time and never finishing, or never seeming to finish

enjoyable /ɪnˈdʒɔɪəbl/ *adj* An enjoyable event or experience gives you pleasure.

environmental /ɪnvaɪərənˈmentəl/ *adj* relating to the environment

famous /ˈfeɪməs/ *adj* known or recognised by many people

faulty /ˈfɔːlti/ *adj* not working correctly

impressive /ɪmˈpresɪv/ *adj* Someone or something that is impressive makes you admire and respect them.

innovative /ˈɪnəvətɪv/ *adj* using new methods or ideas

interactive /ˌɪntərˈæktɪv/ *adj* Interactive computer programs, games, etc. involve the person using them by reacting to the way they use them.

mysterious /mɪsˈtɪəriəs/ *adj* strange or unknown, and not explained or understood

original /əˈrɪdʒənəl/ *adj* describes a piece of work produced by an artist or writer and not a copy

profitable /ˈprɒfɪtəbl/ *adj* making or likely to make a profit

reliable /rɪˈlaɪəbl/ *adj* able to be trusted or believed

seasonal /ˈsiːzənəl/ *adj* happening or existing only at a particular time of the year

spicy /ˈspaɪsi/ *adj* containing strong flavours from spices

thoughtful /ˈθɔːtfəl/ *adj* kind and always thinking about how you can help other people

thoughtless /ˈθɔːtləs/ *adj* not considering how your actions and words might upset someone else

traditional /trəˈdɪʃənəl/ *adj* following the customs or ways of behaving that have continued in a group of people or society for a long time

useful /ˈjuːsfəl/ *adj* helping you to do or achieve something

useless /ˈjuːsləs/ *adj* If something is useless, it does not work well or it has no effect.

UNIT 12

PERSONALITY ADJECTIVES

bad-tempered /bædˈtempəd/ *adj* describes a person who becomes angry and annoyed easily

easy-going /iːziˈgəʊɪŋ/ *adj* usually relaxed and calm, not worried or upset

generous /ˈdʒenərəs/ *adj* willing to give other people money, help, kindness, etc.

impatient /ɪmˈpeɪʃənt/ *adj* easily annoyed by someone's mistakes or because you have to wait

insensitive /ɪnˈsensɪtɪv/ *adj* not noticing or not caring about other people's feelings

mean /miːn/ *adj* A mean person does not like spending money, especially on other people.

optimistic /ɒptɪˈmɪstɪk/ *adj* always believing that good things will happen

patient /ˈpeɪʃənt/ *adj* having patience

pessimistic /pesɪˈmɪstɪk/ *adj* always believing that bad things are likely to happen

reliable /rɪˈlaɪəbl/ *adj* able to be trusted or believed

thoughtful /ˈθɔːtfəl/ *adj* kind and always thinking about how you can help other people

thoughtless /ˈθɔːtləs/ *adj* not considering how your actions and words might upset someone else

unreliable /ʌnrɪˈlaɪəbl/ *adj* not able to be trusted or depended on

ADJECTIVE AND NOUN SUFFIXES

difference /ˈdɪfərəns/ *n* the way in which two people or things are not the same
different /ˈdɪfərənt/ *adj* not the same as someone or something
fit /fɪt/ *adj* healthy and strong, especially as the result of exercise
fitness /ˈfɪtnəs/ *n* the condition of being physically strong and healthy
generosity /dʒenəˈrɒsəti/ *n* the quality of being generous
happiness /ˈhæpɪnəs/ *n* the feeling of being happy
happy /ˈhæpi/ *adj* pleased and in a good mood, especially because something good has happened
importance /ɪmˈpɔːtəns/ *n* how important someone or something is
important /ɪmˈpɔːtənt/ *adj* valuable, useful or necessary
intelligence /ɪnˈtelɪdʒəns/ *n* the ability to learn, understand and think about things
intelligent /ɪnˈtelɪdʒənt/ *adj* showing intelligence, or able to learn and understand things easily
organisation /ɔːgənaɪˈzeɪʃən/ *n* the planning of an activity or event
organised /ˈɔːgənaɪzd/ *adj* planned or arranged
patience /ˈpeɪʃəns/ *n* the quality of being able to stay calm and not get angry, especially when something takes a long time
patient /ˈpeɪʃənt/ *adj* able to stay calm and not get annoyed when something is difficult or takes a long time
qualification /kwɒlɪfɪˈkeɪʃən/ *n* something that you get when you are successful in an exam or course of study
qualified /ˈkwɒlɪfaɪd/ *adj* having passed the exams needed for a particular job
strength /streŋθ/ *n* the ability to do things that need a lot of physical effort or power
strong /strɒŋ/ *adj* A strong person or animal is physically powerful.

UNIT 13

REPORTING NOUNS

confession /kənˈfeʃən/ *n* when you admit that you have done something wrong or illegal
confirmation /kɒnfəˈmeɪʃən/ *n* a statement or proof that something is true
criticism /ˈkrɪtɪsɪzəm/ *n* when you say that something or someone is bad
hint /hɪnt/ *n* when you say something that suggests what you think or want, but not in a direct way
mention /ˈmenʃən/ *n* a brief remark
prediction /prɪˈdɪkʃən/ *n* when you say what will happen in the future
proposal /prəˈpəʊzəl/ *n* a suggestion for a plan
response /rɪˈspɒns/ *n* an answer or reaction to something that has been said or done
rumour /ˈruːmə/ *n* a fact that a lot of people are talking about although they do not know if it is true
statement /ˈsteɪtmənt/ *n* something that someone says or writes officially
threat /θret/ *n* the possibility that something bad will happen
update /ˈʌpdeɪt/ *n* new information

REPORTING VERBS

admit /ədˈmɪt/ *v* to agree that something is true, especially unwillingly
argue /ˈɑːgjuː/ *v* to give reasons to support or oppose an idea, action, etc.
beg /beg/ *v* to make a very strong and urgent request
claim /kleɪm/ *v* to say that something is true or is a fact, although you cannot prove it and other people might not believe it
confirm /kənˈfɜːm/ *v* to say or show that something is true
declare /dɪˈkleə/ *v* to announce something publicly or officially
emphasise /ˈemfəsaɪz/ *v* to show that something is especially important or needs special attention
encourage /ɪnˈkʌrɪdʒ/ *v* to make someone more likely to do something by giving them confidence
propose /prəˈpəʊz/ *v* to suggest a plan or action
remind /rɪˈmaɪnd/ *v* to make someone remember something, or remember to do something
reveal /rɪˈviːl/ *v* to give someone a piece of information that is surprising or that was previously secret
tell /tel/ *v* to say something to someone, usually giving them information

UNIT 14

ACCIDENTS AND EMERGENCIES

be bitten /bi ˈbɪtən/ *v* If you are bitten, an animal uses its teeth to cut into your skin.
bump /bʌmp/ *v* to hurt part of your body by hitting it against something hard
cut yourself /ˈkʌt jəˌself/ *v* to injure yourself with a sharp object which makes you bleed
have an allergic reaction /hæv ən əˌlɜːdʒɪk riˈækʃən/ *phr* If you have an allergic reaction to something, you become sick or develop skin or breathing problems because you have eaten certain foods or been near certain substances.
pass out /pɑːs ˈaʊt/ *pv* to suddenly become unconscious
slip /slɪp/ *v* to slide by accident and fall or almost fall
swallow /ˈswɒləʊ/ *v* to move your throat in order to make food, drink, etc. go down to your stomach
trip over /trɪp ˈəʊvə/ *pv* to fall because you hit your foot on something when you are walking or running
twist /twɪst/ *v* If you twist a part of your body, such as your ankle, you injure it by turning it suddenly.

VOCABULARY LIST

HAVE, MAKE AND *GIVE* + NOUN

have a quarrel /hæv ə ˈkwɒrəl/ *phr* to argue
have the strength /hæv ðə ˈstreŋθ/ *phr* to be strong enough
have a word /hæv ə ˈwɜːd/ *phr* to talk to someone for a short time
make an attempt /meɪk ən əˈtempt/ *phr* If you make an attempt to do something, you try to do it.
make fun of someone/sth /meɪk ˈfʌn əv ˈsʌmʌn/ *phr* to make a joke about someone or something in an unkind way
make a promise /meɪk ə ˈprɒmɪs/ *phr* to say that you will certainly do something
give someone a hand /gɪv ˌsʌmwʌn ə ˈhænd/ *phr* to help someone
give someone a hug /gɪv ˌsʌmwʌn ə ˈhʌg/ *phr* to put your arms round someone and hold them tightly
give a talk /gɪv ə ˈtɔːk/ *phr* to speak to a group of people about a particular subject

UNIT 15

FACIAL EXPRESSIONS

avoid eye contact /əˌvɔɪd ˈaɪ ˌkɒntækt/ *phr* to try not to look at someone's eyes, especially when you're talking to them
bite your lip /baɪt jə ˈlɪp/ *phr* to hold your lower lip under your upper teeth
blink /blɪŋk/ *v* to open and close both of your eyes quickly
blush /blʌʃ/ *v* to become pink in the face, usually from embarrassment
lick your lips /lɪk jə ˈlɪps/ *phr* to move your tongue across the surface of your lips
nod your head /nɒd jə ˈhed/ *phr* to move your head up and down as a way of agreeing, to give someone a sign or to point to something
rub your eyes /rʌb jər ˈaɪz/ *phr* to press your hands or fingers over your eyes and move them backwards and forwards
shake your head /ʃeɪk jə ˈhed/ *phr* to move your head from side to side to mean 'no'
stare /steə/ *v* to look at someone or something for a long time and not move your eyes
yawn /jɔːn/ *v* to take a deep breath with your mouth wide open, because you are tired or bored

-SELF, -SELVES FOR EMPHASIS

We can use *-self* and *-selves* to emphasise the subject or object because we want to draw attention to that person or thing.

We didn't call a plumber – we fixed the leak ourselves.

She didn't want to speak to the shop assistant – she demanded to speak to the manager himself.

UNIT 16

CLIMATE CHANGE

carbon dioxide emissions /kɑːbən daɪˌɒksaɪd iˈmɪʃənz/ *n* the gas formed and released when carbon is burned, or when people or animals breathe out
carbon footprint /ˌkɑːbən ˈfʊtprɪnt/ *n* a measurement of the amount of carbon dioxide produced by the activities of a person, company, organisation, etc.
energy efficient /ˌenədʒi ɪˈfɪʃənt/ *adj* used to describe things that use only as much energy as is needed without wasting any
environmentally friendly /ɪnvaɪərənˌmentəli ˈfrendli/ *adj* not harmful to the environment
exhaust fumes /ɪgˈzɔːst fjuːmz/ *n* the waste gases from a vehicle's engine
fossil fuel /ˈfɒsəl ˌfjuːəl/ *n* a fuel such as coal or oil that is obtained from under the ground
global warming /ˌgləʊbəl ˈwɔːmɪŋ/ *n* an increase in the temperature of the air around the world because of pollution
greenhouse gas /ˈgriːnhaʊs gæs/ *n* a gas that causes the greenhouse effect, especially carbon dioxide (= a gas produced when carbon is burned)
renewable /rɪˈnjuːəbl/ *adj* A renewable form of energy can be produced as quickly as it is used.
solar power /ˌsəʊlə ˈpaʊə/ *n* electricity produced by using the energy from the sun
wind power /ˈwɪnd ˌpaʊə/ *n* electricity produced using wind turbines (= machines with long parts at the top that are turned by the wind)

ALTERNATIVES TO *IF*

as long as /əz ˈlɒŋ əz/ *conj* used to say that something must happen before something else can happen
assuming (that) /əˈsjuːmɪŋ/ *conj* accepting as true without question or proof
even if /ˈiːvən ɪf/ *conj* whether or not
provided that /prəˈvaɪdɪd θət/ *conj* if, or only if

UNIT 17

ADJECTIVES DESCRIBING ART

abstract /ˈæbstrækt/ *adj* Abstract art involves shapes and colours and not images of real things or people.
bizarre /bɪˈzɑː/ *adj* very strange and unusual
classic /ˈklæsɪk/ *adj* A classic book, film, etc. is one that has been popular for a long time and is considered to be of a high quality.
contemporary /kənˈtempərəri/ *adj* modern
controversial /kɒntrəˈvɜːʃəl/ *adj* causing disagreement or discussion
conventional /kənˈvenʃənəl/ *adj* traditional and ordinary
dramatic /drəˈmætɪk/ *adj* exciting and impressive
humorous /ˈhjuːmərəs/ *adj* funny, or making you laugh
powerful /ˈpaʊəfəl/ *adj* having a strong effect on people
remarkable /rɪˈmɑːkəbl/ *adj* very unusual or noticeable in a way that you admire
unique /juːˈniːk/ *adj* different from everyone and everything else

VERBS OFTEN USED IN THE PASSIVE

award /əˈwɔːd/ *v* to give money or a prize following an official decision
be composed of /bi kəmˈpəʊzd əv/ *v* to be the parts that something consists of
devote /dɪˈvəʊt/ *v* to use a space, area or time, etc. for a particular person or thing
elect /ɪˈlekt/ *v* to choose someone for a particular job or position by voting
entitle /ɪnˈtaɪtl/ *v* to give a title to a book, film, event, etc.
establish /ɪˈstæblɪʃ/ *v* to start a company or organisation that is likely to continue for a long time
influence /ˈɪnfluːəns/ *v* to affect or change how someone or something develops, behaves or thinks
prohibit /prəʊˈhɪbɪt/ *v* to officially forbid something
regard /rɪˈgɑːd/ *v* to think of someone or something in a particular way
set /set/ *v* If something is set somewhere, it is in that place or position.

UNIT 18

PERSONAL QUALITIES: NOUNS

ambition /æmˈbɪʃən/ *n* something you want to achieve in your life
bravery /ˈbreɪvəri/ *n* when someone is brave, showing no fear in dangerous or difficult situations
commitment /kəˈmɪtmənt/ *n* when you are willing to give your time and energy to something that you believe in, or a promise or firm decision to do something
courage /ˈkʌrɪdʒ/ *n* the ability to deal with a dangerous or difficult situation without being frightened
determination /dɪtɜːmɪˈneɪʃən/ *n* when someone continues trying to do something, although it is very difficult
drive /draɪv/ *n* energy and determination to achieve things
inspiration /ɪnspɪˈreɪʃən/ *n* If you are an inspiration, you are so good that someone else admires you and is encouraged by your behaviour.
kindness /ˈkaɪndnəs/ *n* kind behaviour
passion /ˈpæʃən/ *n* a strong belief in something or a strong feeling about a subject
sense /sens/ *n* good judgment, especially about practical things
spirit /ˈspɪrɪt/ *n* enthusiasm, energy or courage
strength /streŋθ/ *n* the ability to do things that need a lot of physical or mental effort

PHRASAL VERBS WITH *GET*

get away with /get əˈweɪ wɪð/ *pv* to avoid getting punished for something
get back /get ˈbæk/ *pv* to be given something again that you had before
get into /get ˈɪntuː/ *pv* to succeed in being chosen or elected
get on with /get ˈɒn wɪð/ *pv* to start or continue doing something, especially work
get out of /get ˈaʊt əv/ *pv* to avoid doing something that you do not want to do, especially by giving an excuse
get round to /get ˈraʊnd tə/ *pv* to do something that you have intended to do for a long time
get through /get ˈθruː/ *pv* to deal with a difficult or unpleasant experience successfully

VOCABULARY LIST

UNIT 19

CRIME AND CRIMINALS

burglar /'bɜːglə/ *n* a person who illegally enters buildings and steals things

burglary /'bɜːgləri/ *n* the crime of illegally entering a building and stealing things

burgle /'bɜːgl/ *v* to get into a building illegally and steal things

charge /tʃɑːdʒ/ *v* If the police charge someone, they accuse them officially of a crime.

charge /tʃɑːdʒ/ *n* a formal police statement saying that someone is accused of a crime

commit /kə'mɪt/ *v* to do something that is considered wrong, or that is illegal

court /kɔːt/ *n* the place where a judge decides whether someone is guilty of a crime

deny /dɪ'naɪ/ *v* to say that something is not true

hacker /'hækə/ *n* someone who gets into other people's computer systems or phone system without permission in order to find out information or do something illegal

investigate /ɪn'vestɪgeɪt/ *v* to try to discover all the facts about something, especially a crime or accident

judge /dʒʌdʒ/ *n* someone who controls a trial in court, decides how criminals should be punished and makes decisions about legal matters

jury /'dʒʊəri/ *n* a group of people who have been chosen to listen to all the facts in a trial in a law court and to decide whether a person is guilty or not guilty, or whether a claim has been proved

make an arrest /meɪk ən ə'rest/ *phr* when the police take someone to a police station to ask them about a crime which they might have committed

prisoner /'prɪzənə/ *n* a person who is kept in prison as a punishment

release /rɪ'liːs/ *v* to allow a prisoner to be free

sentence /'sentəns/ *v* to give a punishment to someone who has been found guilty of committing a crime

statement /'steɪtmənt/ *n* something that someone says or writes officially

suspect /'sʌspekt/ *n* someone who may have committed a crime

suspect /sə'spekt/ *v* to think that someone may have committed a crime or done something bad

theft /θeft/ *n* the action or crime of stealing something

victim /'vɪktɪm/ *n* someone who has suffered the effects of a crime

witness /'wɪtnəs/ *n* a person who sees an event happening, especially a crime or an accident

NEGATIVE PREFIXES

disorganised /dɪ'sɔːgənaɪzd/ *adj* not good at planning or organising things

impatient /ɪm'peɪʃənt/ *adj* easily annoyed by someone's mistakes or because you have to wait

impolite /ɪmpə'laɪt/ *adj* not polite, behaving in a way that is rude

inaccurate /ɪn'ækjʊrət/ *adj* not correct or exact

invisible /ɪn'vɪzəbl/ *adj* impossible to see

unclear /ʌn'klɪə/ *adj* not easy to understand

unfair /ʌn'feə/ *adj* not true and morally wrong

unsafe /ʌn'seɪf/ *adj* dangerous

UNIT 20

PLACES

barrier /'bæriə/ *n* a type of fence that prevents people from going into an area

basement /'beɪsmənt/ *n* a room or space that is below ground level in a building

bench /bentʃ/ *n* a long seat for two or more people, usually made of wood or metal

chimney /'tʃɪmni/ *n* a wide pipe that allows smoke from a fire to go out through the roof

community centre /kə'mjuːnəti ˌsentə/ *n* a place where people who live in an area can meet together to play sport, go to classes, etc.

complex /'kɒmpleks/ *n* a group of buildings or rooms that are used for a particular purpose

concrete /'kɒŋkriːt/ *n* a very hard building material made by mixing together cement, sand, small stones and water

frame /freɪm/ *n* the basic structure of a building, vehicle or piece of furniture that other parts are added onto

hut /hʌt/ *n* a small, simple building, often made of wood

ladder /'lædə/ *n* a piece of equipment that is used to reach high places, consisting of short steps fixed between two long sides

rug /rʌg/ *n* a soft piece of material used to cover the floor

shed /ʃed/ *n* a small building used to store things such as tools

shelter /'ʃeltə/ *n* a place that protects you from bad weather or danger

step /step/ *n* one of the surfaces that you walk on when you go up or down stairs

surface /'sɜːfɪs/ *n* the top or outside part of something

COMPOUND ADJECTIVES ENDING IN *-ING*

cost-cutting /ˈkɒst ˌkʌtɪŋ/ *adj* describes actions taken to reduce the amount that is spent on a service or within an organisation

eye-catching /ˈaɪ ˌkætʃɪŋ/ *adj* very attractive or noticeable

heartwarming /ˈhɑːt ˌwɔːmɪŋ/ *adj* (especially of an event, action or story) seeming to be something positive and good and therefore causing feelings of pleasure and happiness

life-threatening /ˈlaɪf ˌθretənɪŋ/ *adj* A life-threatening disease is a very serious one that can cause death.

mouth-watering /ˈmaʊθ ˌwɔːtərɪŋ/ *adj* describes food that looks as if it will taste good

record-breaking /ˈrekɔːd ˌbreɪkɪŋ/ *adj* better, bigger, longer, etc. than anything else before

time-consuming /ˈtaɪm kənˌsjuːmɪŋ/ *adj* needing a lot of time

GRAMMAR REFERENCE AND PRACTICE

UNIT 1 QUESTION FORMS

Yes/No question forms in simple tenses

- Simple tenses use the verb ***do*** + the infinitive when forming *Yes/No* questions.
  You catch the bus. → ***Do*** *you* ***catch*** *the bus?*
  She plays volleyball. → ***Does*** *she* ***play*** *volleyball?*
  They caught the bus. → ***Did*** *they* ***catch*** *the bus?*

Yes/No question forms with *be*

- The verb ***be*** does not use an auxiliary verb to form questions.
  They were at home. → ***Were*** *they at home?*

Yes/No question forms in continuous tenses

I'm winning. → ***Am*** *I winning?*
He was singing. → ***Was*** *he singing?*

Yes/No question forms in perfect tenses

He's made a mistake. → ***Has*** *he made a mistake?*

Yes/No question forms with modal verbs

- Modal verbs can form questions like auxiliary verbs.
  He'd like a drink. → ***Would*** *he like a drink?*
  I can carry the bag. → ***Can*** *I carry the bag?*

Wh- question forms

- Questions with a question word e.g. ***who***, ***what***, ***which***, ***where***, ***why***, ***how***, ***when***, ***how long/much/many/often***, ***what time*** are usually formed in the same way as *Yes/No* questions.
  Where do *you work?* ***What was*** *he singing?*
  Why aren't *they running?* ***How long did*** *it take?*

Subject and object questions

- When the question is about the object of the sentence, the word order is the same as other questions.

Subject		Object	
She	plays	volleyball.	
The bird	is eating	the bread.	
We	've made	a mistake.	
Object		**Subject**	
What	does	she	play?
What	is	it	eating?
What	have	we	made?

- When the question is about the subject of the sentence, the word order is the same as a statement.

Subject		Object
Who	plays	volleyball?
What	is eating	the bread?
Who	has made	a mistake?

Practice

1 **Read the sentences, then write a question for the answer which follows.**

0 My class is starting a drama club this term.
What *is your class starting this term*?
A drama club.

1 Membership costs £5.
How much ______?
£5.

2 We're planning to meet every Friday at six.
What time ______?
Six.

3 We had our first meeting last Friday.
When ______?
Last Friday.

4 Fifteen people came to the party.
How many ______?
Fifteen.

5 Most of them were girls.
______ girls?
Yes, there were only three boys.

6 We should try to get more boys.
______ more boys?
Yes, if possible.

7 We want to do a comedy show at the end of term.
What ______?
A comedy show.

8 Our drama teacher can help us.
Who ______?
Our drama teacher.

2 **Find the mistakes in the questions and correct them.**

1 How much costs this shirt?
______

2 Does your dad sometimes gets angry with you?
______

3 What time the exam finished?
______

4 Where you'd like to go this evening?
______

5 Do we can go out now?
______

6 Which team does support your brother?
______

7 What I should give my friend for her birthday?
______

UNIT 2 PRESENT TENSE REVIEW

Present simple

We use the present simple:

- for habits and routines.
  *We **have** dinner at eight.*
  *Jo **studies** every day.*
- for permanent situations and general facts.
  *They **live** in Tokyo.*
  *A healthy diet **helps** your energy levels.*

Present continuous

We use the present continuous:

- for events happening now.
  *We**'re having** dinner.* (= we're having dinner now)
- for events we plan.
  *We**'re having** dinner at nine this evening.*
  (= we've decided to have dinner at nine)

State verbs

- Some verbs are always simple, not continuous: ***believe***, ***dislike***, ***feel*** (= believe), ***hate***, ***have*** (= possess), ***have got***, ***hear***, ***know***, ***like***, ***look***, ***love***, ***mean***, ***need***, ***prefer***, ***realise***, ***recognise***, ***remember***, ***see***, ***seem***, ***smell***, ***suppose***, ***taste***, ***think***, ***understand***, ***want***, ***weigh***, ***wish***
  *We **feel** that this decision is unfair.*
  *He **has** four phones.*
  *What **does** this message **mean**?*
  *That pizza **smells** wonderful.*
  *I **don't understand** what you want.*
  *She **weighs** 60 kg.*
- Some of these verbs can be continuous when their meaning describes an action: ***feel***, ***have*** (= *eat*, *experience*, *take*, etc.), ***see*** (= meet), ***smell***, ***taste***, ***think*** (= consider), ***weigh***.
  *I**'m not feeling** very well.*
  *She**'s having** a bath.*
  *We**'re seeing** our friends later.*
  *He**'s smelling** the milk to check it's OK.*
  ***Are** you **thinking** about your homework?*

Present perfect with *for/since*

- We use the present perfect for actions which started in the past and are still true. They answer the question *How long …?*
- ***for*** introduces a length of time.
  *I**'ve had** a cold **for** two days.* (= I still have a cold.)
  *I **haven't seen** my cousin **for** two years.*
- ***since*** introduces a point of time in the past.
  *They **haven't done** any homework **since** Friday.*
  *We **have been** here **since** early this morning.*

Practice

1 **Complete the conversations with the present simple, present continuous or present perfect form of the verbs in brackets.**

A

Nick: Hi. Can you talk? I [1] ________ (have) problems with my maths homework.

Maggie: Yes, but can I phone you back in about twenty minutes? I [2] ________ (watch) a match on TV and my team [3] ________ (win)! They [4] ________ (not win) for three weeks.

B

Penny: Look at this advert. [5] ________ (you/recognise) the people in the band?

Elsa: Actually, my brother [6] ________ (know) some of them since they were at school.

Penny: Really? [7] ________ (he/hear) them play since then?

Elsa: Yes, but they [8] ________ (not/play) any concerts in this area for the past year because they [9] ________ (be) abroad on tour. The lead singer's girlfriend [10] ________ (study) at the university here, so I [11] ________ (suppose) they may come back.

Penny: Well, yes, look. They [12] ________ (perform) at our school next month!

C

Rosa: What's all this mess?

Tim: I [13] ________ (make) breakfast. I [14] ________ (be) awake for hours and I'm hungry.

Rosa: What [15] ________ (you/make)? It [16] ________ (smell) rather strange.

Tim: Vegetable omelette. Would you like some?

Rosa: No thanks. I [17] ________ (see) Natalie in half an hour, so I [18] ________ (need) to get dressed now.

2 **Complete the text with the verbs in the box in the present simple, present continuous or present perfect.**

be	come	enjoy	go	go	have	have
have	live	not live	serve	sleep	smell	
not start	take	wake	work			

I [1] ________ with my brother and my mum. We [2] ________ here for very long, but we [3] ________ a nice flat and we [4] ________ living in this part of town. My dad [5] ________ in Canada this year. He [6] ________ home at the end of November.

On weekdays, I [7] ________ up early to get the bus for school. Since my last birthday, I [8] ________ a job in a café on Saturdays. I [9] ________ work until ten, so I [10] ________ till nine. My mum [11] ________ me to work because she [12] ________ to a gym near the café. She [13] ________ a member for quite a long time. On Sundays we [14] ________ to a restaurant for lunch. This Sunday we [15] ________ lunch in a new place. They [16] ________ Mexican food and it [17] ________ great when you walk past the door.

GRAMMAR REFERENCE AND PRACTICE

UNIT 3 PAST TENSE REVIEW

Past simple and past continuous

We use the past simple:

- for completed events in the past.
  *I **visited** China twice **last year**.*
  *I **learned** a few useful phrases **yesterday**.*
- for states in the past related to a particular time.
  *I **didn't know** any Chinese words.*
  ***Did** you **enjoy** your visit?*

We use the past continuous for:

- past events which happen for a relatively long time.
  *He **was sitting** opposite me on the bus.*
- events happening around the time of another past event (in the past simple).
  *I **was doing** my homework when my brother texted.*

Practice

1 Choose the correct form of the verbs.

1 I *fell* / *was falling* off my bike when I *cycled* / *was cycling* home from school.
2 I *dreamt* / *was dreaming* about my favourite football team when my dad *was waking* / *woke* me up.
3 While I *got* / *was getting* ready to go out, I *dropped* / *was dropping* my phone and *broke* / *was breaking* it.
4 My parents *arrived* / *were arriving* home while I *had* / *was having* a shower and my sister *tidied* / *was tidying* the kitchen.
5 Unfortunately, I *didn't have* / *wasn't having* a good view of the band because I *stood* / *was standing* at the back of the hall.

Past perfect

We use the past perfect for events which happened some time before or up to another point in the past.
***I'd phoned** my brother earlier in the day, but he **hadn't answered**.*

Practice

2 Eric runs a café. Look at the list of jobs he has to do before he opens at 8 o'clock. Yesterday he was late. Write sentences about what he had and hadn't done when the café opened.

1 Switch on the coffee machine. ✔
He ______
2 Empty the dishwasher. ✘
He ______
3 Clean the tables. ✘
He ______
4 Put the chairs out. ✔
He ______
5 Open the sunshades. ✘
He ______

used to

We use *used to* for talking about past habits which are not true now.
*I **used to phone** my grandmother every evening*
(= I don't phone her every evening now.)
*They **used to spend** the summer in Florida.*
(= They don't spend the summer in Florida now.)
*We **didn't use to pay** to visit the museum.*
(= It was free, but now we have to pay.)

Practice

3 Complete the sentences with the correct form of *used to* and the verb in brackets.

1 When I was eight, I ______ my little brother all the time. (tease)
2 My sister ______ make-up, but she wears it every day now. (not/wear)
3 ______ coffee when you were little? (you/like)
4 I ______ tea every afternoon for my mum, but I get home too late to do that now. (make)
5 We ______ abroad when we were children, but we now go to the States at least once a year. (not/go)
6 You ______ so happy at school. What's upset you this term? (be)

4 Read the story and choose the correct form of the verbs.

When I was ten my parents [1] *bought* / *had bought* / *were buying* a small sailing boat. My dad [2] *had enjoyed* / *was enjoyed* / *used to enjoy* watersports all his life and when we were children we [3] *were spending* / *had spent* / *used to spend* all our summer holidays by the sea. In fact, my parents [4] *used to meet* / *were meeting* / *had met* each other when they [5] *were both taking* / *both took* / *had both taken* diving lessons.

They [6] *hadn't told* / *weren't telling* / *didn't use to tell* me and my brother about the boat before our holiday, so it was a wonderful surprise for us when we [7] *were seeing* / *had seen* / *saw* it.

After two days, my brother and I [8] *had learned* / *learned* / *were learning* enough to sail the boat around the quiet bay in front of the house where we [9] *used to stay* / *had stayed* / *were staying* that year and we [10] *used to feel* / *felt* / *had felt* quite grown-up. On the third day, we [11] *moved* / *had moved* / *were moving* smoothly across the water when suddenly some dolphins [12] *were appearing* / *used to appear* / *appeared* beside us. We were amazed as we [13] *never saw* / *never used to see* / *had never seen* dolphins before. After that, we [14] *were looking* / *used to look* / *had looked* out for them every day when we [15] *were sailing* / *used to sail* / *sailed*. In fact, they often seemed to be waiting for us. It was a magical experience.

UNIT 4 MAKING COMPARISONS

Comparative structures

We make comparisons using a number of structures:

- comparative adjective + *than*
  colder than ***more powerful than***
- *less* + adjective + *than*
  less cold than ***less powerful than***
- *as* + adjective + *as*
  as cold as ***as powerful as***
- *not as/so* + adjective + *as*
  not as cold as ***not so powerful as***
- the comparative adjective + comma + the comparative adjective
  the higher *you go*, ***the colder*** *it gets.*
- *the more/less* clause + comma + *the more/less* clause
  The more *I listen to this music*, ***the more*** *I like it.*

Adverbs with comparatives and superlatives

- We can modify comparative structures with adverbs and adverbial phrases:
  a little / ***a bit*** / ***a good/great deal*** / ***slightly*** / ***far*** / ***(not) a lot*** / ***(not) much*** + comparative adjective + *than.*
  Scotland is ***a bit colder than*** *England.*
  Winter is usually ***a great deal colder than*** *summer.*
  My motorbike is ***not a lot more powerful than*** *my brother's.*
  almost / ***(not) nearly*** + ***as*** + adjective + ***as.***
  My house is ***almost as big as*** *yours.*
  *My car is****n't nearly as powerful as*** *my dad's.*
- We can modify superlatives with adverbs and adverbial phrases:

easily	+ ***the*** + superlative adjective
by far	
probably	
possibly	

Your house is ***easily the biggest*** *in this road.*
This bike is ***probably the most expensive*** *thing I've ever bought.*

Practice

1 **Choose the correct words.**

1 This jacket looks *more warm* / *warmer*, but the other one is less expensive *as* / *than* this one.
2 My new earphones are *easily* / *slightly* bigger than the old ones and they're *a great deal* / *by far* more powerful.
3 Although my room isn't *so* / *more* comfortable as yours, I think I have *a far* / *a nearly* better view.

2 **Match the sentence halves.**

1 The more I think about it,
2 This hotel is a great deal
3 The buses don't run
4 The fewer friends we invite,
5 The bigger the hotel,
6 John's arrival was

a the better the sports facilities
b the less food we'll have to buy.
c cheaper than the one we stayed in last year.
d by far the best part of the evening.
e nearly as frequently as they used to.
f the less I like the idea of a boat trip.

3 **Do the pairs of sentences mean the same? Mark *S* for same or *D* for different. Explain the differences.**

1 The way you say thank you is less important than the fact that you say it.
It's just as important how you thank someone as the fact that you remember to thank them.

....

....

2 It isn't nearly as difficult to do well in maths as it is in French.
It's easier to do well in maths than it is in French.

....

....

3 Loretta is easily the most selfish friend I have.
My other friends are as selfish as Loretta.

....

....

GRAMMAR REFERENCE AND PRACTICE

UNIT 5 RELATIVE CLAUSES

Defining relative clauses

Defining relative clauses:

- give essential information.
  The game ***that my brother plays*** *is very boring.*
  We need the words *that my brother plays* to understand which game the speaker is referring to.
- include a relative pronoun: ***who*** (for people), ***which*** (for things), ***that*** (for things and people).
  There's the girl ***who*** *sold me the game.*
  She showed me the tablet ***which*** *she uses.*
  I can email the friend ***that*** *I told you about.*
  This is the game ***that*** *I mentioned.*
- can have ***who, which*** or ***that*** as either their subject or object.
  The man ***who/that*** *runs the game shop is very helpful.*
  There's the man ***who/that*** *I told you about.*
  He showed me a website ***which/that*** *he recommends.*
- can begin with ***whose*** (meaning *his/her/their*), ***when*** (for times) and ***where*** (for places).
  Paul is my friend ***whose*** *room is full of computers.*
  I remember the day ***when*** *I got my first computer.*
  The shop ***where*** *I bought this game has a really good selection.*

Practice

1 **Complete the sentences with *who, which, whose, where* or *when*.**

1 The first video game ________ I ever played was called *Racer*.
2 I like talking to people ________ play the same games as me.
3 This the café ________ my friends meet in the evenings.
4 Amy started her blog one day ________ she was on holiday.
5 The friend ________ tablet I borrowed is away on holiday.

2 **Look at the sentences in Exercise 1. Where can you use *that* instead of the word you chose?**

3 **Complete the sentences with your own ideas.**

1 I don't enjoy games which ________
2 A friend is someone who ________
3 I have a classmate whose ________
4 I hate lessons where ________
5 I remember the day when ________

Non-defining relative clauses

Non-defining relative clauses:

- give extra information about things or people.
  This tablet belongs to my brother, ***who*** *plays a lot of video games.*
  If we take out *who plays a lot of video games*, the information in the sentence still makes sense.
- are always separated from the rest of the sentence by commas.
  *My dad***,** *who never plays video games***,** *doesn't understand why I like them.*
- must begin with the relative pronoun ***who*** (for people) or ***which*** (for things) (but never ***that***) as their subject or as their object.
  My brother, ***who*** *is very clever, designs video games.*
  The games, ***which*** *are very exciting, are about a virtual world.*

Practice

4 **Rewrite the pairs of sentences using non-defining relative clauses.**

1 I got my new bike last week. It cost £250.
2 I bought the bike with my own money. I earned it from my Saturday job.
3 I did the job for two years. The job was in a shop.
4 I didn't enjoy the work. The work was quite boring.
5 But most of the staff were very friendly. They weren't much older than me.
6 I've still got a bit of money. I'm going to spend it on a new video game.

5 **Complete the paragraph with *that* if possible, or with *who, which, where* or *when*.**

Hi Claudia,

We finished our exams, [1] ________ were very hard, last week. On the day [2] ________ the exams were all over, I went with my friend Katya to a beach [3] ________ is near my house. Katya is the friend [4] ________ I met last summer at the club [5] ________ I go for tennis lessons.

Katya lost her phone on the beach, [6] ________ was quite busy. It was a new smartphone, [7] ________ her parents gave her only two weeks ago. We thought it had been stolen by some people [8] ________ we saw near us just after we arrived. We moved to another place [9] ________ was less crowded. Later we were walking back past the place [10] ________ we had first been when she realised her phone was in the pocket of her dress! We were so relieved.

What's your news?

Julia xx

UNIT 6 PRESENT PERFECT AND PAST SIMPLE

We use the **present perfect**:

- for actions beginning in the past and continuing into the present.
  *She**'s become** a very good cook.*
- for events before the present where the time is unknown or unimportant.
  *We**'ve made** lots of cakes.*
- for events repeated over a period of time up to the present.
  *He**'s received** six texts in the last ten minutes.*
- With time markers ***just***, ***already***, ***still*** (***not***) and (***not***) ***yet***.
  ***I've just eaten** my sandwich.* (= I ate it a few moments ago.)
  ***I've already eaten** my sandwich.* (= I ate it some time before now.)
  ***I've eaten** my sandwich **already**.* (= I've finished my sandwich.)
  *I **still haven't finished** my sandwich.* (= I'm still eating it now.)
  *I **haven't finished** my sandwich **yet**.* (= I'm still eating it now.)
  ***Have** you **had** lunch **yet**?*

We use the **past simple**:

- for actions which took place in the past, with or without a time reference.
  *She **became** a very good cook.*
  *When she was still a teenager, she **became** a very good cook.*
  *I **didn't finish** my sandwich.*
  *I **didn't finish** my sandwich during my break.*
  *We **made** lots of cakes.*
  *We **made** lots of cakes last weekend.*

Practice

1 **Put the words in brackets in the correct position in each sentence.**

1. Has the film started? (already)
2. We haven't had the results of our exam. (still)
3. Have you decided what to wear to the party? (yet)
4. I've ordered a drink, but I haven't decided what to eat. (already, still)
5. Have you been here a long time or have you arrived? (just)
6. My brother hasn't answered my text. (yet)

2 **Complete the paragraph with the words in the box.**

already	just	since	still	when	yet

Hi Chloe,

How are you? I've [1] ________ changed my room around and it looks really great. I'm going to get a new desk too. I've [2] ________ chosen one and we've ordered it online, but it hasn't arrived [3] ________. I'll probably get a new rug as well, but I [4] ________ haven't decided what colour. I saw a good one [5] ________ I went to town last weekend, but it was rather expensive. I've looked at some others online [6] ________ then, but I haven't seen anything so good.

I'll send you a photo as soon as it's all finished.

Becca xx

3 **Find the mistakes in the sentences and correct them.**

1. Jake ate already three burgers today and now he's having an ice cream.
   ____
2. Michael hasn't still answered my last text.
   ____
3. Stella's English improved a lot since she started that evening class.
   ____
4. Declan has just woken up, so he didn't get dressed yet.
   ____
5. Jan's started learning to drive and she's made already a lot of progress.
   ____

4 **Complete the conversation with the verbs in the past simple or present perfect.**

Emir: Hi, sorry I'm late, I [1] ________ (have) to see the teacher after my last class.
Pat: It's OK. I [2] ________ (already/order) a pizza for us both.
Emir: Oh. Actually, I [3] ________ (eat) a pizza for lunch today. I don't really need another one now.
Pat: Never mind. I [4] ________ (not eat) anything since breakfast so I can probably finish it all myself!

GRAMMAR REFERENCE AND PRACTICE

UNIT 7 MODALS OF ABILITY AND POSSIBILITY AND *MANAGED TO*

	be able to	can/could
Present	am/are/is (not) able to	can/can't (cannot)
Past	was/were (not) able to	could/couldn't
Future	will/won't be able to may/might (not) be able to	*can* sometimes refers to the future, but to make tenses we use *be able to*

managed **(*to*)** is the past tense of ***manage***, a regular verb.

Present

- We use ***can*** or ***be able to*** when we say what someone is capable of.
  *I **can** speak three languages.*
  ***Are** you **able to** finish this work on your own?*
  *She **can't** carry all the bags.*

Past

- We use ***was/were able to*** or ***managed to*** when we describe what someone was capable of in a particular situation.
  ***Were you able to** change the time of your appointment?*
  *I had a puncture, but I **managed to** fix it.*
- We use ***could*** or ***was/were able to*** when we describe what someone was capable of in general.
  *We **could** all ride a bicycle by the time we started school.*
  *I **wasn't able to** tell the time until I was eight.*

Future

- We use ***can*** / ***will be able to*** when we are certain about a possibility in one particular situation.
  *They **can** / They**'ll be able to** meet us at six o'clock.*
  *I **can't** / **won't be able to** watch the match on Tuesday because I've got an exam.*
- We use ***will be able to*** when we are certain about an ability in general.
  *He**'ll be able to** speak good French after six months in Paris.*
  *We **won't be able to** play football if they build on the park.*
- We use ***may/might be able to*** when we are not certain about a future possibility.
  *I **may be able to** go swimming if I finish my homework.*
  *You **might not be able to** see the band if you get cheap seats.*

Practice

1 Complete the sentences with the correct form of *be able to* and the words in brackets.

1 ________ (you/play) in the match next Saturday?
2 We had to cancel our trip to California, but luckily we ________ (get) our money back.
3 I know a little bit of Arabic, so I ________ (translate) that letter if it's not too complicated.
4 I invited my best friend to stay last weekend, but she ________ (not/come).
5 ________ (you/read) before you started school?
6 You have so much energy! I don't know how you ________ (do) all your schoolwork as well as your evening job.
7 I've just realised that we have guests on the day of your barbecue, so I ________ (not/come).
8 I've got important exams this year, so I ________ (not/play) football for the school team this term.

2 Make the sentences into questions using the words in brackets in the correct form.

1 (your brother/be able to/come) ________ to the concert next week?
2 (you/not manage/find) ________ any sandals when you went shopping?
3 (When/Joy/be able to/play) ________ in the band again?
4 (John/be able to/explain) ________ what he wanted?
5 (How far/you/able to/walk) ________ before it started raining?
6 (Elisa/not be able to/help) ________ us with our homework tomorrow?

3 Choose the correct verbs in the report.

Aaron took part in a half-marathon last weekend. As he's 19, this may not sound a great achievement. However, in Aaron's case it was, because last year he was told that he [1] *wasn't able to walk* / *might not be able to walk* again.

Aaron had fallen off his bike when cycling home from school. The street was dark and it was a little icy, and he [2] *couldn't* / *wasn't able to* control his bike. He was left lying on the road with serious injuries. Luckily, Aaron [3] *managed to find* / *could find* his phone and call for an ambulance. He spent several weeks in hospital and he [4] *wasn't able to take* / *couldn't take* an important exam because his injuries meant he [5] *couldn't write* / *didn't manage to write* or use a computer. However, he made an unexpectedly good recovery and after three months he [6] *managed to walk* / *could walk* quite well. When he finished the half-marathon, he told his friends that he hopes he'll be able to run in a full marathon next year.

UNIT 8 FUTURE (1): PLANS AND INTENTIONS

Present simple for timetabled events

We use the present simple:

- for future events which are fixed in a timetable.
  *My flight **leaves** at ten past seven.*
- for future events which are going to take place at a fixed time.
  *The match **starts** at midday.*

Present continuous for future plans

We use the present continuous, usually with the time mentioned:

- for definite plans.
  *My friend Irena **is coming** to stay with me at the end of July.*
  *What **are you doing** at the weekend?*
- for things we've already decided to do.
  *I'**m getting up** early tomorrow.*
  *We'**re not eating** before we go out.*

Going to future

We use ***going to***:

- for plans which have already been made. (This use is similar to the present continuous.)
  *My friend Irena **is going to visit** me at the end of July.*
  *What **are you going to do** at the weekend?*

Will future

We use ***will***:

- for actions which we decide to do as we speak.
  ***I'll look** online for the address I need.*
  ***I'll phone** my dad and see if he can give me a lift.*
  NOTE There is often little difference in meaning between *will* and *going to*, especially when they are used with an adverb such as ***certainly***, ***probably***, ***definitely*** or a phrase such as ***I think***, ***I hope***.

Adverbs in sentences with *going to* and *will*

- Adverb position with ***going to***:
  ***I'm definitely going to watch** the match.*
  ***I'm definitely not going to watch** the match.*
- Adverb position with ***will***:
  ***I'll probably watch** the match.*
  *I **probably won't watch** the match.* (**not** ~~*I won't probably watch the match.*~~)

Practice

1 **Choose the correct forms of the verbs.**

1

Ana: Hi, Sassy. Do you want a coffee? I've already ordered one.
Sassy: Thanks, Ana, but it's a bit hot. I think [1] *I'll have / I have* a cold drink.
Ana: They do good iced coffee here. That's what [2] *I'm having / I'll have.*
Sassy: Oh really? OK, [3] *I'll order / I'm ordering* one too.

2

Soroosh: [1] *Are you having / Do you have* a holiday this summer?
Bobby: Well, [2] *I'm definitely not going to work / I definitely don't work* all the time. [3] *I'll probably visit / I'm probably visiting* my cousins in Germany.
Soroosh: You're lucky to have family abroad. [4] *I'm staying / I'll stay* in a hotel with my parents and my little sister.
Bobby: Why don't you come with me to Germany? [5] *It's only going to cost / It'll only cost* you the price of your plane ticket.
Soroosh: That'd be fantastic. [6] *I'm talking / I'll talk* to my parents tonight.
Bobby: And [7] *I'll check / I'm going to check* the best dates. [8] *I'm going to phone / I'll phone* Germany tomorrow anyway because it's my cousin's birthday.
Soroosh: Thanks, Bobby, that's great.

2 **Put the adverbs in the correct position in each sentence.**

1 We're going to hire a car and drive to the coast. (probably)
2 I won't invite Mark to the barbecue. (definitely)
3 Clara's not going to travel with her brother. (certainly)
4 We'll try the local food in Phnom Penh. (certainly)
5 Hamid won't enjoy the overnight rail journey. (probably)

3 **Complete the paragraph with the present simple, present continuous or *will* future form of the verbs in brackets.**

Hi Misha,

How are you? Here are the final arrangements for our trip next month. You have your ticket. The train [1] .... (leave) Paris at 6 pm. Albert and I [2] .... (meet) outside the Gare du Nord at 5 because I have his ticket. You can meet us there, or we can see you on the train. We definitely [3] .... (not wait) more than five minutes because the security checks [4] .... (probably/take) quite a long time. The train [5] .... (arrive) in London in plenty of time for us to have some food before we go to the hostel. Albert and I [6] .... (take) medium-sized rucksacks and I suggest you do the same. Actually, I [7] .... (send) you a link to the webpage where we found ours, as they're a good make and quite cheap. We're really looking forward to the trip.

Piers

GRAMMAR REFERENCE AND PRACTICE

UNIT 9 FUTURE (2): PREDICTIONS

Predictions with *be going to*

We use ***be going to***:

- for predictions based on physical evidence, usually what we can see as we speak.
  *It's **going to snow**.* (= I can see the snow clouds and it's very cold.)
  *That boy **is going to fall** over his shoelaces.*
  (= I can see his shoelaces aren't fastened.)
  *I'**m going to faint**.* (= I feel ill.)
- for predictions based on what we already know for certain.
  *Millie **is going to run out of** money soon.* (= I know how much money Millie has and I know how fast she's spending it.)
  *You'**re going to enjoy** this music.* (= I know the sort of music you like and I've chosen this for you.)

Predictions with *will*

We use ***will*** for predictions about the future which we believe to be true but can't prove.
*My parents **will probably pay** for me to go to university.*
*The fees **will go up** every year.*
*I'**ll earn** a good salary when I leave university.*

Predictions with future continuous

We use future continuous (***will/won't*** + ***be*** + verb + ***-ing***) for predictions about habits and actions in progress in the future.
*I'**ll be earning** a lot of money this summer.*
***Will you be working** during the school holidays?*
*They **won't be earning** enough to buy a car.*

Predictions with *may* (*not*), *might* (*not*) and *could* + *well*

- ***May***, ***might*** and ***could*** are used to express future possibility that is less certain than ***will*** or the future continuous.
  *I **might earn** a good salary when I leave university.*
  *He **could be earning** a lot of money quite soon.*
  *My parents **may not give** me an allowance.*
- The prediction sounds more certain if ***well*** is added after ***may***, ***might*** and ***could***.
  *The fees **may well go up** every year.*
  *We **could well be working** full-time next year.*
  *They **might well not be earning** enough to buy a car.*
  NOTE ***Could*** + negative does not mean the same as ***may*** and ***might*** in predictions.
  *We **couldn't** be working full-time next year.*
  (*= It's impossible that …*)

Practice

1 **Read the sentences and use the words in brackets to make a prediction using *going to* or the future continuous.**

1 It's six o'clock in the morning and the sun is shining. (It / hot day)
....
2 You and your brother plan to travel round the USA next year. (We / speak / English every day)
....
3 Your friend is riding his bike and drinking from a can at the same time. (He / fall off)
....
4 The school term finishes in three weeks. (After the end of term / I / not study every evening)
....
5 You're waiting for a friend outside the cinema. You hear there's a bad traffic jam on the road from his house. (He / not see / the beginning of the film)
....

2 **Which of the pairs of sentences mean the same and which are different? Mark them *S* for same or *D* for different. Explain the differences.**

1 I'm probably going to buy a new phone.
I may well buy a new phone. ......
2 The shop may not open until the evening.
The shop couldn't open until the evening. ......
3 It's possible I'll get a bigger phone.
I might get a bigger phone. ......
4 I'll be using my new phone tomorrow.
I'll make some calls on my new phone tomorrow. ......
5 I definitely won't text you at lunchtime.
I might well text you at lunchtime. ......

3 **Read about Jack and Joe, then make predictions about their futures. Use *may* (*not*), *might* (*not*) and *could*, and add *well* if appropriate.**

Jack and Joe are brothers. Joe is 10 and Jack is 14. Joe is very bright and is already doing well at school. Jack plays football very well, but he doesn't like school work. However, he likes meeting people and having a good time, whereas Joe is quite shy unless he's with Jack.

1 Jack / not go / university.
....
2 Joe / get very good marks in exams.
....
3 Jack / become a professional football player.
....
4 Jack / earn much more than Joe when he's 25.
....
5 Joe / not be interested in money.
....
6 Joe / get to know famous people through Jack.
....

UNIT 10 THE PASSIVE

The passive: present, past, present perfect

- The passive is formed with a tense of the verb ***to be*** + the past participle of the main verb.

  present simple
  *This room **is used** for dance classes.*

  present continuous
  *My jeans **are being washed**.*

  past simple
  *We **weren't told** what to do.*

  present perfect
  *The room **has been painted**.*
- We use ***by*** to introduce the person or thing that does the action.
  *We're taught Chinese on Saturdays **by Mrs Lee**.*
  *Are you being looked after **by a nurse**?*
  *The window was repaired **by my dad**.*
  *The room has been painted **by the students**.*

The passive: modals

- We form the passive of modal verbs with:
  modal + (*to*) *be* + past participle
  *My sweater **should be washed** at a low temperature.*
  *All these clothes **need to be folded** carefully.*
  *My T-shirts **needn't be ironed**.*
  *The washing machine **might be damaged** by a heavy load.*

The passive: usage

The passive is widely used in English, in both speaking and writing. We use the passive:

- if we do not know who or what does the action.
  *A car **was parked** in the middle of the road.*
  *The window**'s been** broken!*
- if who or what does the action is unimportant.
  *My new bike **is being delivered** today.*
  *These files **should be backed up** regularly.*
- if it is obvious who or what does the action.
  ***I've been asked** to play for my school team.*
  *Your bedroom **needs to be tidied** before you go out.*

Practice

1 Rewrite the sentences using the passive. Do not include *by* and who or what does the action unless it adds important information.

1 A famous footballer has just opened a new sports club in our town.
A new sports club ....

2 A local architect designed the buildings.
The buildings ....

3 Some people held an auction to raise money for the club.
An auction ....

4 Secondary school students are still decorating the inside of the building.
The inside of the building ....

5 They need to finish it by the end of the summer.
It ....

6 Some people have criticised them for working too slowly.
They ....

7 They should offer help instead of criticism.
Help ....

2 Read the description of the sports club, then complete the news report using the same verbs in the passive.

Some thieves have broken into the new sports club and taken valuable equipment. They broke a window, but they didn't set off the alarm. Some local residents saw lights in the club car park last night, but they didn't report them at the time. The thieves damaged several doors. They made holes in the floor when they dragged the heavy equipment across it. The police are investigating the break-in and the insurance company has also inspected the building. The club can replace the equipment immediately, but they need to improve the security lighting in the car park. They should install a gate and someone must lock it every evening. Now that the thieves know what's inside the club, they might steal the new equipment if the club doesn't improve its security.

NEWS — BREAK IN AT LOCAL SPORTS CLUB

The new sports club [1] .... and valuable equipment [2] .... A window [3] .... but the alarm [4] .... Lights [5] .... in the club car park last night but they [6] .... at the time. Several doors [7] .... and holes [8] .... in the floor when the heavy equipment [9] .... across it. The break-in [10] .... and the building [11] .... by the insurance company. The equipment [12] .... immediately but the security lighting in the car park [13] .... A gate [14] .... and it [15] .... every evening. Now that the thieves know what's inside the club, the new equipment [16] .... if security [17] ....

GRAMMAR REFERENCE AND PRACTICE

UNIT 11 PRESENT PERFECT CONTINUOUS

- We form the present perfect continuous in a similar way to the present perfect simple, but we use ***has/have been*** + ***-ing*** verb.

Positive	Negative	Questions
has / have been using	hasn't / haven't been using	has he / have they been using?

- We use the present perfect continuous to talk about:
  - an action that has just stopped.
    *I**'ve been painting** my room. Would you like to see what it looks like?* (It is not clear whether the speaker has completed the action yet.)
  - an action that has not completely finished.
    *I**'ve been painting** my room. It's going to look great when I've finished.*
  - how long the action continued, up to and possibly including the present moment.
    *I**'ve been painting** my room since first thing this morning. I'm really tired.*

Present perfect simple

- We form the present perfect simple with ***has/have*** + the past participle.
- We use the present perfect simple to talk about actions before or up to the present (we do not mention when). These can be:
  - a completed action, especially one which has a present result. (It is clear that the speaker has already completed the action.)
    *I**'ve made** a cake. Would you like a piece?*
  - how often something has happened before now.
    *You**'ve made** a cake every day this week.*
  - with state verbs (*know, love, believe*, etc.).
    *I**'ve known** how to make cakes since I was ten.*

Practice

1 **Complete the sentences with the present perfect continuous form of the verbs in brackets.**

1 The students ________ (use) computers in this school for several years.
2 How long ________ (you/study) electronics?
3 The engineers ________ (not/work) on this problem for long.
4 My sister ________ (make) a list of the things she wants for her birthday.
5 We ________ (design) our ideal house, but we can't agree about the colour scheme.
6 I don't know where my tablet is. I hope my little brother ________ (not/play) games on it.

2 **Write questions, using the words given and putting the verb into the present perfect continuous.**

1 how long / study / this school
____
2 how long / learn / English
____
3 how long / live / here
____
4 how long / do / this exercise
____

3 **Now answer your questions, using the present perfect continuous.**

1 ________
2 ________
3 ________
4 ________

4 **Complete the conversations with the present perfect simple or continuous form of the verbs in brackets.**

1
Kai: I want to make a sandwich, but someone ________ (eat) all the bread.
Zoe: Well, I ________ (make) biscuits. You can have one when they're ready.
Kai: How long will that be? I ________ (play) tennis since two o'clock and I'm starving!

2
Tim: ________ (you/listen) to me or ________ (I/talk) to myself for the past five minutes?
Paul: No, really, I ________ (listen) to everything. And I ________ (already/decide) what we can do about your problem.

3
Francis: I think my brother ________ (wear) my trainers. They're covered in mud.
Sheila: No, he ________ (work) in his room all day. You ________ (not clean) them since you last wore them, that's all.

4
Lucy: The teacher ________ (ask) me three questions this lesson.
Kirsten: She ________ (try) to find out if you understand the text.
Lucy: Well, I ________ (not/understand) any of it up to now!

5
Laurie: My team ________ (not/play) well this season.
Jade: Perhaps they'll do better tomorrow.
Laurie: I doubt it. They ________ (not/have) one good match since the manager left.

UNIT 12 ZERO AND FIRST CONDITIONALS

Zero conditional

- We form the zero conditional with:
  If + present tense + comma + present tense
  OR present tense + ***if*** + present tense.
- ***If*** usually means the same as ***when*** in zero conditional sentences.
  *I always get a headache **if** I'm short of sleep.*
  (= *I always get a headache **when** I'm short of sleep.*)
- In writing, there must be a comma when the ***if-clause*** comes first.
  ***If** you play a musical instrument**,** you get more invitations to parties.*
- We use the zero conditional to state general truths.
  ***If** you **live** in a big city, you **have** lots of shops to choose from.*
- ***You*** often means 'anyone' in sentences like these.
  ***You** get more invitations to parties if **you** play a musical instrument.*

Practice

1 Complete the sentences with suitable verbs.

1 Teenagers ________ bored if they can't spend time with their friends.
2 If you ________ a lot of friends, you always have someone to talk to.
3 If children ________ a musical instrument, they often do better at school.
4 When there are important exams, everyone ________ stressed.

First conditional

- We form the first conditional with:
  If + present tense + comma + future tense
  OR future tense + ***if*** + present tense.
  ***If** you **play** your guitar**, I'll sing**.*
  = ***I'll sing if** you **play** your guitar.*
- ***If*** does **not** mean the same as ***when*** in first conditional sentences. Compare:
  - ***If** my friend **texts** me, **I'll go** to her house.* (= The speaker thinks her friend may text her and invite her.)
  - ***When** my friend **texts** me, **I'll go** to her house.* (= The speaker knows her friend is going to text her and already plans to go to her house.)
- We use the first conditional to describe a real situation and a possible result.
  ***If** I **work** late, **I'll be** too tired to go out.* (= I know from experience that working late makes me too tired to go out.)
- We can use ***may, might*** or ***could*** to make the possibility less certain.
  ***If** I **work** late, I **may be** too tired to go out.* (= I know from experience that working late sometimes makes me too tired to go out.)
  *We **might miss** our friends **if** we **move** to another city.*
  (= I know that we won't see our friends often if we move, so perhaps we'll miss them.)
  ***If** I **don't practise** regularly, I **could fail** my driving test.*
  (= I need to practise regularly, or there's a possibility I'll fail my test.)

Practice

2 Complete the conversation with the correct form of the verbs in brackets.

Kurt: Do you want to go out somewhere this evening?
Jack: I've got some work to do, but if you [1] ________ (not mind) waiting, I'll be free by seven at the latest.
Kurt: That's fine. I've got some shopping to do, but if I finish early, I [2] ________ (go) to the café in the High Street and wait for you there.
Jack: OK. Can we eat there? Is the food good?
Kurt: If you like spicy food, [3] ________ (try) their chilli burger. It's amazing.
Jack: Well, I might not like it if it [4] ________ (be) really hot.
Kurt: Their pizzas are good too. If you [5] ________ (prefer) that kind of thing, they have a good choice.
Jack: Right, see you later. I [6] ________ (text) you if I'm going to be late.

3 Match the sentence halves.

1 You might see some interesting animals
2 If you make a noise,
3 If you come here regularly,
4 You may have to wait several hours
5 If you need to move,
6 If you want to use a camera,

a you learn where to look.
b you'll need permission.
c if you keep very quiet.
d don't do it suddenly.
e if you want to see the new lions.
f you'll frighten the animals away.

4 Complete the sentences with your own ideas.

1 If Anita passes her driving test, her parents might ________________
2 Erfan could get into serious trouble if he ________________
3 If you want to be the most popular person at a party, ________________
4 Malek will have a party if he ________________
5 If Marco works really hard, he may ________________
6 Don't leave your wallet in your desk if ________________

GRAMMAR REFERENCE AND PRACTICE

UNIT 13 REPORTED STATEMENTS

- There are some fixed tense changes when the reporting verb is in the past tense.

Direct speech		**Reported speech**
present simple	→	**past simple**
*'I **enjoy** watching sport on TV.'*		*He said (that) he **enjoyed** watching sport on TV.*
present continuous	→	**past continuous**
*'My team **is playing** well.'*		*She said (that) her team **was playing** well.*
past simple	→	**past perfect**
*'They **played** well last year.'*		*He said (that) they**'d** (**had**) **played** well last year.*
present perfect	→	**past perfect**
*'I **haven't seen** them play live.'*		*She said (that) she **hadn't seen** them play live.*
going to	→	***was going to***
*'They**'re going to** win.'*		*He said (that) they **were going to** win.*
***will* future**	→	***would***
*'I**'ll** be really happy.'*		*She said (that) she**'d (would)** be really happy.*
can	→	***could***
*'The goalie **can** stop any ball.'*		*He said (that) the goalie **could** stop any ball.*
may	→	***might***
*'I **may** go to the final.'*		*She said (that) she **might** go to the final.*
must	→	***had to***
*'I **must** buy a ticket.'*		*He said (that) he **had to** buy a ticket.*

- ***Could***, ***would***, ***should***, ***might***, ***ought to*** and ***used to***, and verbs in the past perfect tense, do not change when reported.
  *'You **could** buy a ticket online.'* → *He said I **could** buy a ticket online.*
  *'They **hadn't won** a match for ages.'* → *She said they **hadn't won** a match for ages.*
- If the information in the reported speech is a permanent situation, or if it is still true, it is not necessary to change the tense of the reported verb.
  *'My team **is playing** well this season.'* → *He said his team **is playing** well this season.* (the season has not ended)
- Pronouns and adverbs often have to change when they are reported.
  *'**I** enjoy watching sport on TV.'* → *She said **she** enjoyed watching sport on TV.*
  *'**You** can watch the match at **my** house **tomorrow**.'* → *He said **I** could watch the match at **his** house **the next day**.*

Practice

1 **Complete the reported sentences.**

1 'I'll get up earlier in future.'
He promised he ______________________

2 'We're looking for some new equipment.'
They told us they ______________________

3 'I enjoy swimming, but I don't like competitions.'
She explained that she ______________________

4 'You didn't listen to my instructions.'
My coach said I ______________________

5 'We must win the match.'
The captain told us that we ______________________

6 'I've played volleyball, but I've never tried basketball.'
Our teacher said she ______________________

2 **Complete the report of what your friend said, changing the verbs as necessary.**

I want to buy a new sports kit. I'm going to look in a shop in the city centre. Last time I looked there, everything was very expensive, but I've heard they're closing down, so I might find a bargain.

She said that she [1] ________ to buy a new sports kit. She [2] ________ look in a shop in the city centre. Last time she [3] ________ there, everything [4] ________ very expensive, but she [5] ________ they [6] ________ down, so she [7] ________ find a bargain.

UNIT 14 REPORTED QUESTIONS

In reported questions:

- the verbs change tense in the same way as in reported statements.
  *'What time **is it**?' → She asked what time **it was**.*
  *'**Are** we **going to** be late?' → She asked if we **were going to** be late.*
- pronouns and adverbs change in the same way as in reported statements.
  *'Where are **you** going **tomorrow**?' → They asked where **we** were going **the next day**.*
- the word order of the reported question is similar to a statement, not a question.
  *'How **can I get** to the sports club**?**' → He asked how **he could get** to the sports club**.***
- the reporting verb ***asked*** is sometimes followed by an object.
  *'What time is it?' → She asked **the driver** what time it was. / She asked what time it was.*
  *'Where are you going?' → They asked **us** where we were going. / They asked where we were going.*

In reported *Wh-* questions:

- the reported question begins with the same question word as the direct question.
- the auxiliary verbs ***do, don't*** (for present simple) and ***did, didn't*** (for past simple) are not used.
  ***Why did** you **call** the police? → I asked **why he had called** the police.*

In reported *Yes/No* questions:

- the reported question begins with ***if*** or ***whether***.
  *Have you seen my front door key? → He asked **whether** I'd seen his front door key.*
  *Did you feed the cat? → She asked me **if** I'd fed the cat.*

REPORTED REQUESTS

- We report a request with the ***to*** infinitive.
  *'**Will you wait** a moment?' → She asked us **to wait** a moment.*
  *'**Can you open** the door, please?' → He asked me **to open** the door.*
- The verbs change tense when the reporting verb is in the past tense in the same way as in reported statements.
- Pronouns and adverbs change in the same way as in reported statements.
- The reporting verb ***asked*** is always followed by a noun or pronoun.
  *'Please **call** the emergency services.' → She asked **me** to call the emergency services.*
- Negative requests are reported with ***not*** + ***to*** infinitive.
  *'Please **don't touch** anything!' → She asked us **not to touch** anything.*

Practice

1 Find and correct five mistakes in the reported questions and requests in the paragraph.

I went to the new sports shop in the shopping centre last week. They have a lot of good kit. When I went in, the shop assistant asked how could she help me. I wanted to know whether they did sell running shoes. The assistant asked me what size shoe I usually wear. She wanted to know did I prefer red or white. I asked if those were the only colours they'd had. She asked me could I wait while she checked with the manager. She then said they didn't have any other colours at that time, so I got these red ones!

2 Change the questions from reported to direct speech.

1 The doctor asked me where the pain was.
The doctor asked, ' ______________________ ?'
2 The nurse asked me why I hadn't phoned for help when the accident happened.
The nurse asked, ' ______________________ ?'
3 They wanted to know how long I had had the problem.
They asked, ' ______________________ ?'
4 My mum asked what she could do to help me.
My mum asked, ' ______________________ ?'
5 My dad wanted to know how many days I was going to be off school.
My dad asked, ' ______________________ ?'

3 Last year, you travelled abroad to do a holiday language course and you had to apply for a visa. Report the questions and requests of the visa clerk.

1 'What is your full name?'
She wanted to know ______________________
2 'Where is the language course held?'
She asked me ______________________
3 'Have you ever visited our country before?'
She asked me ______________________
4 'How are you travelling to the country and how long will you stay there?'
She needed to know ______________________
5 'Do you know the address of where you are staying?'
She asked me ______________________
6 'Have you already paid for your course?'
She wanted to know ______________________
7 'Can you fill in three copies of the application form?'
She asked me ______________________
8 'Please pay the fee in dollars or local currency.'
She asked me ______________________

GRAMMAR REFERENCE AND PRACTICE

UNIT 15 *HAVE/GET SOMETHING DONE; GET SOMEONE TO DO SOMETHING*

- We use ***have/get*** + object + past participle when someone else does something for us.
  *We want to **have** our bikes **mended**.* (= We want someone to ***mend*** our bikes.)
  *I'm going to **get** my hair **coloured**.* (= Someone is going to ***colour*** my hair.)
- ***Get*** is less formal than ***have***.
- We do not usually mention who the person is, unless it's important.
  *I **had/got** my hair **cut**.* (= The hairdresser ***cut*** my hair.)
  *I **had/got** my hair **cut by my sister**.* (emphasises that my sister did it for me)
- We can also use ***have something done*** to describe something unpleasant which happens to us. It usually refers to theft or injury.
  *I **had** my bag **stolen** by a boy on a motorbike.*
  *The security guard **had** his hand **injured** during the robbery.*
- We use ***get someone to do something*** when we ask or persuade someone to do something for us.
  *Max **got** his mum **to cut** his hair for him.*
  *We**'ll get** a trolley **to help** you with your luggage.*

Practice

1 **Find and correct the mistake in each of the sentences.**

1. They got delivered their shopping by a neighbour.
   ……………………………………
2. Can you get this television fixing before the weekend?
   ……………………………………
3. My brother had his arm broke during a rugby match.
   ……………………………………
4. I need to have these trousers mend by someone who can sew well.
   ……………………………………

2 **These people are going to ask someone to do something for them. Complete what they say, using *have/get* + object + past participle of the verb in brackets.**

1. This door is a horrible colour.
   'We're going to ……………………………………' (paint)
2. These new headphones aren't working properly.
   'I'm going to ……………………………………' (replace)
3. This bookcase blocks the light from the window.
   'I'm going to ……………………………………' (move)
4. Our air-conditioning isn't working well.
   'We're going to ……………………………………' (fix)
5. I've taken a great photo of a sunset over the sea.
   'I'm going to ……………………………………' (frame)

3 **A girl you know is attending a school leavers' party soon. Complete the questions you ask her, using *have/get something done* or *get someone to do something*.**

1. Will you do your make-up yourself, or will you ……………………………………?
2. Will your friends make their dresses themselves, or will they ……………………………………?
3. Will you go by bus, or will you ……………………………………?
4. Will Mrs Green, the organiser, cook the food herself, or will she ……………………………………?

4 **Imagine you are the girl in Exercise 3 and someone asked you those questions. Write your answers.**

UNIT 16 SECOND CONDITIONAL

- We form the second conditional with:
  If + past tense + comma + ***would*** + infinitive (without *to*)
  OR ***would*** + infinitive (without *to*) + ***if*** + past tense
  If *I* ***worked*** *late,* ***I'd be*** *too tired to go out.*
  (= I know that working late makes me tired, so I probably won't do it.)
  *You'****d get*** *bored* ***if*** *you* ***didn't have*** *any work to do.*
  (= You probably won't get bored because you have work to do.)
- We use the second conditional with ***would*** to describe an imaginary situation in the present or future.
- We can use ***might*** to make the result of the imaginary situation less certain.
  If + past tense + comma + ***might*** + infinitive (without *to*)
  OR ***might*** + infinitive (without *to*) + ***if*** + past tense
  If *I* ***worked*** *late, I* ***might be*** *too tired to go out.* (I believe that working late may make me tired.)
  You ***might get*** *bored* ***if*** *you* ***didn't have*** *any work to do.*
  (= It's possible that you'd get bored without work to do.)
- We can use ***could*** to talk about ability.
  If + past tense + comma + ***could*** + infinitive (without *to*)
  OR ***could*** + infinitive (without *to*) + ***if*** + past tense
  If *I* ***worked*** *longer hours, I* ***could*** *earn more money.*
  (= I would be able to earn more money.)
  We ***could*** *learn to dive if we* ***went*** *to the seaside for our holiday.* (= We would be able to learn to dive.)
- We sometimes use ***were*** instead of ***was*** after ***If I***.
  If I were *as tall as you, I could run faster.* (= I'm shorter than you, so I can't.)

Practice

1 **Choose the correct form of the verbs.**

1. If I *would have* / *had* a decent bike I *didn't* / *wouldn't* need to ask my mum for a lift so often.
2. Could your family *managed* / *manage* if they *had* / *would have* to use public transport for every journey?
3. You might *get* / *got* fitter as well as saving energy if you *didn't drive* / *didn't drove* everywhere.
4. *Wouldn't* / *Wasn't* it be great if we *don't have* / *didn't have* school tomorrow?
5. Where *could* / *did* we eat if the school *hasn't got* / *didn't have* a café?
6. If you *couldn't* / *didn't* make so much noise, we *might see* / *had seen* some wild deer in these woods.
7. I *would buy* / *had bought* you a better present if there *were* / *might be* more good shops in this area.
8. If I *would be* / *were* as clever as my brother, I *would* / *wouldn't* easily pass my exams.

2 **Complete the conversation using the second conditional. In some cases there is more than one correct answer.**

Alex: This flat isn't in good condition.
Howard: But we could improve it if we [1] ________ (spend) a bit of money. If we [2] ________ (knock) down the wall between the kitchen and the living room, we [3] ________ (have) more space.
Alex: Yes, and anyone working in the kitchen [4] ________ (talk) to the people in the living room. I [5] ________ (be) so happy if we [6] ________ (do) that!
Howard: The bedrooms [7] ________ (be) OK if they just [8] ________ (have) the walls painted.

if only and *wish*

- We use ***wish*** / ***if only*** + past simple or past continuous for a wish about a present situation.
  I wish I knew *the name of that singer.* (= I don't know the name of that singer.)
  If only we had *a car!* (= We don't have a car.)
  I wish I wasn't *so tired.* (= I am tired.)
- We sometimes use ***were*** instead of ***was*** after ***I wish***.
  I wish *I* ***were*** *as tall as you.* (= I'm shorter than you.)
- We use ***wish*** / ***if only*** + ***would/could*** for a wish about the present or future.
  I wish *I* ***could*** *drive.* (= I can't drive.)
  If only *my mum* ***would*** *teach me to drive.* (= She won't teach me.)
- We often use ***wish*** / ***if only*** + ***would(n't)*** when we are annoyed.
  I wish *you* ***wouldn't make*** *such a mess in the bathroom!*

Practice

3 **Read the sentences and complete the wishes.**

1. James's phone doesn't work, so he can't contact his friends.
   'I wish I ____________________ my friends.'
2. Emily wants to do her homework, but her brother's using the computer to play a game.
   'I wish my brother ____________________ the computer when I need it!'
3. Francesca has gone for a run, but it has started to snow.
   'If only it ____________________ so cold.'
4. Miles is feeling ill, so he can't go out.
   'I wish I ____________________ ill.'
5. Archie is doing an exam, but he can't answer most of the questions.
   'If only I ____________________ more questions.'
6. Bettina can't find her best boots. She suspects her sister Ellie has borrowed them.
   'I wish Ellie ____________________ my things.'

GRAMMAR REFERENCE AND PRACTICE

UNIT 17 MODALS OF DEDUCTION: PRESENT

- To talk about probability in the present, we use ***may***, ***may not***, ***might***, ***might not***, ***could***, ***could not***, ***can't***, ***must*** + verb.
- When we think something is possible, but we are not sure, we use ***may***, ***might*** or ***could*** + verb.
  Who knows the code for the alarm?
  *Amy **may know** it.*
  *Amy **could know** it.*
  *Amy **might know** it.*
  (= Perhaps she knows it.)
- We use ***well*** after ***may***, ***might*** and ***could*** when we think something is more probable.
  *Teri **may be** on holiday.* (= Perhaps she's on holiday.)
  *Teri **may well be** on holiday.* (= I think it's very probable that she's on holiday.)
- When we think something is possibly not true, we use ***may not*** or ***might not*** + verb.
  We can ask Amy what the code is.
  *She **may not know** it.*
  *She **might not know** it.*
  (= It's possible that she doesn't know it.)
- When we feel certain that something is true, we use ***must*** + verb.
  Amy lives in the house.
  *She **must know** the code.* (= I'm certain she knows it.)
- The opposite of ***must*** + verb is ***can't/couldn't*** + verb, **not** ~~mustn't + verb~~.
  Ben has never been to the house.
  *He **can't/couldn't know** the code.* (= I'm sure he doesn't know it.)
  not ~~*He mustn't know the code.*~~

Practice

1 **Complete the conversation with *must, might not* or *can't*.**

Marco: All the houses in this road have big gardens. They [1] ________ be very expensive.
Rhona: Yes, and they all have high walls and big gates. They [2] ________ belong to important people.
Marco: Well, I know at least one famous TV star lives around here. But he [3] ________ be at home very often because he works in New York most of the time.
Rhona: Look at that house with the security guard by the gate. I bet that's his.
Marco: The guard [4] ________ have such a boring job: he [5] ________ have anything to do for hours every day.
Rhona: Well, I suppose he [6] ________ mind too much. After all, he [7] ________ meet some celebrities from time to time.

2 **Complete the conversation with *can't, could* or *may well*.**

Amir: Whose bike is that outside Jay's house?
Freddy: It [1] ________ be Zeb's. He often goes to play tennis with Jay.
Amir: Yes, or it [2] ________ be Andy's.
Freddy: No, it [3] ________ be Andy's: he had an argument with Jay last week.
Amir: But they've quarrelled before haven't they? They [4] ________ be friends again by now.
Freddy: That's very true. You [5] ________ be right!

3 **Rewrite the sentences using a modal of deduction. There is more than one correct answer for some of the sentences.**

1 I think perhaps Kari is at a football match.
Kari ________________________________

2 I'm certain this letter is from my school.
This letter ________________________________

3 I'm not really sure if Shamsi studies French as well as German.
Shamsi ________________________________

4 It's possible that Paulo isn't a vegetarian.
Paulo ________________________________

5 I know Rob's not at work because it's his day off.
Rob ________________________________

UNIT 18 THIRD CONDITIONAL

- We form the third conditional with:
  If + past perfect tense + comma + ***would/could/might have*** + past participle OR ***would/could/might have*** + past participle + ***if*** + past tense
  If *you**'d (had) played*** *your guitar, **I'd (would) have sung**.*
  *I **wouldn't have sung if** you **hadn't played** your guitar.*
  If *you **hadn't played** your guitar, I **might not have sung**.*
  Would/Could *you **have sung if** I **hadn't played** my guitar?*
- We use the third conditional with ***would have*** to describe an imaginary situation in the past.
  If I'd (had) worked *late, **I'd have been** too tired to go out.*
  (= I didn't work late, so I was able to go out.)
  *You**'d have been** bored **if** you **hadn't met** your friends.*
  (= You weren't bored because you met your friends.)
- We use ***might*** to make the result of the imaginary situation less certain.
  If I'd (had) worked *late, I **might have been** too tired to go out.*
  *You **might have got** bored **if** you **hadn't met** your friends.*
- We use ***could*** to describe an ability to do something that didn't happen.
  If I'd (had) worked *longer hours**, I could have earned** more money.* (= I didn't work longer hours, so I didn't earn more money.)
  *We **could have learned** to dive if we **had gone** to the seaside for our holiday.* (= We didn't go to the seaside, so we didn't learn to dive.)

Practice

1 Read the story and complete the sentences using *would/might/could* (*not*) *have* + past participle, or the past perfect.

Anna wanted to be a singer in a musical, but she was very nervous so she asked her friend Margot to help her practise her songs. Anna asked Margot to go with her when she tried for a part, but she was too nervous to be able to sing well. The director didn't give the part to any of the girls who applied for it. Then he noticed Margot in the waiting room and thought she looked right for the character. He asked her to sing for him. Luckily she knew the songs because she'd helped Anna to practise them. She didn't think she had a chance of getting the part, so she wasn't nervous. As she had a good voice, she sang very well and got the part.

1 If Anna ________ nervous, she ________ Margot to help her practise her songs.
2 Anna ________ better if she ________ so nervous when she tried for the part.
3 If the director ________ the part to one of the girls who had applied for it, he ________ Margot to sing for him.
4 He ________ her to sing for him if she ________ right for the part.
5 Margot ________ the songs if she ________ Anna to practise them.
6 If Margot ________ she had a chance of getting the part, she ________ nervous.
7 If she ________ well, she ________ the part.

wish + past perfect

- We use ***wish*** + past perfect when we want to express regret about a past situation that we can't change.
  ***I wish** I **had gone** to the concert with you.*
  (= I didn't go and now I regret it.)
  ***She wishes** she **hadn't been** rude to that man.*
  (= She was rude to him and she regrets it.)
  ***I wish** my brother **had come** to the match with me.*
  (= He didn't come with me and I regret it.)

Practice

2 Jake is driving to a party with his friend Brian. Unfortunately, they've run out of petrol a long way from the nearest petrol station. Complete Jake's regrets.

1 We haven't got a phone with us. I lent mine to my sister.
I wish I ________________________________

2 I didn't listen carefully to the directions we were given.
I wish I ________________________________

3 We didn't check how much petrol we had.
I wish we ________________________________

4 I decided to wear boots and my feet hurt.
I wish I ________________________________

5 I shouted at Brian and now he won't speak to me.
I wish I ________________________________

6 I'm hungry. We left our food in the car.
I wish we ________________________________

GRAMMAR REFERENCE AND PRACTICE

UNIT 19 MODALS OF DEDUCTION: PAST

- To talk about possibility in the past, we use modal + ***have*** + past participle.
- When we think something was possible, but we are not sure, we use ***may have***, ***might have*** or ***could have*** + past participle.
  Who knew the code for the alarm?
  *Amy **may have known** it.*
  *Amy **could have known** it.*
  *Amy **might have known** it.*
  (= Perhaps she knew it.)
- When we think something was possibly not true, we use ***may not have*** or ***might not have*** + past participle.
  Perhaps Amy used the code.
  *She **may not have known** it.*
  *She **might not have known** it.*
  (= It's possible that she didn't know it.)
- When we feel certain that something was true, we use ***must have*** + past participle.
  Amy lived in the house.
  *She **must have known** the code.* (= I'm certain she knew it.)
- The opposite of ***must have*** + past participle is ***can't/ couldn't have*** + past participle, **not** ~~mustn't have + past participle~~.
  Ben had never been to the house.
  *He **can't have known** the code.*
  *He **couldn't have known** the code.*
  not ~~*He **mustn't have known** the code.*~~ (= I'm sure he didn't know it.)

Practice

1 **On a school trip to London, two boys became separated from their teacher and classmates for several hours. Complete what the other students said, using the phrases in the box. Use each phrase once only.**

can't have listened	could have left
may have disappeared	may have thought
must have been	must have got off
must have switched off	

1 'The trains were very crowded and the boys were separated from the rest of us, so they .... at the wrong station.'
2 'They .... to the teacher's instructions.'
3 'They both wanted to do some shopping, so they .... on purpose.'
4 'The teacher .... very worried about them.'
5 'We tried to text them, but they .... their phones.'
6 'The boys .... it was very funny, but they were lucky to find the group again.'
7 'We .... without them and then they would really have been in trouble.'

2 **Choose the correct verbs in the conversations.**

1
Sonny: I haven't got my sunglasses. I know I had them when we came out!
Cheryl: You [1] *must have / couldn't have* left them on the beach. Shall we go and look for them?

2
Carlo: Benny asked me to lend him £20, but I didn't have enough money. I was so embarrassed.
Suzy: He [2] *might not have / may have* realised that you left your wallet at home.

3
Della: Did you see Emma got full marks in the chemistry exam?
Freya: Really? She [3] *must have / may have* worked incredibly hard.
Della: Yes. Or she [4] *might have / couldn't have* cheated.
Freya: I don't believe that. She's such an honest person – she [5] *can't have / may not have* done anything dishonest.

3 **Rewrite the sentences using a past modal of deduction. There is more than one correct answer for some of the sentences.**

1 Perhaps Andy forgot to charge his phone.
Andy ....
....
2 We are sure that Dan texted his parents last night.
Dan ....
....
3 It's not possible that Adrienne forgot to book tickets for the film.
Adrienne ....
....
4 I can see that Sima didn't enjoy her meal.
Sima ....
....
5 Perhaps Marcus didn't travel by train.
Marcus ....
....
6 I think it's possible that Donna passed her driving test, but I'm not sure.
Donna ....
....

UNIT 20 *-ING* FORMS

- The ***-ing*** form (sometimes called the *present participle* or the *gerund*) is regular: ***being***, ***knowing***, ***seeing***, ***having***, ***running***, etc.
- ***-ing*** forms are used very often in English. We use them:
  - as the subject of a clause.
    Cooking *can be fun.*
  - as the object of a clause.
    When did you finish ***cooking****?*
  - with other words following the -***ing*** form as part of the subject or object.
    Cooking for friends *can be fun.*
    When did you finish ***cooking the meal****?*
  - after verbs and phrases that express likes and dislikes.
    I ***love cooking*** *for friends.*
    I ***don't enjoy clearing up*** *the kitchen.*
  - after prepositions.
    I learned to cook ***by watching*** *TV programmes.*
    Do you use this spoon ***for making*** *the sauce?*
  - after adjective + preposition.
    My brother's ***good at chopping*** *vegetables.*
    My dad gets ***anxious about lighting*** *the barbecue.*
    My mum's ***famous for making*** *kebabs.*

Practice

1 **Complete the second sentence so that it has a similar meaning to the first sentence. Use the words in brackets + *-ing*.**

1 Poppy knows how to find information online really quickly. (brilliant at)
Poppy is ....

2 Luke didn't want to sing in public because he thought he might look stupid. (afraid of)
Luke didn't want to sing in public because he was
....

3 Nora apologised to us after she broke the chair. (sorry for)
Nora said she was ....

4 Oliver felt very happy when he heard he'd won the art prize. (pleased about)
Oliver was ....

5 Riki just can't keep her room tidy. (hopeless at)
Riki is ....

6 Mary didn't speak in class because she thought she might make mistakes. (nervous about)
Mary didn't speak in class because she was
....

Participle clauses

- The ***-ing*** form can introduce a participle clause.
- We can use the participle clause instead of making a new sentence.
- The participle clause can be negative (***not*** + ***-ing***).
- The participle clause can:
  - add information.
    I saw my sister ***standing*** *at the bus stop.* (= I saw my sister. + My sister was standing at the bus stop.)
    Being *short of money, I don't often eat out.* (= I'm short of money. + I don't often eat out.)
    Not having *much money, I don't often eat out.*
  - describe another action happening at the same time as the action of the main verb.
    Walking *home from school, I saw a crowd of people in the square.*
    Wondering *what had happened, I ran across the road.*
    Not looking *where I was going, I nearly bumped into a car.*
- In sentences which describe two actions happening at the same time, the subject of the main verb **must** be the same as the subject in the participle clause.
  Walking *quickly across the road, I nearly bumped into a car.*
  not ~~*Walking quickly across the road, a car nearly hit me.*~~
  (This would mean that the car was walking quickly across the road!)

Practice

2 **Combine the sentences into one. Use a participle clause.**

1 Yesterday I found a small box. The box was lying in front of my door.
....

2 I didn't know what it contained. I opened it very carefully.
....

3 I removed some pieces of newspaper. I was amazed to find two beautiful old glasses.
....

4 I wanted to know what they were. I did some research online.
....

5 They may be quite valuable. They are 200 years old.
....

6 They look beautiful. They stand where the light shines through them.
....

7 I have no idea who sent them to me. I can't say thank you for them.
....

LIST OF IRREGULAR VERBS

Infinitive	Past simple	Past participle
be	was, were	been
become	became	become
begin	began	begun
break	broke	broken
bring	brought	brought
build	built	built
burn	burned/burnt	burned/burnt
buy	bought	bought
catch	caught	caught
choose	chose	chosen
come	came	come
cost	cost	cost
cut	cut	cut
do	did	done
draw	drew	drawn
dream	dreamed/dreamt	dreamed/dreamt
drink	drank	drunk
drive	drove	driven
eat	ate	eaten
fall	fell	fallen
feel	felt	felt
find	found	found
fly	flew	flown
forget	forgot	forgotten
get	got	got
give	gave	given
go	went	gone/been
grow	grew	grown
have	had	had
hear	heard	heard
hit	hit	hit
hold	held	held
hurt	hurt	hurt
keep	kept	kept
know	knew	known
learn	learned/learnt	learned/learnt
leave	left	left

Infinitive	Past simple	Past participle
lend	lent	lent
lie	lay	lain
lose	lost	lost
make	made	made
mean	meant	meant
meet	met	met
pay	paid	paid
put	put	put
read	read /red/	read /red/
ride	rode	ridden
ring	rang	rung
run	ran	run
say	said	said
see	saw	seen
sell	sold	sold
send	sent	sent
show	showed	shown
shut	shut	shut
sing	sang	sung
sit	sat	sat
sleep	slept	slept
speak	spoke	spoken
spell	spelled/spelt	spelled/spelt
spend	spent	spent
stand	stood	stood
steal	stole	stolen
swim	swam	swum
take	took	taken
teach	taught	taught
tell	told	told
think	thought	thought
throw	threw	thrown
understand	understood	understood
wake	woke	woken
wear	wore	worn
win	won	won
write	wrote	written

Acknowledgements

The authors would like to thank everyone who worked on the first edition of *Prepare*, and also Robert Vernon and Alyson Maskell for their hard work on the second edition. James Styring dedicates this book to Jude Robert Alver Styring. Nicholas Tims thanks Clare, Ismay and Elodie for their endless support.

The authors and publishers are grateful to the following for reviewing the material during the writing process:

Italy: Ilaria Longhi; Spain: John Hayward and Isabel Sobrino

The authors and publishers acknowledge the following sources of copyright material and are grateful for the permissions granted. While every effort has been made, it has not always been possible to identify the sources of all the material used, or to trace all copyright holders. If any omissions are brought to our notice, we will be happy to include the appropriate acknowledgements on reprinting and in the next update to the digital edition, as applicable.

Key: U = Unit, LS = Life Skills, C = Culture, EA = Extra Activities, R = Review.

Text
U6: Text about Alessandra Peters. Copyright © Alessandra Peters. Reproduced with kind permission.; Text about Elijah Quashie. Copyright © Elijah Quashie. Reproduced with permission of Richmond Quashie; **U7**: Text about Beth Reekles. Copyright © Beth Reekles. Reproduced with kind permission; **U19:** Text adapted from 'French woman accused of disguising herself as daughter to sit exam' by Angelique Chrisafis. The Guardian, 20/6/13. Copyright © Guardian News & Media 2013; **U20:** Text adapted from 'Youngsters build the ultimate two-storey treehouse 85ft high with spiral staircase and viewing platform... but have to tear it down because of health and safety fears' by Dan Bloom, *Daily Mail* 27/3/14. Copyright © Daily Mail; Text adapted from 'South Whidbey teen builds tiny transportable house' 10/2/2012, South Whidbey Record. Copyright © South Whidbey Record/IKONIK.

Photography
The following images are sourced from Getty Images.

U1: JGI/Jamie Grill; **U2**: gehringj/E+; Christopher Polk/Getty Images for DirecTV/Getty Images Entertainment; Kevin Mazur/Getty Images for Global Citizen; Jeff Kravitz/Getty Images for iHeartMedia; Kevin Mazur/WireImage; Luca Teuchmann/Getty Images Entertainment; Rick Kern/WireImage; Jose Luis Pelaez/The Image Bank/Getty Images Plus; JGI/Jamie Grill; Hoxton/Tom Merton; **C1**: Kevin Mazur/Getty Images for Billboard; Samir Hussein/Redferns; **U3:** sahpictures/Corbis; Andersen Ross/DigitalVision; Tetra Images; JackF/iStock/Getty Images Plus; Michael Kelley/Stone/Getty Images Plus; Mark Webster/Cultura; Jordan Mansfield/Getty Images for LTA; Steve Debenport/E+; **U4:** Westend61; Tom Pfeiffer/VolcanoDiscovery/Photographer's Choice/Getty Images Plus; Sdubi/iStock/Getty Images Plus; Marc Ward/Stocktrek Images; mantaphoto/E+; Debbie Egan-Chin/NY Daily News Archive; STR/AFP; Toshi Sasaki/Photographer's Choice/Getty Images Plus; **LS1:** Brian Stablyk/Photographer's Choice; AlexRaths/iStock/Getty Images Plus; Mark-W-R/iStock/Getty Images Plus; Norasit Kaewsai/iStock/Getty Images Plus; **U5:** 3000ad/iStock/Getty Images Plus; **U6:** Claudia Goepperl/Photodisc; Echo/Juice Images; Mint Images; **C2:** David J. Becker/Getty Images Sport; JOSEP LAGO/AFP; Christian Petersen/Getty Images News; Thomas Lohnes/Getty Images News; **U7:** Lisbeth Hjort/Cultura; **U8:** juliedeshaies/iStock/Getty Images Plus; GCShutter/iStock/Getty Images Plus; Bernd Opitz/Taxi/Getty Images Plus; Cavan Images/Cavan; Soft_Light/iStock/Getty Images Plus; Iñigo Fdz de Pinedo/Moment; artherng/RooM; buzbuzzer/E+; ElOjoTorpe/Moment; Patrick J. Endres/Corbis NX/Getty Images Plus; Michael Hall/Taxi; **LS2:** pixdeluxe/E+; Westend61; **R2:** bmcent1/iStock/Getty Images Plus; alashi/DigitalVision Vectors; **U9:** JackF/iStock/Getty Images Plus; Fuse/Corbis; PrzemyslawKlos/EyeEm; FatCamera/E+; Jose Luis Pelaez Inc/Digital Vision; PhotoAlto/Laurence Mouton/BrandX Pictures; Corbis/VCG; Wdnet/iStock/Getty Images Plus; Caiaimage/Rob Daly/Caiaimage; **U10:** kate_sept2004/E+; Yasser Chalid/Moment; MIXA; Michele Tantussi; Olly Curtis/MacFormat Magazine; TOBIAS SCHWARZ/AFP; Jasmin Merdan/Moment; Sergei_Tremasov/iStock/Getty Images Plus; Vera Ivanchenko/EyeEm; Ismailciydem/iStock/Getty Images Plus; Johnny Greig/iStock/Getty Images Plus; Bryan Hainer; **C3:** Zhang Peng/LightRocket; Westend61; rsampedro1976/iStock/Getty Images Plus; **U11:** FatCamera/E+; Francesco Carta fotografo/Moment; VitaliiPhoto/iStock/Getty Images Plus; PeopleImages/E+; d3sign/Moment; Classen Rafael/EyeEm; metamorworks/iStock/Getty Images Plus; Westend61; krisanapong detraphiphat/Moment; luismmolina/E+; luchschen/iStock/Getty Images Plus; REMKO DE WAAL/AFP; Ociacia/iStock/Getty Images Plus; SolStock/E+; **U12:** DigitalVision; Johnny Greig/E+; Caiaimage/Sam Edwards/OJO+; JGI/Jamie Gril ; VioletaStoimenova/E+; Luxy Images; Hoxton/Tom Merton; **LS3:** Wavebreakmedia/iStock/Getty Images Plus; filo/DigitalVision Vectors; Hill Street StudiosLLC/DigitalVision; **R3:** Hero Image; **U13:** Shaun Botterill; Stu Forster; courtneyk/E+; FatCamera/E+; Michae lBlann/The Image Bank; David Cannon; nattrass/E+; **U14:** Schulte Productions/E+; Jené Gonzales/EyeEm; iloveimages/Juice Images; Science Photo Library; Jose Luis Stephens/EyeEm; Peopleimages/E+; Rawpixel/iStock/Getty Images Plus; Andrew Bret Wallis/Photodisc; martin-dm/iStock/Getty Images Plus; Piccell/Photographer's Choice; laflor/E+; TanyaLittle/RooM; Mihajlo Maricic/EyeEm; **C4:** sarotepruksachat/Moment; PASCALPOCHARD-CASABIANCA/AFP; Westend61; Hero Images; **U15:** wingedwolf; Nicholas Free/E+; omersukrugoksu/E+; Jamie Garbutt/Taxi; Paul Bradbury/Caiaimage; Dougal Waters/Photodisc; Matthieu Spohn/PhotoAlto Agency RF Collections; PeopleImages/E+; LeoPatrizi/E+; Allen Donikowski/Moment; Robert Recker/Corbis; xua/iStock/Getty Images Plus; Sproetniek/iStock/Getty Images Plus; Charly_Morlock/iStock/Getty Images Plus; JAG IMAGES/Cultura; Doug Byrnes/Corbis/Getty Images Plus; Hazmi Che man/Moment; **U16:** Toa55/iStock/Getty Images Plus; republica/iStock/Getty Images Plus; Westend61; CHAIWATPHOTOS/iStock/Getty Images Plus; Maskot; inhauscreative/E+; Universal History Archive/UIG; Brit Worgan/The Image Bank; acilo/iStock/Getty Images Plus; Backyard Production/iStock Editorial/Getty Images Plus; **LS4:** DANNYHU/Moment; gustavofrazao/iStock/Getty Images Plus; Hero Images; **R4:** Pete Rowbottom/Moment; **U17:** WOLFGANG KUMM/Getty Images; EducationImages/UIG; Tim Graham; Photography by Ria Novosti, Daisy-Daisy/iStock/Getty Images Plus; sam74100/iStock/Getty Images Plus; EdReschke/Photodisc; Debi Dalio/Moment; Ha lBeral/Corbis; Patrick Fraser/DigitalVision; Michael H/DigitalVision; Sunset Avenue Productions/DigitalVision; Serge; **U18:** Diedra Laird/Charlotte Observer/MCT/Tribune News Service; Marc Bryan-Brown/WireImage; PeteSaloutos/Blend Images; Flashpop/Stone; **C5:** François BIBAL/Gamma-Rapho; Tim Graham/Getty Images News; View Pictures/Universal Images Group; **U19:** Daniel Allan/Photographer's Choice; Juanmonino/E+; KatarzynaBialasiewicz/iStock/Getty Images Plus; Matthias Tunger/Photodisc; UpperCutImages; Monty Rakusen/Cultura; Chris Ryan/OJO Images; **U20:** QUIQUE GARCIA/AFP; **LS5:** Jutta Klee/The Image Bank; Hero Images; JGI/Tom Grill; asiseeit/E+; InPicturesLtd./Corbis; **R5:** Pixelchrome Inc/DigitalVision; Alexander Spatari/Moment; **EA:** Hero Images; Sirinapa Wannapat/EyeEm; Soltan Frédéric/CorbisDocumentary; Andrew Benge/Getty Images Entertainment; Tao Zhang; Kaveh Kazemi/Getty Images News; Elea Dumas/Photolibrary; DGLimages/iStock/Getty Images Plus; Cultura RM Exclusive/Alan Graf/Cultura Exclusive; Cultura RM Exclusive/Stefano Gilera.

The following photographs have been sourced from other library/sources.

U4: AJP/Shutterstock; **R1**: © Bad Buildings 2014; **U5:** Courtesy of Codemasters; Courtesy of Epic Games; Courtesy of Mojang; Overcooked 2. Developed by Team17 Digital Ltd and Ghost Town Games Ltd © 2019. Published by Team17 Digital Ltd. Team17 is a trademarks of Team17 Digital Limited. All other trademarks, copyrights and logos are property of their respective owners; Tinxi/Shutterstock; **U6**: Copyright © Elijah Quashie; Andrew Crowley/© Telegraph Media Group Limited 2016;

C2: angkrit/Shutterstock; **U7:** © Rolf Marriott Photography; Nick Ansell/PA Archive/Press Association Images; Nick Ansell/ PA Archive/Press Association Images; **U8**: Ange/Alamy Stock Photo; **C3:** Adam van Bunnens/Alamy Stock Photo; **U11:** Matjaz Tancic/Alamy Stock Photo; **U13:** Christian Palma/PA Wire/Press Association Images; Paige Holden; **U16:** ICE AGE: COLLISION COURSE © 2016 Twentieth Century Fox. All rights reserved; THE DAY AFTER TOMORROW © 2004 Twentieth Century Fox. All rights reserved; **U17:** WENN Ltd/Alamy Stock Photo; T Photography/Shutterstock; Camera Press London; Lewis Tse Pui Lung/Shutterstock; Adam Gasson/Alamy Stock Photo; **U18:** JeffG/ Alamy Stock Photo; Stephen Cooper/Newspix; PAUL RUHTER/ AP/Press Association Images; Australian of the Year Awards/ Ahmed Dini; **C5:** ©Tate, London 2019; © Association Marcel Duchamp/ADAGP, Paris and DACS, London 2019; © FMGB Guggenheim Bilbao Museoa; Tate Modern from St Paul's. 2016. Tate, London, 2019. Photo ©Tate; **U20:** CarolineSchiff/Photodisc; AlpamayoPhoto/E+; Peter Wattendorff/Corbis; Copyright © Celina Dill; Image & Stories/Alamy Stock Photo; Angelo Cavalli/Alamy Stock Photo.

Front cover photography by Klaus Vedfelt/DigitalVision/Getty Images.

Illustration
Ludovic Salle (Advocate Art), Mark Duffin

Audio
All audios are sourced from Getty Images.

The Hot Rocks/SoundExpress; Atlas/SoundExpress; harbottle/ SoundExpress; Marcus Bressler/SoundExpress; Erika Gonzalez/ SoundExpress; CT/SoundExpress; Richard Neumann/ SoundExpress.

The publishers are grateful to the following contributors: cover design and design concept: restless; typesetting: emc design Ltd; audio recordings: produced by Leon Chambers and recorded at The SoundHouse Studios, London; Life Skills and Culture sections: Will Varney; Grammar reference section: Louise Hashemi; project management: Carol Goodwright.